A FLOOD OF EVIDENCE

40 REASONS NoaH AND THE ArK STILL MATTER

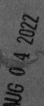
KEN HAM AND BODIE HODGE

First printing: September 2016
Seventh printing: August 2021

ISBN: 978-0-89051-978-3
ISBN: 978-1-61458-561-9 (digital)
Library of Congress Number: 2016913219

Cover by John Taylor

Photo and image credits: Thanks to Dan Lietha, Maria Murphy, Bodie Hodge, Ken Ham, Answers in Genesis, Wikipedia Commons, Renton Maclachlan (Te Wairoa items), Dr. Tommy Mitchell, Dan Stelzer, and Larry Smith.

Please consider requesting that a copy of this volume be purchased by your local library system.

Printed in the United States of America

Please visit our website for other great titles:
www.masterbooks.com

For information regarding author interviews,
please contact the publicity department at (870) 438-5288.

Master
Books®
A Division of New Leaf Publishing Group
www.masterbooks.com

contents

preface

Bodie Hodge and Ken Ham

WHY ANOTHER BOOK ON THE FLOOD AND THE ARK?

There are hosts of books, videos, film, and Internet information about Noah's ark. Some of it is quite good. Much of it is miserable! Some are blatantly inaccurate and unbiblical (consider the *Noah* film with Russell Crowe and directed by Darren Aronofsky, which was primarily an attack on the Bible). Some ark and Flood information is too technical for many readers. Some ark and Flood resources are so basic that readers lose interest.

What this book was designed to do was filter through the massive amounts of information and give you *what you need to know*. We tried to do it in a way that keeps you from getting caught up in too much technical data and debates, and yet gives you some "meat to chew on" without being too basic. If you wanted to move on to a deeper level of technical debate after this book (which builds on some of the chapters), then at least you would have a foundation to dive into the subjects further.

Also, we wanted this to be a book that stands on the *authority of the Bible* as our absolute and final standard on issues. We didn't want a book to rest on the *opinions of men* like so many resources do, but to treat the Bible for what it is — the truth. We are unashamed of this and up-front about this as you can see.

In doing so, we hope this book also points you to the Lord Jesus Christ of which the Flood (the first part of the book) and Noah's ark (the second part of the book) is a picture. The Flood was a judgment on sin and the ark was a means of salvation from that catastrophe. All you had to do was enter the door of the ark to be saved.

In the same way, Jesus Christ ultimately judges sin for all eternity. Yet Jesus Christ describes Himself as *the door* by which all must enter to be saved from their sin. The shed blood of Jesus Christ, who took the punishment for sin upon Himself, is the *only* means of salvation.

> Nor is there salvation in any other, for there is no other name under heaven given among men by which we must be saved (Acts 4:12).

Introduction

1 | THE FLOOD AND NOAH'S ARK: AN INTRODUCTION – GETTING DOWN TO THE BASICS

Ken Ham AND Bodie Hodge

INTRODUCTION

> That there was a flood 4,000 years ago is not provable. In fact, the evidence, for me at least, as a reasonable man, is overwhelming that it couldn't possibly have happened; there's no evidence for it. — Bill Nye[1]

Evolutionist Bill Nye repeatedly attacked the global Flood recorded in the Bible at the historic debate with Ken Ham over creation-evolution at the Creation Museum on February 4, 2014. Did you ever wonder why he did this? The reason was simple. He *had* to. In fact, anyone who believes in an old earth, Christian or secular, cannot believe in a global Flood.

In any scenario that involved millions and billions of years of earth history, a catastrophe like the Flood of Noah's day would be devastating! Thinking clearly, the secular idea of millions of years is used in an attempt to explain rock layers (that contain fossils). The fossil layers were supposedly laid down slowly over long periods of time *without any major catastrophes.*

Yet the global Flood of Noah's day would account for the majority of those rock layers quickly.[2] So millions of years would vanish in light of a catastrophe like that! This is why Bill Nye (and anyone else) arguing for an old earth must fight against the famous Flood of biblical proportions!

---

1. Ken Ham and Bodie Hodge, *Inside the Nye-Ham Debate* (Green Forest, AR: Master Books, 2014), p. 344.
2. Of course we have had some rock layers form since that time from volcanoes, local floods, and so on, but the bulk of the rock layers that contain fossils came from Noah's Flood.

IMPOrTance OF THE FLOOD

Is the issue of Noah's Flood important? Absolutely. It may be one of the key battles in the authority of Scripture in our day and age. Sadly, even certain Christians join with non-Christians to attack the truth of a global Flood. For example, popular old-earth Christian Dr. Hugh Ross attacks the ark and the global Flood by saying:

> Not even an ark of steel armor plate could survive the rigors of a Flood gone global in Forty Days nor of the devastating effects of tens of thousands of feet of erosion in forty days and similar uplift within a year's time.[3]

> No viable scientific evidence has ever been found for a recent, global Flood.[4]

Surprising to many, the attacks on the ark and Noah's worldwide Flood are coming from both *outside* the Church and *inside* the Church. So the Flood is an important issue. Join with us on this adventure to investigate issues and questions surrounding the Flood and ark of Noah to help lay to rest these erroneous claims.

THE CHURCH anD a GLOBaL FLOOD

It is not enough to merely teach a global Flood — we need to teach the next generation how to defend it (this dives into the field of apologetics[5] — defending the faith). The Flood is documented and discussed in the Bible in Genesis 6–8 as well as other portions of Scripture (that refer back to the Flood event) quoting Jesus Christ or Paul the Apostle or a Psalmist. The universal Flood really occurred, and Scripture clearly teaches this truth.

The secular culture has been taught to deny the global Flood of Noah, however, many people in our churches (and culture) now struggle with the fact of the world-covering Flood! To put it bluntly, the churchgoer has been influenced by the secular belief system — evolutionism — that opposes the reality of the biblical Flood. Many in the Church succumb to this secular peer pressure and deny the global Flood.

---

3. Hugh Ross, *The Genesis Question* (Colorado Springs, CO: NavPress, 1998), p. 156.
4. Ibid., p. 157.
5. Apologetics is derived from the Greek word *apologia,* which means "to give a defense or give an answer."

Therefore, *in the churches* across the Western world, there is a significant problem. Consider the original study of the general public by America's Research Group led by Britt Beemer in 2015 to help estimate and prepare for the number of people who would visit the Ark Encounter in Kentucky.

For instance, when asked "Do you believe Noah's ark was actually built or only a legend?" the results for those who said, "Yes , it was actually built" were as follows (by age group):

60s — 86%

50s — 74%

40s — 81%

30s — 81%

20s — 52%[6]

Notice how the generation currently in their 20s overwhelmingly dropped! This is the impact of secular schooling, most media and secular museums, and their insistence on millions of years and a denial of the Flood.

What about church attendees? As far back as the year 2000, George Barna, who works with church statistics, revealed that the number of people who do not believe in absolute truth in the pews was staggering. One writer concluded:

Can you believe that 27% of all the people who attend an evangelical church do not believe in absolute truth?[7]

Consider this statistic. God is the absolute truth and so is the Bible (his written revelation) . . . including the account of Noah's ark and the Flood! And yet, over 1 in 4 in our evangelical churches do not really believe it. More recently, Britt Beemer, of America's Research Group, found that:

One in six said their pastor said something to make them believe that the Book of Genesis contained myths and legends that we know are untrue.[8]

Over 20% (one in five) said their pastors taught that there is no problem, biblically speaking, if Christians believe in an earth that is millions or billions of years old.[9]

6. Ken Ham with Jeff Kinley, research by Britt Beemer, *Ready to Return* (Green Forest, AR: Master Books, 2015), p. 103–104.
7. Carl Kerby, "WDJS, not just WWJD," May 11, 2000, based on research by George Barna, https://answersingenesis.org/jesus-christ/wdjs-not-just-wwjd/.
8. Ham with Kinley, *Ready to Return*, p. 30.
9. Ibid., p. 30.

Keep in mind that the idea that the earth is millions of years old comes from rejecting the idea of a *global* Flood of Noah's day. Then all the Flood sediment is seen as evidence of slow gradual accumulations over millions of years! Regarding kids who attended church, Beemer found that:

> Eighty-three percent said their science teachers taught them that the earth was millions or billions of years old.[10]

What this means is that the secular, atheistic world is being more effective at training the church kids than the Church! It is time to reverse this trend! Approximately 90 percent of kids in church homes attend state schools where they are indoctrinated with secular thought (think naturalism and atheism) for about 40 hours a week — including secular morality (moral relativism)! Churches are doing well if they are allowed to teach kids within their doors for 3 hours a week!

Essentially, many Christians are sending their children to be taught a different religion in state school systems and then we wonder why our kids walk away from Church! Is there any doubt as to why the next generation is walking after the religion of secular humanism (think atheism, agnosticism, secularism, naturalism, etc.) and its evil tenants, and leaving the Church?

You need to understand that the foundation of Christianity is under attack in our day and age. These attacks are focused on Genesis 1–11, including the Flood and Noah's ark — in state schools, secular media, and secular museums . . . and even in many churches and Christian schools! We need to be prepared for the secular claims so that we can be ready to give a defense for the hope that is in us for our Christian faith surrounding the Flood and Noah's ark (e.g., 2 Corinthians 10:4–5[11]; 1 Peter 3:15[12]). Now let us embark on this journey of *what you need to know.*

---

10. Ibid., p. 28.
11. For the weapons of our warfare are not carnal but mighty in God for pulling down strongholds, casting down arguments and every high thing that exalts itself against the knowledge of God, bringing every thought into captivity to the obedience of Christ.
12. But sanctify the Lord God in your hearts, and always be ready to give a defense to everyone who asks you a reason for the hope that is in you, with meekness and fear.

2 | THE GENESIS ACCOUNT OF THE FLOOD

BODIE HODGE

Genesis 6:1–9:20 with a few clarifying comments for the reader.

Genesis 6

1 Now it came to pass, when men began to multiply on the face of the earth, and daughters were born to them,

2 that the sons of God saw the daughters of men, that they were beautiful; and they took wives for themselves of all whom they chose.

3 And the LORD said, "My Spirit shall not strive with man forever, for he is indeed flesh; yet his days shall be one hundred and twenty years." [**This is not a longevity limitation, as many people lived well beyond this for a thousand years, but is instead the countdown to the Flood.**]

4 There were giants [**Hebrew:** *nephilim*, **which is related to the verb "to fall"; not necessarily giants here as context simply doesn't tell us; all we know is that the later** *nephilim* **in Numbers 13:33**[1] **were giant in stature by their immediate context and their placement with other giant peoples in the land of Canaan**] on the earth in those days, and also afterward, when the sons of God came in to the daughters of men and they bore children to them. Those were the mighty men who were of old, men of renown.

---

1. "There we saw the giants (the descendants of Anak came from the giants); and we were like grasshoppers in our own sight, and so we were in their sight."

5 Then the LORD saw that the wickedness of man was great in the earth, and that every intent of the thoughts of his heart was only evil continually.

6 And the LORD was sorry that He had made man on the earth, and He was grieved in His heart [**not that God was sorry in His unchanging nature or** *will*, **but of his state of** *work* **with man. Matthew Poole rightly asserts about this figure of speech that it is "a common figure called** *anthropopathia*, **whereby also eyes, ears, hands, nose, &c. are ascribed to God; and it signifies an alienation of God's heart and affections from men for their wickedness"**].

7 So the LORD said, "I will destroy man whom I have created from the face of the earth, both man and beast, creeping thing and birds of the air, for I am sorry that I have made them."

8 But Noah found grace in the eyes of the LORD.

9 This is the genealogy of Noah. Noah was a just man, perfect in his generations. Noah walked with God.

10 And Noah begot three sons: Shem, Ham, and Japheth.

11 The earth also was corrupt before God, and the earth was filled with violence.

12 So God looked upon the earth, and indeed it was corrupt; for all flesh had corrupted their way on the earth [**both man and land-dependent animals**].

13 And God said to Noah, "The end of all flesh has come before Me, for the earth is filled with violence through them; and behold, I will destroy them with the earth.

14 "Make yourself an ark of gopherwood [**either a type of wood or a way the wood was worked (think of plywood or pressed wood or a planking style)**]; make rooms in the ark, and cover it inside and outside with pitch [**likely sap/plant-based as opposed to petroleum based, which is largely a product from the Flood**].

15 "And this is how you shall make it: The length of the ark shall be three hundred cubits, its width fifty cubits, and its height thirty cubits [**ancient cubits tended to vary from about 18 inches (short cubits) to 21 inches (long cubits)**].

16 "You shall make a window for the ark [**Hebrew** *tsohar*, **even though it is translated as window, it actually means "noon"**

or "midday." It was a feature that runs the length of the top and middle of the ark to allow lighting and ventilation like a "ridge vent" on a house today], and you shall finish it to a cubit from above; and set the door of the ark in its side. You shall make it with lower, second, and third decks.

17 "And behold, I Myself am bringing floodwaters on the earth, to destroy from under heaven all flesh in which is the breath of life; everything that is on the earth shall die.

18 "But I will establish My covenant with you; and you shall go into the ark — you, your sons, your wife, and your sons' wives with you. [This is a guarantee to Noah that his family would survive the persecution he would receive for following the Lord to be faithful at building the ark and being a preacher of righteousness.]

19 "And of every living thing of all flesh you shall bring two of every sort into the ark, to keep them alive with you; they shall be male and female.

20 "Of the birds after their kind, of animals after their kind, and of every creeping thing of the earth after its kind, two of every kind will come to you to keep them alive. [Kinds are not necessarily to be equated with our modern concept of species, but in most instances are *family* level (or *genus* or *species* in some instances) or in rare cases, an *order* level.]

21 "And you shall take for yourself of all food that is eaten, and you shall gather it to yourself; and it shall be food for you and for them."

22 Thus Noah did; according to all that God commanded him, so he did.

Genesis 7

1 Then the Lord said to Noah, "Come into the ark, you and all your household, because I have seen that you are righteous before Me in this generation.

2 "You shall take with you seven each of every clean animal, a male and his female; two each of animals that are unclean, a male and his female;

3 "also seven each of birds of the air, male and female, to keep the species alive on the face of all the earth.

4 "For after seven more days I will cause it to rain on the earth forty days and forty nights, and I will destroy from the face of the earth all living things that I have made."

5 And Noah did according to all that the LORD commanded him.

6 Noah was six hundred years old when the floodwaters were on the earth.

7 So Noah, with his sons, his wife, and his sons' wives, went into the ark because of the waters of the flood.

8 Of clean animals, of animals that are unclean, of birds, and of everything that creeps on the earth,

9 two by two they went into the ark to Noah, male and female, as God had commanded Noah.

10 And it came to pass after seven days that the waters of the flood were on the earth.

11 In the six hundredth year of Noah's life, in the second month, the seventeenth day of the month, on that day all the fountains of the great deep were broken up, and the windows of heaven were opened.

12 And the rain was on the earth forty days and forty nights. **[Any rain, after this and until the 150th day when the rain was restrained per Genesis 8:2, was not *on the earth*, which was now submerged for a time but the rain was falling on the waters that were currently covering the earth.]**

13 On the very same day Noah and Noah's sons, Shem, Ham, and Japheth, and Noah's wife and the three wives of his sons with them, entered the ark —

14 they and every beast after its kind, all cattle after their kind, every creeping thing that creeps on the earth after its kind, and every bird after its kind, every bird of every sort.

15 And they went into the ark to Noah, two by two, of all flesh in which is the breath of life.

16 So those that entered, male and female of all flesh, went in as God had commanded him; and the LORD shut him in.

17 Now the flood was on the earth forty days. The waters increased and lifted up the ark, and it rose high above the earth.

18 The waters prevailed and greatly increased on the earth, and the ark moved about on the surface of the waters.

19 And the waters prevailed exceedingly on the earth, and all the high hills under the whole heaven were covered.

20 The waters prevailed fifteen cubits upward, and the mountains were covered. [**Clearly, this is a global Flood.**]

21 And all flesh died that moved on the earth: birds and cattle and beasts and every creeping thing that creeps on the earth, and every man.

22 All in whose nostrils was the breath of the spirit of life, all that was on the dry land, died [**that is, all land-dwelling, air-breathing animals that were not on board the ark had died**].

23 So He destroyed all living things which were on the face of the ground: both man and cattle, creeping thing and bird of the air. They were destroyed from the earth. Only Noah and those who were with him in the ark remained alive.

24 And the waters prevailed on the earth one hundred and fifty days.

Genesis 8

1 Then God remembered Noah, and every living thing, and all the animals that were with him in the ark. [**Not that an all-knowing God forgot, but this is** *standing against* **those that died in the Flood in the context immediately above — Genesis 7:21–23.**] And God made a wind to pass over the earth, and the waters subsided.

2 The fountains of the deep and the windows of heaven were also stopped, and the rain from heaven was restrained.

3 And the waters receded continually from the earth. At the end of the hundred and fifty days the waters decreased.

4 Then the ark rested in the seventh month, the seventeenth day of the month, on the mountains of Ararat. [**Take note that this is not necessarily Mt. Ararat, the active volcano that we know today.**]

5 And the waters decreased continually until the tenth month. In the tenth month, on the first day of the month, the tops of the

mountains were seen [*visible*; by either water level reducing and/ or vapor/fog clearing or perhaps a combination of both].

6 So it came to pass, at the end of forty days, that Noah opened the window of the ark which he had made.

7 Then he sent out a raven, which kept going to and fro until the waters had dried up from the earth [a hardy bird that can survive the rough conditions that were still present outside the ark].

8 He also sent out from himself a dove, to see if the waters had receded from the face of the ground.

9 But the dove found no resting place for the sole of her foot, and she returned into the ark to him, for the waters were on the face of the whole earth. So he put out his hand and took her, and drew her into the ark to himself.

10 And he waited yet another seven days, and again he sent the dove out from the ark.

11 Then the dove came to him in the evening, and behold, a freshly plucked olive leaf was in her mouth; and Noah knew that the waters had receded from the earth.

12 So he waited yet another seven days and sent out the dove, which did not return again to him anymore.

13 And it came to pass in the six hundred and first year, in the first month, the first day of the month, that the waters were dried up from the earth; and Noah removed the covering of the ark and looked, and indeed the surface of the ground was dry [note this is just the surface of the ground].

14 And in the second month, on the twenty-seventh day of the month, the earth was dried [note this is the whole earth].

15 Then God spoke to Noah, saying,

16 "Go out of the ark, you and your wife, and your sons and your sons' wives with you.

17 "Bring out with you every living thing of all flesh that is with you: birds and cattle and every creeping thing that creeps on the earth, so that they may abound on the earth, and be fruitful and multiply on the earth."

18 So Noah went out, and his sons and his wife and his sons' wives with him.

19 Every animal, every creeping thing, every bird, and whatever creeps on the earth, according to their families, went out of the ark. [**They did not come out two-by-two, but now by their** *families*, **so there probably was some breeding on the ark — this may be where the term "breed like rabbits" originates!**]

20 Then Noah built an altar to the LORD, and took of every clean animal and of every clean bird, and offered burnt offerings on the altar [**interestingly, this leaves a breeding stock of male and female clean animals for each of Noah's three sons**].

21 And the LORD smelled a soothing aroma. Then the LORD said in His heart, "I will never again curse the ground for man's sake, although the imagination of man's heart is evil from his youth; [**note the differences between this and Genesis 6:5**] nor will I again destroy every living thing as I have done.

22 "While the earth remains, seedtime and harvest, cold and heat, winter and summer, and day and night shall not cease."

Genesis 9:1–20

1 So God blessed Noah and his sons, and said to them: "Be fruitful and multiply, and fill the earth. [**Knowing that God blessed Noah's sons here, which included Ham, could be one of the reasons Noah didn't curse Ham, but instead Ham's son Canaan later in Genesis 9:25.**[2]]

2 "And the fear of you and the dread of you shall be on every beast of the earth, on every bird of the air, on all that move on the earth, and on all the fish of the sea. They are given into your hand.

3 "Every moving thing that lives shall be food for you. I have given you all things, even as the green herbs. [**The original diet was changed. Now God first permits meat to be eaten.**]

4 "But you shall not eat flesh with its life, that is, its blood.

5 "Surely for your lifeblood I will demand a reckoning; from the hand of every beast I will require it, and from the hand of man. From the hand of every man's brother I will require the life of man.

6 "Whoever sheds man's blood, by man his blood shall be shed; for in the image of God He made man.

---

2. Then he said: "Cursed be Canaan; a servant of servants he shall be to his brethren."

7 And as for you, be fruitful and multiply; bring forth abundantly in the earth and multiply in it."

8 Then God spoke to Noah and to his sons with him, saying:

9 "And as for Me, behold, I establish My covenant with you and with your descendants after you,

10 "and with every living creature that is with you: the birds, the cattle, and every beast of the earth with you, of all that go out of the ark, every beast of the earth.

11 "Thus I establish My covenant with you: Never again shall all flesh be cut off by the waters of the flood; never again shall there be a flood to destroy the earth." [**Again, this shows it was a unique event — a global flood, as we have local floods all the time.**]

12 And God said: "This is the sign of the covenant which I make between Me and you, and every living creature that is with you, for perpetual generations:

13 "I set My rainbow in the cloud, and it shall be for the sign of the covenant between Me and the earth.

14 "It shall be, when I bring a cloud over the earth, that the rainbow shall be seen in the cloud; [**not that rainbows were impossible before this, but like bread used in communion, it now has significance and meaning**]

15 "and I will remember My covenant which is between Me and you and every living creature of all flesh; the waters shall never again become a flood to destroy all flesh.

16 "The rainbow shall be in the cloud, and I will look on it to remember the everlasting covenant between God and every living creature of all flesh that is on the earth." [**The rainbow now became a symbol and reminder, like bread and wine for communion.**]

17 And God said to Noah, "This is the sign of the covenant which I have established between Me and all flesh that is on the earth."

18 Now the sons of Noah who went out of the ark were Shem, Ham, and Japheth. And Ham was the father of Canaan.

19 These three were the sons of Noah, and from these the whole earth was populated.

20 And Noah began to be a farmer, and he planted a vineyard.

The Flood and the History of "Millions of Years"

3 | WHY WAS IT NECESSARY TO KILL ALL THOSE *innocent* PEOPLE IN THE FLOOD?

KEN HAM AND BODIE HODGE

Have you heard these questions or even asked them yourself?

- Why would God send a Flood to kill all those people — they weren't that bad?

- How could God kill the innocent children in the Flood — they didn't do anything wrong?

- Why would God kill the animals because of man's actions?

We are surprised how often we have heard these questions. Even within the Church, people struggle with the fact that God sent a Flood to kill everybody (except Noah's family). There are some views floating around that the pre-Flood people really weren't that bad and that God overreacted to judge the world with a global Flood. Let's look at these serious questions in more detail.

Diorama at the Creation Museum showing people stranded as the ark is floating.

were people innocent at the time of the flood?

There is this idea that people are "basically good" and "basically innocent." If you have been in this camp, get ready for a shocking statement — no one is basically good or innocent! Only God is good (Luke 18:19[1]). But why? Couldn't a good God have created a good world?

God *did* make a good world. It was perfect (Deuteronomy 32:4[2]) and very good (Genesis 1:31[3]). But we no longer live in *that* world, but instead, we live in a world that has been cursed due to sin and we have to deal with death and suffering — which is the punishment for sin! This occurred in Genesis 3 (see also Romans 8:19–22[4]). This is why death, suffering, natural evils (disasters like tornadoes, earthquakes, and hurricanes), and atrocities happens. It is a result of judgment on sin. Essentially, we have been given *a taste* of what life is like without God.

When Adam (and Eve) sinned, the punishment was ultimately death (Genesis 2:17,[5] 3:19[6]). Because of this, we all sin too as we were in Adam when he sinned and so we have sin nature (yes, we all came from Adam). This is why we are prone to sin too. We have sinful flesh (Romans 8:3[7]) and sinful minds from the moment we are conceived/fertilized (Genesis 8:21,[8] Psalm 51:5,[9] Jeremiah 17:9,[10] Colossians 1:21,[11] etc.).

---

1. So Jesus said to him, "Why do you call Me good? No one is good but One, that is, God."
2. He is the Rock, His work is perfect; for all His ways are justice, a God of truth and without injustice; righteous and upright is He.
3. Then God saw everything that He had made, and indeed it was very good. So the evening and the morning were the sixth day.
4. For the earnest expectation of the creation eagerly waits for the revealing of the sons of God. For the creation was subjected to futility, not willingly, but because of Him who subjected it in hope; because the creation itself also will be delivered from the bondage of corruption into the glorious liberty of the children of God. For we know that the whole creation groans and labors with birth pangs together until now.
5. "But of the tree of the knowledge of good and evil you shall not eat, for in the day that you eat of it you shall surely die."
6. "In the sweat of your face you shall eat bread till you return to the ground, for out of it you were taken; for dust you are, and to dust you shall return."
7. For what the law could not do in that it was weak through the flesh, God did by sending His own Son in the likeness of sinful flesh, on account of sin: He condemned sin in the flesh.
8. And the LORD smelled a soothing aroma. Then the LORD said in His heart, "I will never again curse the ground for man's sake, although the imagination of man's heart is evil from his youth; nor will I again destroy every living thing as I have done."
9. Behold, I was brought forth in iniquity, and in sin my mother conceived me.
10. The heart is deceitful above all things, and desperately wicked; who can know it?
11. And you, who once were alienated and enemies in your mind by wicked works, yet now He has reconciled.

And this is why everyone eventually dies. Really, when people ask why God judged the people of Noah's day with death, it's the wrong question — the point is everyone is under the judgment of death. The right question to ask is why it was the time for these people of Noah's day to die.

Ever since sin with Adam and Eve in the Garden of Eden, people have been prone to evil and sin. So is anyone innocent because we are all sinners? No. This is confirmed in Romans 3:23[12] as well, since we have all sinned and fallen short of the glory of God.

With this foundation in mind, what were the people like before the Flood? God tells us:

> Then the LORD saw that the wickedness of man was great in the earth, and that every intent of the thoughts of his heart was only evil continually (Genesis 6:5).

> The earth also was corrupt before God, and the earth was filled with violence. So God looked upon the earth, and indeed it was corrupt; for all flesh had corrupted their way on the earth (Genesis 6:11–12).

No one was innocent in the sight of God anyway. Now imagine the cannibalism, rape, murder, child sacrifice, and so on. Yet God was patient. He gave a 120-year countdown to the Flood (Genesis 6:3[13]) and even sent a preacher of righteousness (2 Peter 2:5[14]). There was no excuse not to repent. The judgment was righteous.

BUT WHAT ABOUT THE CHILDREN — AREN'T THEY INNOCENT?

A Christian lady once pleaded with me that she, "just couldn't see how God could send the Flood knowing that innocent children would die in the Flood." As we have seen before, none are innocent (Romans 3:23[15]). The punishment for sin is death, and even at conception a baby can die as we sadly see quite often with miscarriages and rampant abortion in today's secular culture. We have to remember that we are all already judged with death.

---

12. For all have sinned and fall short of the glory of God.
13. And the LORD said, "My Spirit shall not strive with man forever, for he is indeed flesh; yet his days shall be one hundred and twenty years."
14. And did not spare the ancient world, but saved Noah, one of eight people, a preacher of righteousness, bringing in the flood on the world of the ungodly.
15. For all have sinned and fall short of the glory of God.

It would be impossible for someone who is sinless to die — even our sinless Christ could not have died had He not taken our sin upon Him. Christ became sin for us (2 Corinthians 5:21[16]) and bore the punishment that we deserve for sin on the Cross — through His shed blood (1 Peter 2:24[17]).

There is a misconception that children are innocent of sin, but this is not true. They can be wicked, violent, corrupt, and have evil thoughts all the time. Parents often concur that this is true! This is why parents are so important when training their children. But we know from the Bible that all were corrupt, evil, violent, and so on. This includes children. And children can further develop these habits from their parents if not trained in righteousness. If the Word of God was not impressed upon children, then false humanistic views were impressed upon the kids (Deuteronomy 11:19[18])!

But let's just consider for a moment a theoretical situation. *If* there were righteous children — why would they not be on the ark? Noah was the only one found righteous at the onset of the Flood (Genesis 7:1[19]). But further, who was it who kept these children from entering the door of the ark? It was their unrighteous parents or guardians. So one should not misplace the responsibility of the parents/guardians and try to say God was the one who didn't send a means of salvation for the children! Keep in mind that the children were not innocent by the time the Flood came. And their parents, being unrighteous themselves, were surely encouraging them in their sin!

God did send a means of salvation with the ark for the righteous. But it was the parents of those children who were so unrighteous, that they refused to even give their children an opportunity but impressed upon them sin as well — that is what we expect from those whose every thought is evil all the time.

Consider another issue. How many children were alive at the time of the Flood? When a civilization becomes evil, who usually pays the price first? It

---

16. For He made Him who knew no sin to be sin for us, that we might become the righteousness of God in Him.

17. Who Himself bore our sins in His own body on the tree, that we, having died to sins, might live for righteousness — by whose stripes you were healed.

18. You shall teach them to your children, speaking of them when you sit in your house, when you walk by the way, when you lie down, and when you rise up.

19. Then the LORD said to Noah, "Come into the ark, you and all your household, because I have seen that you are righteous before Me in this generation."

is the children and babies. How many ancient cultures killed or sacrificed children? Far too many!

In the Bible, we find evil people like Pharaoh of Egypt trying to kill baby boys through the midwives when they were born. Then Pharaoh threw them into the Nile — little did Pharaoh know that his own son and his army of Egyptians would later be drowned by God in the Red Sea! Herod murdered children. Canaanites (Leviticus 18) and later the Israelites (Jeremiah 32:35[20]) sacrificed their children to Molech, a false god. A few others include Carthage and the Incan and Aztec cultures.

In our own evil day, the German Nazis, led by Adolf Hitler, killed adults and children in terrible manners to build their "thousand-year Reich." And even the USA, China, England, France, and many other countries regularly practice abortion, the sacrifice of babies for their own selfish purposes in hopes to make their own lives better, which is exactly what ancient sacrifices were supposed to do too! Many of those who accuse the Christian God of being a "genocidal god" because of the Flood, support the genocidal killing of millions of children in their mother's wombs, which is a double standard fallacy!

With a broken heart, we see sacrifice of children in our day all the time, and yet the culture before the Flood was so bad that God judged them with the Flood. Were there even any children left? People were trying to make a name for *themselves*, not their children (Genesis 6:4,[21] "men of renown")! If the whole world were murderers, the population of the world cuts in half in one day, and who were prime targets? The children most likely were the first to receive the brunt of this attack! Evil people rarely want the responsibility of raising children; the kids often get in their way.

Regardless, our Creator God, who is a just God, had every right to enact His judgment as He determined.

WHY DID ANIMALS GET JUDGED?

We often believe that animals are entirely innocent creatures to their actions. But are they? The serpent in the Garden of Eden, an instrument of Satan,

---

20. And they built the high places of Baal which are in the Valley of the Son of Hinnom, to cause their sons and their daughters to pass through the fire to Molech, which I did not command them, nor did it come into My mind that they should do this abomination, to cause Judah to sin.

21. There were giants on the earth in those days, and also afterward, when the sons of God came in to the daughters of men and they bore children to them. Those were the mighty men who were of old, men of renown.

was still cursed for its involvement (Genesis 3:14[22]). In the Law of Moses, if a man or woman had sexual relations with an animal, both they and the animal were to be put to death (e.g., Leviticus 20:15–16[23]). If an ox kills someone in Mosaic Law, the animal must be put to death (Exodus 21:28–29[24]). Let us put it this way: animals get their due as well.

The Bible says:

> So God looked upon the earth, and indeed it was corrupt;
> for all flesh had corrupted their way on the earth (Genesis 6:12).

This means that all animals (i.e., all flesh) *had* corrupted themselves on the earth, not just humanity. Animals were originally to be vegetarian (Genesis 1:30[25]), and many were likely corrupting themselves by being meat eaters. Many animals may have been corrupted to be homosexual in their actions (defying their ordinance to be fruitful and multiply in Genesis 1) or attacking people (some of these corruptions could be by the influence of demons, consider Mark 5:12[26]).

Let us also not forget that man had dominion over the animals (Genesis 1:26–28[27]). So if the dominion of man falls, so do the things under that dominion. When Hitler made a decision to begin WWII, that decision affected his whole dominion. Did that mean that the animals within Hitler's dominion were not affected by his decision? By no means. When those who

---

22. So the LORD God said to the serpent: "Because you have done this, you are cursed more than all cattle, and more than every beast of the field; on your belly you shall go, and you shall eat dust all the days of your life."

23. If a man mates with an animal, he shall surely be put to death, and you shall kill the animal. If a woman approaches any animal and mates with it, you shall kill the woman and the animal. They shall surely be put to death. Their blood is upon them.

24. If an ox gores a man or a woman to death, then the ox shall surely be stoned, and its flesh shall not be eaten; but the owner of the ox shall be acquitted. But if the ox tended to thrust with its horn in times past, and it has been made known to his owner, and he has not kept it confined, so that it has killed a man or a woman, the ox shall be stoned and its owner also shall be put to death.

25. "Also, to every beast of the earth, to every bird of the air, and to everything that creeps on the earth, in which there is life, I have given every green herb for food"; and it was so.

26. So all the demons begged Him, saying, "Send us to the swine, that we may enter them."

27. Then God said, "Let Us make man in Our image, according to Our likeness; let them have dominion over the fish of the sea, over the birds of the air, and over the cattle, over all the earth and over every creeping thing that creeps on the earth." So God created man in His own image; in the image of God He created him; male and female He created them. Then God blessed them, and God said to them, "Be fruitful and multiply; fill the earth and subdue it; have dominion over the fish of the sea, over the birds of the air, and over every living thing that moves on the earth."

had dominion (man) were to be judged with the global Flood, their whole dominion fell (including animals). But consider this oft-overlooked point: the animal kinds aboard the ark were saved from judgment too.

CONCLUSION

Keep in mind that God is a righteous judge. He knew the hearts of everyone who was judged in the Flood and it was a *righteous* judgment. Who are we to proclaim, in any measure, that the judgment on wicked and violent people prior to the Flood was unjust? And by what standard would we be judging? It would be our own arbitrary, fallible, sinful standard.

> I see the treacherous, and am disgusted, because they do not keep Your word. Consider how I love Your precepts; revive me, O Lord, according to Your lovingkindness. The entirety of Your word is truth, and every one of Your righteous judgments endures forever (Psalm 119:158–160).

So was the Flood necessary? Yes! And it was a *righteous* judgment on sinners who refused to repent and wallowed in their sin. They loved sin more than they loved God, so there was no longer any reason for them to continue to reap the good benefits from a good God. A very violent group of anti-God people were met with a very violent Flood . . . a fitting means of cleansing vindication for those they killed and harmed for so long.

4 | FLOOD LEGENDS

BODIE HODGE

When we start with the Bible, the Flood of Noah's day was an actual historical event about 4,350 years ago. Outside the Bible, do we expect that cultures around the world retained this history to one degree or another? Yes we do. Let me start with some context.

BABEL

After the Flood, there was another significant event when God confused the language of the whole world, because people were trying to defy God. They were refusing to listen to God's command to fill the earth (Genesis 9:1[1]). Instead they came together and built a city and tower at Babel to try to keep them from filling the earth (Genesis 11:4[2]).

So God came down and confused their language, and different families came out of Babel speaking differently. These language families continued to change into the various languages we have today.[3]

But what is significant about the splitting at Babel with regard to the Flood? It simply means that people went in various directions, taking their history of the world (Genesis 1–11) to different parts of the globe.

---

1. So God blessed Noah and his sons, and said to them: "Be fruitful and multiply, and fill the earth."
2. And they said, "Come, let us build ourselves a city, and a tower whose top is in the heavens; let us make a name for ourselves, lest we be scattered abroad over the face of the whole earth."
3. For more on this subject see Bodie Hodge, *Tower of Babel* (Green Forest, AR: Master Books, 2013).

We expect details of this history to be lost in some instances, embellished in some instances, major events lost all together, names changed (it was language change, after all), local animals to be inserted (e.g., duck instead of a dove as in Genesis 8:11[4]), local mountains to replace the mountains of Ararat (Genesis 8:4[5]), etc. to replace places in the accounts and so on.

Thus, we expect that these cultures retain some of the true history of the Flood one way or another. But we seriously doubt they will have kept the entire account error free. Of course, the Bible records the true account because the Holy Spirit, who is God, inspired the account through Moses.[6]

HOW MANY FLOOD LEGENDS?

So what do have? There are somewhere between 300 and 500 Flood legends worldwide. I prefer to say "over 300," and you'll see why in a moment. But why the range in the first place? Simply put, we keep finding more.

Allow me to explain. You can research and easily find about 200 Flood legends without extensive research. Dr. John Morris of the Institute for Creation Research has done this.[7] So has Japanese researcher Nozomi Osanai for her Master's thesis at Wesley Biblical Seminary.[8] In fact, *I've* done this too! Though there were more, I read over 200 flood accounts when researching a family book that I co-authored with Laura Welch on flood legends (*The Flood of Noah, Legends and Lore of Survival,* Master Books, 2014).

In years past, various researchers would tally a few of these together in books on Native American history, Aboriginal Australian culture, or various other regional cultures. In other cases, you would find one legend here or there. You need to understand that we are just now living in an era when many of these are being tallied together. Few books and resources were

---

4. Then the dove came to him in the evening, and behold, a freshly plucked olive leaf was in her mouth; and Noah knew that the waters had receded from the earth.

5. Then the ark rested in the seventh month, the seventeenth day of the month, on the mountains of Ararat.

6. Terry Mortenson and Bodie Hodge, "Did Moses Write Genesis?" in *How Do We Know the Bible Is True? Volume 1*, Ken Ham and Bodie Hodge, gen. eds. (Green Forest, AR: Master Books, 2011), p. 85–102.

7. John Morris, "Why Does Nearly Every Culture Have a Tradition of a Global Flood?" *Acts & Facts* 30 (9), 2001, http://www.icr.org/article/why-does-nearly-every-culture-have-tradition-globa/.

8. Nozomi Osanai, "A Comparative Study of the Flood Accounts in the Gilgamesh Epic and Genesis," Wesley Biblical Seminary, reprinted on Answers in Genesis, August, 3, 2005, https://answersingenesis.org/the-flood/flood-legends/flood-gilgamesh-epic/.

all-encompassing when it comes to Flood legends. And this makes sense as more come to light each year.

For example, I met two missionaries who visited the Creation Museum while on furlough from their missions work. They are missionaries who are the first contact with certain tribes in the Amazon. At the time, they were the first in contact with two different tribes. I asked if those tribes had a Flood or creation legend. They said the tribes did and they even had a legend where the languages split apart too! The missionaries told me that they were unaware if any of their co-missionaries with these tribes had documented this yet. Of course, I encouraged them to make sure to do so in the future so there is a record of it. But this outlines that new Flood legends (as well as Babel and creation legends) are still being ascertained even now.

Even though people did tally some Flood accounts in the past (1918 and 1931),[9] let's just look at more modern numbers. In 1961, researchers Drs. Henry Morris and John Whitcomb looked into this subject saying there were "scores and hundreds"[10] of these legends. Later, others used round numbers like 200. Even later, as research afforded, people recorded what they could find as actual numbers. For example, Dr. Duane Gish and Gloria Clanin, researching for children's books, were confident enough to state 270 Flood stories in 1992[11] and 1996.[12]

Since this time, numbers have gone up again to a point that Laura Welch (Senior Editor for Christian publisher Master Books) and I were able to confidently state from over 300 to upward of 500 legends in the family book on Flood legends. Even evolutionists have concurred that the number of Flood stories could be as high as 500.[13]

Our preference is to be safer with the count and say "over 300" as opposed to say "nearly 500." Why, you might ask? The reason is that most of the legends I found clearly spoke of a *global* Flood. But there were a handful that we could not discern if they were speaking of a global Flood or a local Flood. So it wouldn't surprise me if a small portion of Flood legends are discussing a

9. For example, Bryan Nelson, *The Deluge Story in Stone* (Augsburg, MN, 1931) or Sir James Frazer, *Folk-Lore in the Old Testament* (London, England: Macmillan & Co., Ltd., 1918).

10. John Whitcomb and Henry Morris, *The Genesis Flood* (Phillipsburg, NJ: P&R Publishing, 1961), p. 48.

11. Duane Gish, *Dinosaurs by Design* (Green Forest, AR: Master Books, 1992), p. 74.

12. Gloria Clanin, *In the days of Noah* (Green Forest, AR: Master Books, 1996), p. 60.

13. Robert Schoch, *Voyages of the Pyramid Builders* (New York, NY: Jeremy P. Tarcher/Penguin, 2003), p. 249.

flood in their history, but not necessarily the deviated accounts of the Flood of Noah. So I prefer to err on the side of a conservative number, not the maximum number. I would encourage others to be diligent in this as well.

WHAT ARE SOME OF THESE FLOOD LEGENDS?

Whole volumes of books could be written if we put every account into one volume. Many accounts are nearly chapter-length in duration! So instead, here are excerpts and recounts from a few shorter examples from various parts of the world to "whet your appetite."

Aztec Legend of the Flood

> A man named Tapi lived a long time ago. Tapi was a very pious man. The creator told Tapi to build a boat that he would live in. He was told that he should take his wife, a pair of every animal that was alive into this boat. Naturally everyone thought he was crazy. Then the rain started and the flood came. The men and animals tried to climb the mountains but the mountains became flooded as well. Finally the rain ended. Tapi decided that the water had dried up when he let a dove loose that did not return.[14]

Hawaiian Legend of the Flood

> Hawaiians have a flood story that tells of a time when, long after the death of the first man, the world became a wicked, terrible place. Only one good man was left, and his name was Nu-u. He made a great canoe with a house on it and filled it with animals. In this story, the waters came up over all the earth and killed all the people; only Nu-u and his family were saved.[15]

Chinese Legend of the Flood

> Another flood story is from China. It records that Fuhi, his wife, three sons, and three daughters escaped a great flood and were the only people alive on earth. After the great flood, they repopulated the world.[16]

---

14. Flood Legends from around the world, http://www.nwcreation.net/noahlegends.html.
15. Monty White, "Flood Legends," March 29, 2007, https://answersingenesis.org/the-flood/flood-legends/flood-legends/.
16. Ibid.

Miao Legend of the Flood

So it poured forty days in sheets and in torrents.
Then fifty-five days of misting and drizzle.
The waters surmounted the mountains and ranges.
The deluge ascending leapt valley and hollow.
An earth with no earth upon which to take refuge!
A world with no foothold where one might subsist!
The people were baffled, impotent and ruined,
Despairing, horror stricken, diminished and finished.
But the Patriarch Nuah was righteous.
The Matriarch Gaw Bo-lu-en upright.
Built a boat very wide. Made a ship very vast.
Their household entire got aboard and were floated,
The family complete rode the deluge in safety.
The animals with him were female and male.
The birds went along and were mated in pairs.
When the time was fulfilled, God commanded the waters.
The day had arrived, the flood waters receded.
Then Nuah liberated a dove from their refuge,
Sent a bird to go forth and bring again tidings.
The flood had gone down into lake and to ocean;
The mud was confined to the pools and the hollows."
There was land once again where a man might reside;
There was a place in the earth now to rear habitations.
Buffalo then were brought, an oblation to God,
Fatter cattle became sacrifice to the Mighty.
The Divine One then gave them His blessing;
Their God then bestowed His good graces.[17]

Tanzania Legend of the Flood

Once upon a time the rivers began to flood. The god told two
people to get into a ship. He told them to take lots of seed and to
take lots of animals. The water of the flood eventually covered the
mountains. Finally the flood stopped. Then one of the men, wanting to know if the water had dried up let a dove loose. The dove

17. Ernest Truax, "Genesis According to the Miao People," *Acts & Facts* 20 (4) 1991, http://
www.icr.org/article/genesis-according-miao-people/.

returned. Later he let loose a hawk which did not return. Then the men left the boat and took the animals and the seeds with them.[18]

NaMeS OF NOaH . . . anD HIS WIFe?

Another fascinating aspect of Flood legends is to see the various names of Noah and his wife. Recall that after Babel many patriarchs at Babel often had new names applied to them from the various languages that came out of Babel. Here are 20 (of the many) of variants of Noah's name.

Names of Noah in Various Ancient Cultures

	Name	Culture	Authority/Reference
1	Noah*	Israel	Genesis 6–9.
2	Noes/Noe	Germany and Scandinavia	Wright, ed., *Reliiquae Antiquae*, 1841–1845, copy at London's Guildhall Library, Aldermanbury, p. 173.**
3	Noeh	Ireland	Annals of Clonmacnois
4	Nuah	Maio (China)	E.A. Truax, "Genesis According to the Miao People," *Acts & Facts*. 20 (4) 1991.
5	Deucalion	Greece	e.g., Apollodorus, 1.7.2.
6	Titan	Celtic	B. Sproul, *Primal Myths* (New York: HarperOne Publisher, 1979).
7	Ziusudra	Sumeria	D. Hammerly-Dupuy, *Some Observations on the Assyro-Babylonian and Sumerian Flood Stories* (Lima, Peru: Colegio Union, 1968).
8	Atrahasis	Babylonia	S. Dalley, *Myths from Mesopotamia* (Oxford: Oxford University Press, 1989).
9	Xisuthrus	Chaldea	G. Smith, "The Chaldean Account of the Deluge," *Transactions of the Society of Biblical Archaeology*, 2:213–34. 1873.

---

18. "Flood Legends from Around the World," http://www.nwcreation.net/noahlegends.html.

10	Tumbainot (and wife Naipande)	East Africa (Masai people)	J.G. Frazier, *The Golden Bough* (Hertfordshire: Wordsworth Editions Ltd., 1993).
11	Nama	Central Asia	U. Holmburg, "Finno-Ugric, Siberian," in C.J.A. MacCulloch, ed., *The Mythology of All Races v. IV* (Boston, MA: Marshall Jones, 1927).
12	Manu	India	T.H. Gaster, *Myth, Legend, and Custom in the Old Testament* (New York, NY: Harper & Row, 1969).
13	Nol	Pacific Island (Loyalty Islands)	Gaster, p. 107.
14	Nu'u	Hawaii	D.B. Barrere, *The Kumuhonua Legends: A Study of Late 19th Century Hawaiian Stories of Creation and Origins,* Pacific Anthropological Records, No. 3, Bishop Museum, Honolulu, HI, 1969, p. 19–21.
15	Kunyan	Alaska	Gaster, p. 117–118.
16	Wissaketchak	Cree (Native Americans)	Frazier, p. 309–310.
17	Nanaboujou	Ottawa (Native Americans)	Frazier, p. 308.
18	Montezuma	Papago (Native Americans)	Gaster, p. 114–115.
19	Tezpi	Mexico (Michoacan)	Gaster, p. 122.
20	Marerewana	Guyana (South America)	Gaster, p. 126.

* Several cultures actually still retained the name "Noah."

** See also: MS. Cotton, Otho. B. XI., cit. Magoun, p. 249; Assersius, *De Rebus Gestis Alfredi* (Ed. Stevenson, Oxford, 1904), Cap I; Vetustissima Regum Septentrionis Series Langfethgatal dicta, *Scriptores Rerum Danicarum Medii AEvi*, Ed., Jacobus Langebek, Vol. I, Hafniae, 1772, p. 1–6.

We even find names of Noah's wife in some instances. There are well over 100 accounts that give a name for Noah's wife.[19] Keep in mind that the Bible doesn't specifically reveal Noah's wife's name. Listed below are a few examples of Noah's wife's name given in Flood legends. In some cases, you can recognize similarities (e.g., Emzara, Amzurah, and Noyemzar; or Haykêl and Haikal).

Names of Noah's Wife in Various Ancient Cultures

	Name	Culture	Reference/ Authority
1	*Emzara*, daughter of Rake'el, son of Methu-selah	Judea	*Book of Jubilees*
2	*Haykêl*, the daughter of Namûs (or Namousa), the daughter of Enoch, the brother of Methu-selah	Arabia	*Kitab al-Magall* (the Book of Rolls)
3	*Noyemzar* (variants: Nemzar, or Noyanzar)	Armenia	The Bible Cyclope-dia*
4	Set	Latium (Italy)	*Inventiones Nomi-num*
5	*Naamah*, the daughter of Lamech and sister of Tubal-Cain (from Gene-sis 4:22**)	Judea	*Genesis Rabba* midrash
6	*Haykêl*, the daughter of Namûs (or Namousa), the daughter of Enoch, the brother of Methu-selah	Syria	*Book of the Cave of Treasures*
7	*Dalila* (Variant *Dalida*)	Angles and Sax-ons (Germany and England)	Dialogue of *Solo-mon and Saturn*
8	*Haikal*, the daughter of Abaraz, of the daugh-ters of the sons of Enos	Ethiopia/Cush	*Conflict of Adam and Eve with Satan*

19. E.g., Francis Lee Utley, "The One Hundred and Three Names of Noah's Wife," The University of Chicago Press, *Speculum*, Vol. 16, No. 4 (Oct., 1941), p. 426–452.

9	*Gaw Bo-lu-en*	China (Maio)	Edgar Truax on Maio recitations***
10	*Haykêl, the daughter of Namûs (or Namousa), the daughter of Enoch, the brother of Methuselah*	Upper Egypt	*Patriarch Eutychius of Alexandria*
11	*Phiapphara*	Angles and Saxons (Germany and England)	Ælfric of Eynsham's translation of the first 7 books of the Bible (Heptateuch)
12	*Amzurah, the daughter of Barakil, another son of Mehujael*	Persia (Iran)	Persian historian Muhammad ibn Jarir al-Tabari
13	*Percoba*	Ireland	*Codex Junius*

   * *The Bible Cyclopedia*, Volume 2 (London: Harrison and Co.; John W. Parker, 1843), p. 735.

  ** "And as for Zillah, she also bore Tubal-Cain, an instructor of every craftsman in bronze and iron. And the sister of Tubal-Cain was Naamah."

 *** E.A. Truax, "Genesis According to the Miao People," *Acts & Facts*, 20 (4) 1991.

Conclusion

Flood legends are an excellent confirmation of what we expected to find in a biblical worldview. Consider the converse. In an evolutionary story with millions of years where there was supposedly no global flood, there shouldn't be any global flood stories. So why would *anyone* have a massive global flood account in their history? Is it because they live near a river and see little floods? This gets even more troubling when you realize that many of these legends are by cultures in super dry deserts and mountainous regions where Floods simply do not occur!

Flood legends are also useful in witnessing the true history of the world as a foundation to the Gospel. You can use these Flood, creation, or Tower of Babel legends[20] from cultures' own histories as a steppingstone to the truth in Genesis. Commend these people's ancestors for trying to hold on to that foundational history, as it is important to set the foundation of the Gospel.

20. For more Tower of Babel legends see Bodie Hodge, *Tower of Babel* (Green Forest, AR: Master Books, 2013), p. 221–226.

It is a powerful way to witness to people as a foundation to point to the work of Christ on the Cross. Genesis can be used as a steppingstone to reveal that we are all connected to our Creator who came to save us from sin and death that was founded in that same history from our common grandparents, Adam and Eve.

5 | A CHANGING VIEW OF THE FLOOD EVIDENCE

KEN HAM AND BODIE HODGE

ANALOGY TO GET STARTED

Let's say you eyewitnessed a catastrophe such as a volcano blowing its top — like Mount St. Helens did in 1980 (and erupting again in 1982). Then you, being a trustworthy and qualified person, documented it properly (wrote down what happened in detail). You documented that the eruption laid down rock layers quickly in a matter of hours for example or that it carved out canyons in a subsequent eruption in 1982 in about one day.

Now let's say that 100 years later, geologists decide that Mount St. Helens never did erupt and there was no catastrophe that affected things around it. Then these same scientists decide to report that the rock layers (from the eruption) were *not* laid down by an eruption but instead were laid down slowly over long periods of time . . . perhaps millions of years.

Furthermore, they decide the canyons were actually evidence of slow gradual erosion, but definitely not from volcanic action! After all, they don't see Mount St. Helens erupting, so they assume it never had.

Then they criticize you for "making up fairy tales about Mount St. Helens" when you "*falsely*" claim that it actually erupted! Let's say they go so far as to get laws passed to refuse to allow anyone to consider that Mount St. Helens actually did erupt in 1980 in public arenas like state schools or museums that are state funded.

Sounds ludicrous, doesn't it? Do you realize this follows exactly what happened with regard to God's eyewitness account of the Flood of Noah and its evidence in our modern time? Let's take a look.

41

HOW DID PEOPLE VIEW THE FLOOD PRIOR TO THE 1800S?

God's account is the eyewitness account of the Flood. This Flood finds its confirmation all over the world in historical accounts. Having seen immense Flood legends in the historical accounts of cultures all over the world, it is rather safe to say that cultures all over the world held to a global Flood in their past. This is expected since the Bible is true.[1] As Noah's descendants scattered across the globe (Genesis 11:1–9), these people took their history of the Flood with them and it varied and deviated due to the effects of sin.

Ancient historians like Josephus the Jew, Berosus the Chaldean, Hieronymus the Egyptian, Mnaseas, and Nicolaus of Damascus (Josephus even mentions these last four) discussed a powerful flood that occurred in their past.

Ancient Greek historians like Xenophanes, Herodotus, Eratosthenes, and Strabo all commented on fossils being from a significant *water* event in the past (not always to the extent of biblical proportions but they understood the point). Naturally, Christians and Jews (and even Muslims) were still following what Genesis says occurred in the past regarding a global Flood, and likewise held to the Flood as the mechanism for the bulk of the fossil formation.

The connections between fossils and the Flood are obvious. From a biblical perspective, we expect to find trillions of things buried by a water-based sediment in the rock layers. For thousands of years, Flood layers were readily viewed as just that . . . Flood layers. Rock layers that contain fossils are primarily from the Flood of Noah and this was not really in much dispute in ages past.

Now, we want to add a caveat. Did you notice that we said "rock layers that contain fossils are *primarily* from the Flood"? Why did we say that? The reason is that we have had some fossil layers *since* the time of the Flood. There have been local catastrophes that have added layers of fossils in some local regions. This could be from local floods, tsunamis, volcanoes, earthquakes, and so on. Of course, the bulk came from the judgment of the Flood in Noah's day.

Due to respect and authority for Genesis, it was readily seen throughout the Western World, Middle East, and many other places as the true

---

1. Keep in mind that if an evolutionary history was true, there should be *no* global flood legends!

source of history including the Flood. But even though the majority readily recognized that the Flood easily explains rock layers that contained fossils, something major happened! All of this was about to change.

The Great Turning Point

In the late 1700s and early 1800s, there was a movement to leave the Bible out of the subject of rock layers. In other words, they wanted to leave God out of it. God is the ultimate eyewitness. Not only did He create all things, knows all things, upholds all things, and has always been there, but He cannot lie either! What greater person to document things of the past than God? Through Moses, God the Holy Spirit recorded the events of the past regarding the Flood.

Certain people attacked God and said not to trust what God said. Instead, they rejected that a global Flood occurred by appealing to fallible and imperfect ideas of man making guesses about the past.

When the debate had simmered down, the predominant thought in the 1800s was that all the fossil rock layers were laid down slowly and gradually (without any catastrophes) over millions of years. They said the fossil layers were made by slow accumulations throughout supposed long ages. This is called "uniformitarianism." This is because things supposedly formed in a *uniform* fashion, without catastrophes (i.e., slowly over a long time).

In other words, these people said to reject God's eyewitness account (making man out to be greater than God, by the way) and say that Noah's Flood is a farce (not true). Having seen many geological catastrophes in my own lifetime, it is a *hard pill to swallow* to believe that there were no catastrophes in the past. But nonetheless, people actually fell for this strange idea!

Believe it or not, the secularists have even succeeded in passing laws that forbid the freedom of teaching about the global Flood in the state classroom or by state-sponsored places for fear of getting fired and sued! Sounds ludicrous, but this has occurred! The secularists did to the Flood exactly what occurred in our example at the opening of this chapter about Mount St. Helens!

So, to summarize, fossils layers from the Flood of Noah's day came under attack and people arbitrarily decided there were no major catastrophes (and certainly not a global flood) in the past. They decided that these rock layers that have fossils (fossiliferous) were laid down slowly and gradually over millions of years.

The secularists openly claimed God got it wrong and then pushed for legislation that made it illegal for the state or state schools or state-sponsored places to teach the global Flood from the Bible. Does this mean that the rock layers really were laid down slowly over millions of years and there was no global Flood? By no means! It just means some people are forced to teach only the secular humanistic religion (the common religion of the day that teaches that man supersedes God).

Furthermore, it means that many kids are not allowed to hear the truth, but only a false religious view that is being imposed on generations of unsuspecting kids. The rest of us (i.e., Christians) are not so limited, but have an obligation and freedom to teach the truth. It is time to get back to the truth and stop worrying about the false secular religion that has permeated our society.

6 | BIBLICALLY, HOW OLD IS THE EARTH?

BODIE HODGE

The question of the age of the earth has produced heated discussions on Internet debate boards, classrooms, TV, radio, and in many churches, Christian colleges, and seminaries. The primary sides are:

- Young-earth proponents (biblical age of the earth and universe of about 6,000 years)[1]

- Old-earth proponents (secular age of the earth of about 4.5 billion years and a universe about 14 billion years old)[2]

The difference is immense! Let's give a little history of where the *biblical calculation* came from. We will discuss the old earth development in the subsequent chapter.

WHERE DID A YOUNG-EARTH WORLDVIEW COME FROM?

Simply put, it came from the Bible. Of course, the Bible doesn't say explicitly anywhere, "The earth is 6,000 years old." Good thing it doesn't; otherwise it would be out of date the following year. But we wouldn't expect an all-knowing God to make that kind of a mistake.

God gave us something better. In essence, He gave us a "birth certificate." For example, using a personal birth certificate, a person can calculate

---

1. Not all young-earth creationists agree on this age. Some have slight variation to this number.
2. Some of these old-earth proponents accept molecules-to-man biological evolution and so are called theistic evolutionists. Others reject neo-Darwinian evolution but accept the evolutionary timescale for astronomical and geological evolution, and hence agree with the evolutionary order of events in history.

how old he is at any point. It is similar with the earth. Genesis 1 says that the earth was created on the first day of creation (Genesis 1:1–5). From there, we can begin to calculate the age of the earth.

Let's do a rough calculation to show how this works. The age of the earth can be estimated by taking the first five days of creation (from earth's creation to Adam), then following the genealogies from Adam to Abraham in Genesis 5 and 11, then adding in the time from Abraham to today.

Adam was created on day 6, so there were five days before him. If we add up the dates from Adam to Abraham, we get about 2,000 years, using the Masoretic Hebrew text of Genesis 5 and 11.[3] Whether Christian or secular, most scholars would agree that Abraham lived about 2,000 B.C. (4,000 years ago). So a simple calculation is:

$$
\begin{array}{r}
5 \text{ days} \\
+ \sim 2000 \text{ years} \\
+ \sim 4000 \text{ years} \\
\hline
\sim 6000 \text{ years}
\end{array}
$$

At this point, the first five days are negligible. Quite a few people have done this calculation using the Masoretic text (which is what most English translations are based on) and, with careful attention to the biblical details, have arrived at the same time frame of about 6,000 years, or about 4000 B.C. Two of the most popular, and perhaps best, are a recent work by Floyd Jones[4] and a much earlier book by James Ussher[5] (1581–1656). See table 1.

Table 1: Jones and Ussher

Name	Age Calculated	Reference and Date
James Ussher	4004 B.C.	*The Annals of the World,* A.D. 1658
Floyd Nolan Jones	4004 B.C.	*The Chronology of the Old Testament*, A.D. 1993

The misconception exists that Ussher and Jones were the only ones to arrive at a date of 4000 B.C.; however, this is not the case at all. Jones[6] lists several

3. Bodie Hodge, "Ancient Patriarchs in Genesis," Answers in Genesis, https://answersingenesis. org/bible-characters/ancient-patriarchs-in-genesis/.

4. Floyd Nolan Jones, *Chronology of the Old Testament* (Green Forest, AR: Master Books, 2005).

5. James Ussher, *The Annals of the World* (Green Forest, AR: Master Books, 2003), translated by Larry and Marion Pierce.

6. Jones, *Chronology of the Old Testament*, p. 26.

chronologists who have undertaken the task of calculating the age of the earth based on the Bible, and their calculations range from 5501 to 3836 B.C. A few are listed in table 2 with a couple of newer ones and their references.

Table 2: Chronologists' Calculations

Chronologist	When Calculated?	Date B.C.
Julius Africanus	**c. 240**	**5501**
George Syncellus	**c. 810**	**5492**
John Jackson	**1752**	**5426**
Dr William Hales	**c. 1830**	**5411**
Eusebius	c. 330	5199
Benjamin Shaw	2004	* 4954
Marianus Scotus	c. 1070	4192
L. Condomanus	n/a	4141
Jim Liles	2013	** 4115
Thomas Lydiat	c. 1600	4103
M. Michael Maestlinus	c. 1600	4079
J. Ricciolus	n/a	4062
Jacob Salianus	c. 1600	4053
H. Spondanus	c. 1600	4051
Martin Anstey	1913	4042
W. Lange	n/a	4041
E. Reinholt	n/a	4021
J. Cappellus	c. 1600	4005
E. Greswell	1830	4004
E. Faulstich	1986	4001
D. Petavius	c. 1627	3983
Frank Klassen	1975	3975
Becke	n/a	3974
Krentzeim	n/a	3971
W. Dolen	2003	3971
E. Reusnerus	n/a	3970

J. Claverius	n/a	3968
C. Longomontanus	c. 1600	3966
P. Melanchthon	c. 1550	3964
J. Haynlinus	n/a	3963
A. Salmeron	d. 1585	3958
J. Scaliger	d. 1609	3949
M. Beroaldus	c. 1575	3927
A. Helwigius	c. 1630	3836

   * Benjamin Shaw, "The Genealogies of Genesis 5 and 11 and their Significance for Chronology," BJU, December, 2004. Dr. Shaw states the date as "about 5000 B.C." in Appendix I, but the specific date is derived from adding 1,656 years (the time from creation to the Flood) to his date of the Flood, which is stated as 3298 B.C. on p. 222.

  ** Jim Liles, Earth's Sacred Calendar (Tarzana, CA: Bible Timeline, 2013).

As you will likely note from table 2, the dates are not all 4004 B.C. There are several reasons chronologists have different dates,[7] but two primary reasons:

1. Some used the Septuagint or another early translation, instead of the Hebrew Masoretic text. The Septuagint is a Greek translation of the Hebrew Old Testament, done about 250 B.C. by about 70 Jewish scholars (hence it is often cited as the LXX). It is good in most places, but appears to have a number of inaccuracies. For example, one relates to the Genesis chronologies where the LXX indicates that Methuselah would have lived past the Flood, without being on the ark!

2. Several points in the biblical timeline are not straightforward to calculate. They require very careful study of more than one passage. These include exactly how much time the Israelites were in Egypt and what Terah's age was when Abraham was born. (See Jones' and Ussher's books for a detailed discussion of these difficulties.)

The first four in table 2 (bolded) are calculated from the Septuagint (others give certain favoritism to the LXX too), which gives ages for the patriarchs' firstborn much higher than the Masoretic text or the Samarian Pentateuch (a version of the Old Testament from the Jews in Samaria just before Christ). Because of this, the Septuagint adds in extra time. Though

---

7. Others would include gaps in the chronology based on the presences of an extra Cainan in Luke 3:36. But there are good reasons this should be left out.

the Samarian and Masoretic texts are much closer, they still have a few differences. See table 3.

Table 3: Septuagint, Masoretic, and Samarian Early Patriarchal Ages at the Birth of the Following Son

Name	Masoretic	Samarian Pentateuch	Septuagint
Adam	130	130	230
Seth	105	105	205
Enosh	90	90	190
Cainan	70	70	170
Mahalaleel	65	65	165
Jared	162	62	162
Enoch	65	65	165
Methuselah	187	67	167
Lamech	182	53	188
Noah	500	500	500

Using data from table 2 (excluding the Septuagint calculations and including Jones and Ussher), the average date of the creation of the earth is 4045 B.C. This still yields an average of about 6,000 years for the age of the earth.

Extra-biblical Calculations for the Age of the Earth

Cultures throughout the world have kept track of history as well. From a biblical perspective, we would expect the dates given for creation of the earth to align much closer to the biblical date than billions of years.

This is expected since everyone was descended from Noah and scattered from the Tower of Babel. Another expectation is that there should be some discrepancies about the age of the earth among people as they scattered throughout the world, taking their uninspired records or oral history to different parts of the globe.

Under the entry "creation," *Young's Analytical Concordance of the Bible*[8] lists William Hales' accumulation of dates of creation from many cultures, and in most cases Hales says which authority gave the date. See table 4.

8. Robert Young, *Young's Analytical Concordance to the Bible* (Peadoby, MA: Hendrickson, 1996), referring to William Hales, *A New Analysis of Chronology and Geography, History and Prophecy*, Vol. 1 (1830), p. 210.

Table 4: Selected Dates for the Age of the Earth by Various Cultures

Culture	Age, B.C.	Authority listed by Hales
Spain by Alfonso X	6984	Muller
Spain by Alfonso X	6484	Strauchius
India	6204	Gentil
India	6174	Arab Records
Babylon	6158	Bailly
Chinese	6157	Bailly
Greece by Diogenes Laertius	6138	Playfair
Egypt	6081	Bailly
Persia	5507	Bailly
Israel/Judea by Josephus	5555	Playfair
Israel/Judea by Josephus	5481	Jackson
Israel/Judea by Josephus	5402	Hales
Israel/Judea by Josephus	4698	University History
India	5369	Megasthenes
Babylon (Talmud)	5344	Petrus Alliacens
Vatican (Catholic using the Septuagint)	5270	N/A
Samaria	4427	Scaliger
German, Holy Roman Empire by Johannes Kepler*	3993	Playfair
German, reformer by Martin Luther	3961	N/A
Israel/Judea by computation	3760	Strauchius
Israel/Judea by Rabbi Lipman	3616	University History

* Luther, Kepler, Lipman, and the Jewish computation likely used biblical texts to determine the date.

Historian Bill Cooper's research in *After the Flood* provides dates from several ancient cultures.[9] The first is that of the Anglo-Saxons, whose history has 5,200 years from creation to Christ, according to the Laud and Parker Chronicles. Cooper's research also indicated that Nennius' record of the

---

9. Bill Cooper, *After the Flood* (UK: New Wine Press, 1995), p. 122–129.

ancient British history has 5,228 years from creation to Christ. The Irish chronology has a date of about 4000 B.C. for creation, which is surprisingly close to Ussher and Jones! Even the Mayans had a date for the Flood of 3113 B.C.

This meticulous work of many historians should not be ignored. Their dates of only thousands of years are good support for the biblical date somewhere in the neighborhood of about 6,000 years, but not the supposed billions of years claimed by many today.

7 | Origin of the Old-Earth Worldview

Ken Ham and Bodie Hodge

Knowing this first: that scoffers will come in the last days, walking according to their own lusts, and saying, "Where is the promise of His coming? For since the fathers fell asleep, all things continue as they were from the beginning of creation." For this they willfully forget: that by the word of God the heavens were of old, and the earth standing out of water and in the water, by which the world that then existed perished, being flooded with water (2 Peter 3:3–6).

ATTACKING THE FLOOD

Prior to the late 1700s, precious few believed in an old earth. The approximate 6,000-year age for the earth was challenged only rather recently, beginning in the late 18th century. These opponents of the biblical chronology essentially left God out of the picture. Three of the old-earth advocates included Comte de Buffon, who thought the earth was at least 75,000 years old. Pièrre LaPlace imagined an indefinite but very long history, and Jean Lamarck also proposed long ages.[1]

However, the idea of millions of years really took hold in geology when men like Abraham Werner, James Hutton, William Smith, Georges Cuvier, and Charles Lyell used their interpretations of geology as the standard,

---

1. Terry Mortenson, "The Origin of Old-earth Geology and its Ramifications for Life in the 21st Century," *TJ* 18, no. 1 (2004): 22–26, online at www.answersingenesis.org/tj/v18/i1/oldearth.asp.

rather than the Bible. Werner estimated the age of the earth at about one million years. Smith and Cuvier believed untold ages were needed for the formation of rock layers. Hutton said he could see no geological evidence of a beginning of the earth; and building on Hutton's thinking, Lyell advocated "millions of years."

From these men and others came the secular consensus view that the geologic layers were laid down slowly over long periods of time based on the rates at which we see them accumulating today. Hutton said:

> The past history of our globe must be explained by what can be seen to be happening now. . . . No powers are to be employed that are not natural to the globe, no action to be admitted except those of which we know the principle.[2]

This viewpoint is called *naturalistic uniformitarianism*, and it excludes any major catastrophes such as Noah's Flood. Though some, such as Cuvier and Smith, believed in multiple catastrophes separated by long periods of time, the uniformitarian concept became the ruling dogma in geology.

Thinking biblically, we can see that the global Flood in Genesis 6–8 would wipe away the concept of millions of years, for this Flood would explain massive amounts of fossil layers. Most Christians fail to realize that a global Flood could rip up many of the previous rock layers and redeposit them elsewhere, destroying the previous fragile contents. This would destroy any evidence of alleged millions of years anyway. So the rock layers can theoretically represent the evidence of either millions of years or a global Flood, but not both. Sadly, by about 1840 even most of the Church elite had accepted the dogmatic claims of the secular geologists and rejected the global Flood and the biblical age of the earth.

After Lyell, in 1899 Lord Kelvin (William Thomson) calculated the age of the earth, based on the cooling rate of a molten sphere instead of water (Genesis 1:2[3]). He calculated it to be a maximum of about 20–40 million years (this was revised from his earlier calculation of 100 million years in 1862).[4]

---

2. James Hutton, *Theory of the Earth* (trans. of Roy. Soc. of Edinburgh, 1785); quoted in A. Holmes, *Principles of Physical Geology* (UK: Thomas Nelson & Sons Ltd., 1965), p. 43–44.

3. The earth was without form, and void; and darkness was on the face of the deep. And the Spirit of God was hovering over the face of the waters.

4. Mark McCartney, "William Thompson: King of Victorian Physics," *Physics World*, December 2002, physicsworld.com/cws/article/print/16484.

With the development of radiometric dating in the early 20th century, the age of the earth expanded radically. In 1913, Arthur Holmes' book, *The Age of the Earth*, gave an age of 1.6 billion years.[5] Since then, the supposed age of the earth has expanded to its present estimate of about 4.5 billion years (and about 14 billion years for the universe). But there is growing scientific evidence that radiometric dating methods are completely unreliable (more on this in subsequent chapters).[6]

Table 1 Summary of the Old-Earth Proponents for Long Ages

Who?	Age of the Earth	When Was This?
Comte de Buffon	78 thousand years old	1779
Abraham Werner	1 million years	1786
James Hutton	Perhaps eternal, long ages	1795
Pièrre LaPlace	Long ages	1796
Jean Lamarck	Long ages	1809
William Smith	Long ages	1835
Georges Cuvier	Long ages	1812
Charles Lyell	Millions of years	1830–1833
Lord Kelvin	20–100 million years	1862–1899
Arthur Holmes	1.6 billion years	1913
Clair Patterson	4.5 billion years	1956

Christians who have felt compelled to accept the millions of years as fact and try to fit them into the Bible need to become aware of this evidence. Today, secular geologists will allow some catastrophic events into their thinking as an explanation for what they see in the rocks. But uniformitarian thinking is still widespread and secular geologists will seemingly never entertain the idea of the global catastrophic Flood of Noah's day.

---

5. Terry Mortenson, "The History of the Development of the Geological Column," in *The Geologic Column*, eds. Michael Oard and John Reed (Chino Valley, AZ: Creation Research Society, 2006).

6. For articles at the layman's level, see www.answersingenesis.org/home/area/faq/dating.asp. For a technical discussion, see Larry Vardiman, Andrew Snelling, and Eugene Chaffin, eds., *Radioisotopes and the Age of the Earth*, Vol. 1 and 2 (El Cajon, CA: Institute for Creation Research; Chino Valley, Arizona: Creation Research Society, 2000 and 2005). See also "Half-Life Heresy," *New Scientist*, October 21 2006, p. 36–39, abstract online at www.newscientist.com/channel/fundamentals/mg19225741.100-halflife-heresy-accelerating-radioactive-decay.html.

The age of the earth debate ultimately comes down to this foundational question: Are we trusting man's imperfect and changing ideas and assumptions about the past? Or are we trusting God's perfectly accurate eyewitness account of the past, including the creation of the world, Noah's global Flood, and the age of the earth?

CONCLUSION

When we start our thinking with God's Word, we can calculate that the world is about 6,000 years old.

The age of the earth ultimately comes down to a matter of trust — it's a worldview issue. Will you trust what an all-knowing God says on the subject or will you trust imperfect man's assumptions and imaginations about the past that regularly are changing?

Age of the Earth Battle: Millions of Years or a Global Flood

Ken Ham and Bodie Hodge

Introduction

Who would have thought that rock layers would be the source of such an immense debate? After all, they are just rock layers, right? But this is really what the age of the earth debate boils down to — a global Flood or slow, gradual millions of years. We look at the same evidence — rock layers — but we look at them from two different viewpoints.

When it comes to the age of the earth debate, many think that it has something to do with radiometric dating. But dating methods are a new idea that people have tried to use as a secondary point to back up this idea (belief) of rock layers being evidence of millions of years — more on this in the next chapter.

But there are two opposing timescales based on these two opposing views of the rock layers. Let's dive into this.

Timescale

Geological timescales are everywhere! You can hardly miss them. They are in children's books, textbooks, laymen books, technical journals, and so on. They typically look like the one on the following page.

Naturally, there are some that can get technical. But take note that they assume certain layers took millions of years to form. Early geological scales, in the 1800s for example, did not have a time stamped on them.

Even timescales in the past look different from the ones today. Once they started saying these rock layers were "eras of time" they started putting age

GEOLOGIC TIMESCALE

ERA	PERIOD	EPOCH	SUCCESSION OF LIFE
CENOZOIC recent life	QUATERNARY 0-1 Million Years	Recent Pleisto-cene	
	TERTIARY 62 Million Years	Pliocene Miocene Oligocene Eocene	
MESOZOIC middle life	CRETACEOUS 72 Million Years		
	JURASSIC 46 Million Years		
	TRIASSIC 49 Million Years		
PALEOZOIC ancient life	PERMIAN 50 Million Years		
	PENNSYLVANIAN 30 Million Years (Carboniferous)		
	MISSISSIPPIAN 35 Million Years		
	DEVONIAN 60 Million Years		
	SILURIAN 20 Million Years		
	ORDOVICIAN 75 Million Years		
	CAMBRIAN 100 Million Years		
	PRECAMBRIAN		

© 2007 Answers in Genesis USA

dates on them. Then they kept adjusting the dates to get older and older ones. They kept pushing earth's age back further and further to get more time in hopes that they would have enough time for biological evolution. Even with the time they have today, it still isn't even enough time (as molecules-to-man evolution is impossible anyway), but they have slowed down changing it in our day and age. But this doesn't mean it won't change tomorrow!

Timescale Discussion

Keep in mind that secular timescales are based on the idea that there were no significant catastrophes that occurred in the past. They further assume that these rock layers are formed because of slow deposition over millions and billions of years. We don't accept this assumption that there were no major catastrophes in the past — especially in light of the global Flood in Genesis 6–8. This assumption of no catastrophes (particularly no global Flood) is just a bad arbitrary guess — and really a deliberate ploy in an attempt to discredit the Bible.

For the moment, consider what would happen if a massive catastrophe did occur like a global Flood or an asteroid strike. The entire timescale would be called into question, as previous rock layers would be eradicated and new rock layers would occur quickly. So it would not match this idea of slow gradual changes. This is why any major catastrophe would be rejected in the secular world, because it would destroy the idea of millions and billions of years. They have to have this long timescale to even attempt to propose their biological evolutionary ideas.

You need to understand that when people reject major catastrophes like the Flood, they assume that the rock layers formed slowly based on uniform rates we see *today*. This is called "uniformitarianism" or "gradualism." For example, they say rock layers form when dust, sand, or dirt slowly accumulates over the course of a year or sediment from a river or the edge of a sea accumulates into a layer over the course of a year. Then these layers add up over the course of long ages and capture living creatures to form rock layers with fossils.

In the same way, they assume that a river carves out a canyon at a slow rate like what we see on a typical day, and over long ages it finally carves out these canyons to a significant degree. Any catastrophes would upset this, and even though we see catastrophes today (tsunamis, local floods, earthquakes, volcanoes, etc.), these are largely ignored to develop the long timescales.

Do Creationists Agree with the Rock Layers on the Timescale?

Believe it or not, creationists and evolutionists actually agree on something. We agree on the actual rock layers that exist. That is not in dispute. We all agree on the rock layers and that they can be divided into types in much the same way. Our disagreement rises with the *timing* of the formation of these rock layers!

Where the evolutionists say the fossiliferous rock layers "were laid down slowly over millions of years without any major catastrophes," the creationists say that "most of these rock layers were deposited by the Flood of Noah's day." So it is the same evidence based on the same observations, but we simply have two different interpretations of that evidence. Creationists start with God's Word, which informs us of the global Flood (e.g., Genesis 7:19–20[1]) that was a major catastrophe about 4,300 years ago. A creationist's geologic timescale would be much closer to the one on the following page.

---

1. And the waters prevailed exceedingly on the earth, and all the high hills under the whole heaven were covered. The waters prevailed fifteen cubits upward, and the mountains were covered.

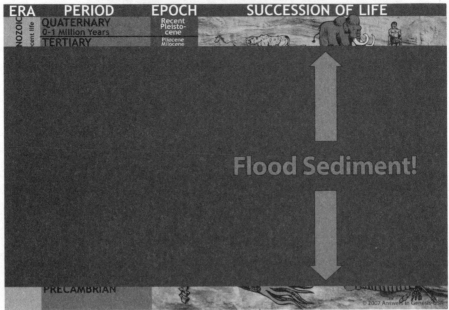

Now there would be rock layers formed *since* the Flood (not over millions of years) from tsunamis, local floods, volcanoes, etc., but most of the rock layers that have fossils come from the global Flood of Noah's day. So we agree on the rock layers, but the *timing* is different.

CATASTROPHISM

In the 1800s, there were people in the secular world who held to what is called "catastrophism." They disagreed with the uniformitarians' ideas that there were no catastrophes, and yet they disagreed with the Bible that discussed the biblical global Flood. They held that there *were* major catastrophes from time to time, like a multitude of global or massive floods. But they had these separated out by eons of time. This view all but died a tragic death and uniformitarian ideas dominated until recently with a new revival of this view.

Just now — in our day and age — we have secular geologists who entertain the idea that there may have been several major catastrophes in the past. These ideas are again becoming popular. For example, many secular geologists (scientists who study rock layers) and paleontologists (scientists who study fossils) have been asserting this idea of a *mass extinction event* about "65 million years ago" that finished off the dinosaurs. Furthermore, they will often discuss several major extinction events — many including water.

The good thing is that these geologists recognize that a catastrophe best explains the fossiliferous rock layers. The bad thing is that they refuse to acknowledge that the Genesis Flood was that event. Furthermore, few notice the implication of how even a single catastrophe in the past *destroys the geologic timescale*. The rock layers are still the rock layers, but the *timing* then must be in error if you have a major catastrophe to lay down a particular rock layer instead of millions of years!

In other words, catastrophists who believe in multiple catastrophes over the course of millions of years *cannot have millions of years* in the rock layers themselves, by which they try to appeal for long ages! A catastrophe destroys the idea of rock layers being slowly and gradually formed over millions of years. And yet, many catastrophists are more than willing to continue to use the geologic timescale that their own view refutes! This is a major inconsistency!

Grand Canyon

When talking about rock layers and timing, it is difficult to avoid the Grand Canyon and the Grand Staircase (which extends farther out and above the immediate Grand Canyon layers). This is an ideal example of the debate over timing. Was the canyon formed:

1. slowly and gradually over millions of years and then carved out by the Colorado River slowly over millions of years or

2. by a catastrophe that laid down the rock layers and a catastrophe that carved out the rock layers?

The uniformitarian would argue it was a lot of time and a little bit of water, whereas the creationist would argue it was a lot of water and little bit of time! We have the same rock layers, same fossils, same Grand Canyon, but two different interpretations of that evidence. The Flood makes sense of depositing and carving those rock layers quickly.

Slow, gradual accumulations make little sense because many of the rock layers at the Grand Canyon have no evidence of erosion between the rock layers, which in some cases supposedly have millions of years separating

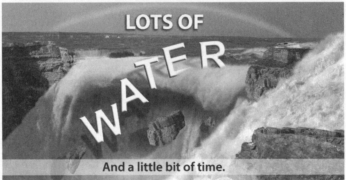

these rock layers. For example, the flat boundary between Hermit Shale and the Coconino Sandstone are supposed to have millions of years of erosion between them, but they don't.

Now as a note, creationists disagree over when the Grand Canyon was officially carved out. Both positions agree that the canyon was carved via a catastrophe; but where many have this at the end stages of the Flood, others have it as the result of a breached dam either at the end of the Flood[2] or during the early post-Flood era. Either way, it was formed as a consequence of the global Flood.

---

2. For more on the Grand Canyon formation please see Andrew Snelling and Tom Vail, "When and How Did the Grand Canyon Form?" *The New Answers Book 3*, Ken Ham, gen. ed. (Green Forest, AR: Master Books, 2010), p. 173–186.

A Lesson in Radiometric Dating – Semi-Technical

Bodie Hodge

Introduction

We've seen how the secularists have used rock layers that have fossils to build the geologic timescale and how that relates to the age of the earth. Radiometric dating was the next installment that took the age of the earth from the supposed *millions of years* to the *billions of years*! But is radiometric dating the knockout punch for the age of the earth? Not at all, though many seem to falsely think so. Let's break this idea down.

Uniformitarian Methods for Dating the Age of the Earth

Radiometric dating methods are one particular form of *uniformitarian* dating method. Don't let the word uniformitarian scare you! Uniformitarian dating methods are simply assuming something (i.e., a rate) has been uniform in the past; that is, unchanging. For example, if we wanted to estimate how old the earth was by one of the many uniformitarian methods, we might select sodium influx into the oceans. Here is how it works:

A. We assume there was no sodium (e.g., salt) in the oceans to begin with.

B. We measure how much sodium is eroding into the oceans today by rivers, volcanoes, and so on.

C. We measure how much sodium is leaving the oceans (like sea spray from ocean storms that come inland and leave some sodium inland).

D. We assume that there has never been any *significant* catastrophes in the past to make major changes to sodium influx into the oceans (in other words we assume these rates have always been the same).

E. Then we calculate how long it would take for the oceans to arrive at their sodium level today (how salty the ocean has become).

In this example, we really made some wild assumptions didn't we? We assume there were no catastrophes in the past. And next, we assumed that the ocean had no salt to begin with. Of course, these assumptions are in error. When God gathered the seas on day 3 and let dry land appear (Genesis 1:9–10[1]), He could well have made sure they had a certain degree of sodium or saltiness. This would immediately upset this dating method.

Furthermore, the global Flood in Genesis 6–8 was a significant catastrophe that surely increased the sodium influx tremendously. Let's not forget about famines and droughts that plagued the Old Testament world that surely played a role as well, such as reducing influx of sodium or reducing the sea spray. The point is that catastrophes have been an important part of our past that throws a "monkey wrench" into *any* uniformitarian dating method.

Radiometric Dating

Radiometric dating, perhaps the most popular form of uniformitarian dating, was the culminating factor that led to the belief in *billions* of years for earth history for the secular humanists. A radiometric dating method requires a radioactive (an element that wants to break down into another element) material A (the parent) into material B (the daughter). For example, a radioactive form of potassium (the parent) wants to break down into argon (the daughter).

Any radiometric dating model or other uniformitarian dating method can and does have problems as referenced before dealing with their assumptions. All uniformitarian dating methods require assumptions for extrapolating present-day processes back into the past. The assumptions related to radiometric dating can specifically be seen in these questions:

- Initial amounts?
- Was any parent amount added?

---

1. Then God said, "Let the waters under the heavens be gathered together into one place, and let the dry land appear"; and it was so. And God called the dry land Earth, and the gathering together of the waters He called Seas. And God saw that it was good.

- Was any daughter amount added?
- Was any parent amount removed?
- Was any daughter amount removed?
- Has the rate of decay changed?

If the assumptions are accurate, then uniformitarian dates should agree with radiometric dating across the board for the same event. However, radiometric dates often disagree with one another or do not match other uniformitarian dating methods for the age of the earth, such as the influx of salts into the ocean, the rate of decay of the earth's magnetic field, and the growth rate of human population.[2]

The late Dr. Henry Morris compiled a list of 68 uniformitarian estimates for the age of the earth by Christian and secular sources.[3] The current accepted secular age of the earth is about 4.54 billion years, based on radiometric dating of a group of meteorites,[4] so keep this in mind when viewing Table 1.

Table 1: Uniformitarian Estimates Other than Radiometric Dating Estimates for Earth's Age Compiled by Morris

	0 – 10,000 years	>10,000 – 100,000 years	>100,000 – 1 million years	>1 million – 500 million years	>500 million – 4 billion years	>4 billion – 5 billion years
Number of uniformitarian methods*	23	10	11	23	0	0

* When a range of ages is given, the maximum age was used to be generous to the evolutionists. In one case, the date was uncertain, so it was not used in this tally, so the total estimates used were 67. A few on the list had reference to Saturn, the sun, etc., but since biblically the earth is older than these, dates related to them were used.

As you can see from Table 1, uniformitarian maximum ages for the earth obtained from other methods are nowhere near the 4.5 billion years esti-

---

2. Russell Humphrey, "Evidence for a Young World," *Impact*, June 2005, online at http://www.answersingenesis.org/docs/4005.asp.
3. Henry M. Morris, *The New Defender's Study Bible* (Nashville, TN: World Publishing, 2006), p. 2076–2079.
4. C.C. Patterson, "Age of Meteorites and the age of the Earth," *Geochemica et Cosmochemica Acta*, 10(1956):230–237.

mated by radiometric dating; of the other methods, only two calculated dates were as much as 500 million years. So they do not match up and most methods disagree with the age of the earth being 4.5 billion years!

So why do people reject most radiometric and uniformitarian dates, and only trust the dates that give extremely long ages (like potassium argon, uranium-lead, or rubidium-strontium)? It is because of their presupposition to billions of years before they even look at the subject.

CARBON DATING

Right up front, carbon-14 (^{14}C) cannot give dates of millions or billions of years as many think. This is a common misconception in the general public. It can only give calculations of thousands of years (50,000–100,000 years as a theoretical maximum). The results from some radiometric dating methods completely undermine those from the other radiometric methods; ^{14}C dating is one such example.

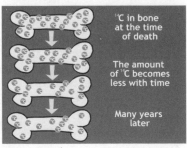

How does ^{14}C work? As long as an organism is alive it takes in ^{14}C and ^{12}C (normal carbon) from the atmosphere (where it is assumed to be constant) through breathing and diet; however, when it dies, the carbon intake stops. Since ^{14}C is radioactive (decays into ^{14}N), the amount of ^{14}C in a dead organism gets less and less over time.

At death, carbon intake STOPS!

Carbon-14 dates are determined from the measured ratio of radioactive carbon-14

^{14}C in bone at the time of death

The amount of ^{14}C becomes less with time

Many years later

to normal carbon-12 ($^{14}C/^{12}C$). Used on samples that came from once living or growing creatures, such as wood or bone, the measured $^{14}C/^{12}C$ ratio is compared with the ratio in things today. Carbon-14 has a derived half-life of 5,730 years (again an estimate based on lab experiments), so the ^{14}C in any organic material supposedly 100,000 years old should have decayed into nitrogen.[5]

Some things, such as wood trapped and encased in lava flows, said to be millions of years old by other radiometric dating methods, still have ^{14}C in them per geologist Dr. Andrew Snelling's research.[6] If the items were millions of years old, then they shouldn't have any traces of ^{14}C.

Coal and diamonds, which are found in or sandwiched between rock layers allegedly millions and billions of years old, have been shown to have ^{14}C ages of only tens of thousands of years.[7] So which date, if any, is correct? The older date should immediately be thrown out. The diamonds or coal can't be millions of years old if they have any traces of ^{14}C still in them. This shows that these dating methods are completely unreliable and indicates that the presumed assumptions in the methods are erroneous.

Potassium-Argon Dating

Similar kinds of problems are seen in the case of potassium-argon dating, which has been considered one of the most reliable methods. When a lava flow solidifies, it is supposed to start the radiometric-dating clock. We know when many lava flows occurred — the exact year in fact. Dr. Andrew Snelling points out several of these problems with potassium-argon, as seen in Table 2 with volcanoes when we knew their exact eruption year.[8]

---

5. This does not mean that a ^{14}C date of 50,000 or 100,000 would be entirely trustworthy. I am only using this to highlight the mistaken assumptions behind uniformitarian dating methods.

6. Andrew Snelling, "Conflicting 'Ages' of Tertiary Basalt and Contained Fossilized Wood, Crinum, Central Queensland Australia," *Technical Journal* 14, no. 2 (2005): 99–122.

7. John Baumgardner, "^{14}C Evidence for a Recent Global Flood and a Young Earth," in *Radioisotopes and the Age of the Earth: Results of a Young-Earth Creationist Research Initiative*, ed. Vardiman et al. (Santee, CA: Institute for Creation Research; Chino Valley, AZ: Creation Research Society, 2005), p.587–630.

8. Andrew Snelling, "Excess Argon: The 'Achilles' Heel' of Potassium-Argon and Argon-Argon Dating of Volcanic Rocks," *Impact*, January 1999, online at www.icr.org/index.php?module=articles&action=view&ID=436.

Table 2: Potassium-argon (K-Ar) Dates in Error

Volcanic Eruption	When the Rock Formed	Date by (K-Ar) Radiometric Dating
Mt. Etna basalt, Sicily	122 B.C.	170,000–330,000 years old
Mt. Etna basalt, Sicily	A.D. 1972	210,000–490,000 years old
Mount St. Helens, Washington	A.D.1986	Up to 2.8 million years old
Hualalai basalt, Hawaii	A.D.1800–1801	1.32–1.76 million years old
Mt Ngauruhoe, New Zealand	A.D.1954	Up to 3.5 million years old
Kilauea Iki basalt, Hawaii	A.D.1959	1.7–15.3 million years old

These dates simply don't even come close! If we cannot trust the dates on known volcanoes, why trust the method elsewhere?

RUBIDIUM STRONTIUM DATING

One popular method used for *really old* age dating is rubidium-strontium, where a radioactive element (rubidium; Rb) changes into another element (strontium; Sr).[9] More specifically, it is the specific isotopes of ^{87}Rb and ^{87}Sr or ^{86}Sr. For the lay reader, don't let this terminology scare you — it is simply a form of rubidium (the parent element) that changes into strontium (the daughter element).

It is claimed that the half-life of this change from Rb to Sr is about 48–49 billion years. In other words, it is claimed that for half of the Rb to change into Sr, it would take about 49 billion years. Yes, you read this correctly; it would take about 3 times the estimated age of the universe to change half of the Rb in the universe to Sr. So it is curious where all the strontium came from in the universe since only minute amounts could have been generated from Rb if the universe is only 13–15 billions years. Strontium is, after all, the 15th most common element on earth, yet rubidium is the 23rd most common element.[10] But this problem is not an issue for a God who created the universe element rich.

---

9. Strontium is named for a village in Scotland, where it was first discovered.
10. K.K. Turekian and K.H. Wedepohl, "Distribution of the Elements in Some Major Units of the Earth's Crust," *Geological Society of America Bulletin* 72 (2): 175–192, 1961; W.C. Butterman and R.G. Reese, "Mineral Commodity Profiles: Rubidium," accessed June 23, 2014, http://pubs.usgs.gov/of/2003/of03-045/of03-045.pdf.

Obviously, an experiment cannot be observed or repeated to verify this half-life in its fullness, so where did this *guess* come from? After all, there are other isotopes of Rb like ^{83}Rb or ^{86}Rb and in total there are about 32 isotopes, though only two are naturally occurring. But these other isotopes decay in days — that is, a few have observable half-lives of less than 90 days, some even less than 35 days, and in many cases less than one day. So why is it assumed that the half-life of ^{87}Rb is about 48–49 billion years?

Simple — they observe in a lab how much ^{87}Rb is there one day and then measure how much ^{87}Rb is there another day and then calculate the half-life by extrapolating. For the technical person that is $[t_{1/2} = t * \ln(2)/\ln(N_0/N_t)]$; where t is time between observations, N_0 is how much was there originally and N_t is the amount of the substance after this amount of time.

But the problem here is simple: how do we know that the half-life really is this long (claimed to be 48–49 billion years)? We really should not detect many decay changes (alpha and beta particle discharges, for example) over days, weeks, and a few years by observation. And yet this is extrapolated from tens to the power of 8! This would not be acceptable in other disciplines.

Allow me to use a layman example. If I polled 5 people on a question and then extrapolated that to say all 6–7 billion people on earth agree . . . would that be acceptable? Not at all! Even if we had a few years of observations, this amount of time is still far too short to give us a reasonable sampling of N_t, let alone to calculate a proper rate. But there are further problems.

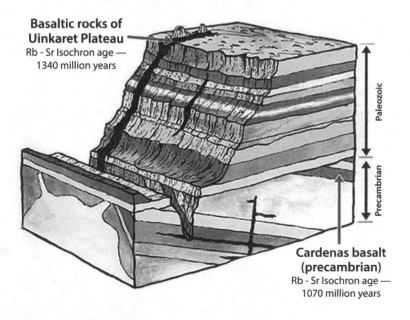

Basaltic rocks of Uinkaret Plateau
Rb - Sr Isochron age — 1340 million years

Paleozoic

Precambrian

Cardenas basalt (precambrian)
Rb - Sr Isochron age — 1070 million years

Rubidium-Strontium gives dates we know are wrong. A great example is at the Grand Canyon. At the bottom of the Grand Canyon is a rock layer that is Precambrian called the Cardenas Basalt. It obviously existed before the fossiliferous rock layers of the Grand Canyon were deposited well above it. At the top of the Grand Canyon there is a lava flow that ran down the canyon into the Colorado River. This lava flow is clearly a later, recent formation.

These two volcanic layers have been dated using Rb-Sr. This lava flow on top of the Grand Canyon (calculated at 1.34 billion years) came out to be over 250 million years older than the basalt at the bottom (calculated at 1.07 billion years)![11] This is blatantly impossible. Not that these ages are remotely close, as the volcano is sitting on top of rock layers from the Flood of Noah and is less than 4,500 years old! So the Rb-Sr date is off by more than a billion years! And yet to make things worse, Native Americans may have witnessed this eruption according to some accounts and yet they are not billions of years old!

conclusion

There are other radiometric methods like uranium-lead, thorium-lead, or samarium-neodymium that secularists try to use to profess certain dates, but they all run into the same problems derived from their assumptions. This brief look at these methods here raises a critical question. If radiometric dating fails to get an accurate date on something of which we *do* know the true age, then how can it be trusted to give us the correct age for rocks that had no human observers to record when they formed?

If the methods don't work on rocks of known age, it is most unreasonable to trust that they work on rocks of unknown age. It is better to trust the Word of the God who created the world, knows its history perfectly, and has revealed sufficient information in the Bible for us to understand that history and the age of the creation.

11. Steve Austin, ed., *Grand Canyon Monument to Catastrophe* (Santee, CA: Institute for Creation Research, 1994), p. 111–131.

CAN'T CHRISTIANS JUST TAKE THE IDEA OF 'LONG AGES' AND INSERT THEM INTO THE BIBLE SOMEWHERE?

KEN HAM AND BODIE HODGE

INTRODUCTION

Many Christians mix their religion based on God's Word with the secular humanistic religion (man's word), particularly regarding the supposed millions of years for earth's history. They are really taking aspects of the false religion and mixing it with their Christianity.

In most cases, this is done by taking the secular beliefs about origins like big bang, millions of years, and biological evolution, and reinterpreting God's Word in an attempt to "fit them in." Regrettably, many Christians accept man's views of evolution (in geology, biology, astronomy, chemistry, etc.) and try to mix it with Scripture.

THE FOUR 'EVOLUTIONS'

Let me clarify something. Most people, when they hear the word "evolution," really think of the *general theory of evolution (GTE)* or, in laymen's terms, "molecules-to-man," "electron-to-engineer," or "goo-to-you." But there are really four types of evolution that make up that word:

> *Cosmological/Astronomical evolution:* including big-bang models (essentially everything evolved from nothing)[1]
> *Geological evolution:* millions of years of slow, gradual accumulations of rock layers (instead of mostly being rock layers from the Flood)

---

1. Some may hold to other variant evolutionary forms like an infinitely regressive universe or steady-state model but most adhere to one of the big-bang models.

Chemical evolution: life came from matter (non-life), otherwise called "abiogenesis"

Biological evolution: a single, simple life form gave rise to all other life forms down through the ages

Within the Church, there are those who try to fit astronomical evolution, geological evolution, chemical evolution, or biological evolution into the Bible. Some Christians accept one, some, or all of these in their attempts to accommodate the secular beliefs with God's Word. Usually, it is geological evolution. This acceptance undermines the authority of the Word of God as it takes man's ideas about the past to supersede God's Word in Genesis. This is ultimately undermining the Gospel too, as it undercuts the WORD from which the Gospel comes.

WHERE DO PEOPLE TRY TO PUT MILLIONS OF YEARS?

Virtually all Christians who have bought into an old earth (that is millions and billions of years of long ages) place the millions of years *prior* to Adam.

We have genealogical lists that connect Adam to Christ (e.g., Luke 3). For the *old-earth Christians*, it would be blatantly absurd to try to insert millions and billions of years into these genealogies and say that Adam and Eve were made at the beginning of creation.[2]

Instead, old-earth creationists (as they are often denoted[3]) take these long ages and insert them somewhere prior to Adam; hence creation week has been a divisive point in Christianity ever since the idea of long ages such as millions of years became popular in the 1800s. Here are some of the differing positions within the Church — but all have one common factor — endeavoring to somehow fit millions of years into the Bible.

Gap Theories (incorporating geological and astronomical evolution)

1. **Pre-time gap.** This view adds long ages prior to God creating in Genesis 1:1.[4] The pre-time gap falls short for a number of

---

2. In Mark 10:6, Jesus says: "But from the beginning of the creation, God 'made them male and female.' "
3. In many other cases, those Christians who adhere to long ages are called "compromised Christians" since they are compromising by mixing these two religions' origins accounts (humanism and Christianity). Properly, this is syncretism, where they synchronize the religions of Christianity and humanism into one blended religion.
4. In the beginning God created the heavens and the earth.

reasons, such as having death before sin (discussed in detail in the next chapter), allowance of man's ideas about millions of years to supersede God's Word, having *time* before time existed, and the like. As another example, how can one have millions of years of time prior to the creation of time? It is quite illogical.

2. **Ruin-reconstruction gap.** This is the most popular gap idea, which adds long ages between Genesis 1:1[5] and Genesis 1:2.[6] Scottish pastor Thomas Chalmers popularized it in the early 1800s as a response to long ages, which was becoming popular. This idea is promoted in the Scofield and Dake Study Bibles and is often associated with a Luciferian fall and flood — but that would make Lucifer (Satan) in his sinful state very good and perfect. After God created Adam, God said everything He made was "very good" (Deuteronomy 32:4[7]; Genesis 1:31[8]).[9]

3. **Modified gap/precreation chaos gap.** This view adds long ages between Genesis 1:2[10] and 1:3,[11] and it is primarily addressed in the International Conference on Creation.[12] It has many of the same problems already mentioned in the first two gaps already discussed.

4. **Soft gap.** This also includes a gap between Genesis 1:2[13] and 1:3,[14] but unlike previous views, it has no catastrophic events or destruction of a previous state. Furthermore, it merely proposes that God

---

5. Ibid.

6. The earth was without form, and void; and darkness was on the face of the deep. And the Spirit of God was hovering over the face of the waters.

7. He is the Rock, His work is perfect; for all His ways are justice, a God of truth and without injustice; righteous and upright is He.

8. Then God saw everything that He had made, and indeed it was very good.

9. K. Ham, "What About the Gap & Ruin-Reconstruction Theories?" in *The New Answers Book*, K. Ham, gen. ed. (Green Forest, AR: Master Books, 2006); for a technical response see also, W. Fields, *Unformed and Unfilled* (Collinsville, IL: Burgener Enterprises, 1997).

10. The earth was without form, and void; and darkness was on the face of the deep. And the Spirit of God was hovering over the face of the waters.

11. Then God said, "Let there be light"; and there was light.

12. One refutation of this view is in Andrew Snelling, ed., *Proceedings of the Sixth International Conference on Creationism* (Dallas, TX: Institute for Creation Research, 2008), "A Critique of the Precreation Chaos Gap Theory," by John Zoschke.

13. The earth was without form, and void; and darkness was on the face of the deep. And the Spirit of God was hovering over the face of the waters.

14. Then God said, "Let there be light"; and there was light.

created the world this way and left it for long periods of time in an effort to get starlight here. In essence, this view has a young earth and an old universe. The problem is that stars were created after the proposed gap (day 4), and it is unnecessary to make accommodations for long ages to solve the so-called starlight problem. Getting distant starlight to earth is not a problem for an all-powerful God. It is only a problem in a strict naturalistic view.

5. **Late gap.** This view has a gap between chapters 2 and 3 of Genesis. In other words, some believe that Adam and Eve lived in the Garden for long ages before sin. This view has problems too. For example, Adam and Eve were told by God to be "fruitful and multiply" in Genesis 1:28,[15] and waiting long ages to do so would have been disobeying God's Word. This doesn't make sense. In addition, there is the problem of Adam only living 930 years as recorded in Genesis (Genesis 5:5[16]).[17]

When someone tries to put a large gap of time in the Scriptures when it is not warranted by the text, this should throw up a red flag to any Christian. In many gap theory models, Satan allegedly rebels between Genesis 1:1–2[18] (or otherwise in the first three verses of Scripture). Consider the theological problem of Satan, in his sinful state being called "very good" in Genesis 1:31.[19] This would make an evil Satan very good. In fact, this would make *sin* very good too. Satan could not have fallen into sin until after this declaration in Genesis 1:31.[20]

Day Age Models (each model adheres to geological and astronomical evolution)

1. **Day-age.** This idea was popularized by Hugh Miller in the early 1800s after walking away from Thomas Chalmers' idea of

---

15. Then God blessed them, and God said to them, "Be fruitful and multiply; fill the earth and subdue it; have dominion over the fish of the sea, over the birds of the air, and over every living thing that moves on the earth."

16. So all the days that Adam lived were nine hundred and thirty years; and he died.

17. Bodie Hodge, *The Fall of Satan* (Green Forest, AR: Master Books, 2011), p. 23–26, https://answersingenesis.org/bible-characters/adam-and-eve/when-did-adam-and-eve-rebel/.

18. In the beginning God created the heavens and the earth. The earth was without form, and void; and darkness was on the face of the deep. And the Spirit of God was hovering over the face of the waters.

19. Then God saw everything that He had made, and indeed it was very good. So the evening and the morning were the sixth day.

20. Ibid.

the gap theory, and prior to his suicide. This model basically stretched the days of creation out to be millions of years long. Of course, lengthening the days in Genesis to accommodate the secular evolutionist view of history simply doesn't match up with what is stated in Genesis 1.[21]

2. **Progressive creation.** This is a modified form of the day-age idea (really in many ways it's similar to theistic evolution) led by Dr. Hugh Ross, head of an organization called Reasons to Believe. He appeals to nature (actually the secular interpretations of nature) as the supposed 67th book of the Bible, and then uses these interpretations to supersede what the Bible says. Recall that nature is cursed according to Genesis 3 and Romans 8. Dr. John Ankerberg is also a leading supporter of this viewpoint.[22] This view proposes that living creatures go extinct repeatedly over millions of years, but God, from time to time, makes new kinds and new species all fitting with a (geologically and cosmological/astronomically) evolutionary view of history.[23] Things are out of order in creation week in the progressive creation view, and death before sin is devastating to this position.

Theistic Evolutionary Models (each variant basically adheres to geological, astronomical, and biological evolution)

1. **Theistic evolution (evolutionary creation).** Basically, the idea of Genesis 1–11 is thrown out or heavily reinterpreted to allow for evolutionary ideas to supersede the Scriptures. Harvard botany professor Asa Gray was a contemporary of Darwin and promoted this idea, but Darwin opposed Gray's mixing of Christianity with evolution since they were two opposing views. They wrote several letters to one another. Charles Hodge and Benjamin B. Warfield of Princeton Theological Seminary in the mid-to-late

---

21. T. Mortenson, "Evolution vs. Creation: The Order of Events Matters!" *Answers in Genesis*, April 4, 2006, https://answersingenesis.org/why-does-creation-matter/evolution-vs-creation-the-order-of-events-matters/.
22. J. Seegert, "Responding to the Compromise Views of John Ankerberg," *Answers in Genesis*, March 2, 2005, https://answersingenesis.org/reviews/tv/responding-to-the-compromise-views-of-john-ankerberg/.
23. K. Ham and T. Mortenson, "What's Wrong with Progressive Creation?" in K. Ham, gen. ed., *The New Answers Book 2* (Green Forest, AR: Master Book, 2008), p. 123–134.

1800s also advocated the mixing of Christianity with evolution. Today, this view is heavily promoted by a group called BioLogos. Basically, they accept the prevailing evolutionist (false) history including the big bang and then add a demoted form of God to it. BioLogos writers have different ways of wildly reinterpreting Genesis to accommodate evolution into Scripture.

2. **Framework hypothesis.** Dr. Meredith Kline (1922–2007), who accepted many evolutionary ideas, popularized this view in America.[24] It is very common in many seminaries today. Those who hold to framework treat Genesis 1 as a literary device (think poetic or semi-poetic), with the first three days paralleling and equating to the last three days of creation. These days are not seen as 24-hour days but are taken as metaphorical or allegorical to allow for ideas like evolution/millions of years to be entertained. Hence, Genesis 1 is treated as merely being a literary device to teach that God created everything (essentially in 3 days[25]).[26] However, Genesis 1 is not written as poetry but as literal history.[27]

3. **Cosmic Temple.** Dr. John Walton agrees the language of Genesis 1 means ordinary days, but since he believes in evolution had to do something about it. Walton proposes that Genesis 1 has nothing to do with material origins but instead is referring to

---

24. It was originally developed in 1924 by Professor Arnie Noordtzij in Europe, which was a couple of decades before Dr. Kline jumped on board with framework hypothesis.

25. "For in six days the LORD made the heavens and the earth, the sea, and all that is in them, and rested the seventh day. Therefore the LORD blessed the Sabbath day and hallowed it" (Exodus 20:11). "It is a sign between Me and the children of Israel forever; for in six days the LORD made the heavens and the earth, and on the seventh day He rested and was refreshed" (Exodus 31:17).

26. T. Chaffey and B. McCabe, "What is Wrong with the Framework Hypothesis?" *Answers in Genesis*, June 11, 2011, https://answersingenesis.org/creationism/old-earth/whats-wrong-with-the-framework-hypothesis/.

27. Hebrew expert Dr. Steven Boyd writes: "For Genesis 1:1–2:3, this probability is between 0.999942 and 0.999987 at a 99.5% confidence level. Thus, we conclude with statistical certainty that this text is narrative, not poetry. It is therefore statistically indefensible to argue that it is poetry. The hermeneutical implication of this finding is that this text should be read as other historical narratives." Dr. Steven Boyd, Associate Professor of Bible, The Master's College, *Radioisotopes and the Age of the Earth*, Volume II, Editors Larry Vardiman, Andrew Snelling, and Eugene Chaffin (Dallas, TX: Institute for Creation Research, 2005), p. 632. We would go one step further than Dr. Boyd, who left open the slim possibility of Genesis not being historical narrative, and say it *is* historical narrative and all doctrines of theology, directly or indirectly, are founded in the early pages of Genesis — though we appreciated Dr. Boyd's research.

what he calls "God's Cosmic Temple." By relegating Genesis 1 to be disconnected from material origins of earth, then he is free to believe in evolution and millions of years.

CONCLUSION

Note that each compromise position has one common factor — attempting to fit millions of years into the Bible. That's why there are so many such compromise positions, with very creative ways of attempting to add in the supposed long ages. The only position that works is the one in which Genesis is taken as literal history!

Each old-earth Christian worldview has no choice but to demote a global Flood to a local flood in order to accommodate the alleged millions of years (geological evolution) of rock layers (a global Flood would have destroyed these layers and laid down new ones).[28]

Also, the compromise views that accept the big-bang idea have accepted a view that contradicts Scripture. They have adopted a model to explain the universe without God (which is what the big bang is — a model that requires no God). So if God is added to the big-bang idea, then really . . . God didn't do anything because the big bang dictates that the universe really created itself.[29]

Each old-earth view also has an insurmountable problem in regard to the issue of death before sin (discussed in the next chapter) that undermines both the authority of God's Word and the gospel.[30] The idea of millions of years came out of naturalism — the belief that the fossil-bearing rock layers were laid down slowly and gradually over millions of years before man.

This idea of long ages was meant to do away with the belief that Noah's Flood was responsible for most of the fossil-bearing sedimentary layers. There is no reason for Christians to adopt the atheistic, naturalism religious view (secular humanism) and mix it with their Christianity.

28. J. Lisle and T. Chaffey, "Defense — A Local Flood?" in *Old Earth Creation on Trial* (Green Forest, AR: Master Books, 2008), p. 93–106, https://answersingenesis.org/the-flood/global/defensea-local-flood/.

29. J. Lisle, "Does the Big Bang Fit with the Bible?" in K. Ham, gen. ed., *The New Answers Book 2* (Green Forest, AR: Master Books, 2008), p. 103–110, https://answersingenesis.org/big-bang/does-the-big-bang-fit-with-the-bible/.

30. B. Hodge, *The Fall of Satan* (Green Forest, AR: Master Books, 2011), p. 68–76.

11 | BIBLICALLY, COULD DEATH HAVE EXISTED BEFORE SIN?

KEN HAM AND BODIE HODGE

Death and sin — these are two things today's society seems to want to avoid in a conversation! In today's secular culture, kids have been taught for generations that death goes back for millions of years. But there is a huge contrast when you open the pages of Scripture beginning in Genesis.

There is no greater authority than God on any issue (consider Hebrews 6:13[1]). Since God is the authority regarding the past (as well as the authority on all matters), then it is logical that the Bible should be the authority on the issue of death and its relationship with sin. Let's get a big picture of sin and death and how they are related in the Bible.

EVERYTHING WAS PERFECT ORIGINALLY

> Then God saw everything that He had made, and indeed it was very good. So the evening and the morning were the sixth day (Genesis 1:31).

> He is the Rock, His work is perfect; for all His ways are justice, a God of truth and without injustice; righteous and upright is He (Deuteronomy 32:4).

When God finished creating at the end of day 6, God declared everything "very good." It was very good — it was perfect. God's work of creation is perfect and this is verified in Deuteronomy 32:4. We would expect nothing less of a perfect God.

---

1. For when God made a promise to Abraham, because He could swear by no one greater, He swore by Himself.

What was this "perfect" or "very good" creation like? Were animals dying? Was man dying? Let's look more closely at what the Bible teaches.

very good!

A very good creation

EVERYTHING WAS VEGETARIAN ORIGINALLY

> And God said, "See, I have given you every herb that yields seed which is on the face of all the earth, and every tree whose fruit yields seed; to you it shall be for food. Also, to every beast of the earth, to every bird of the air, and to everything that creeps on the earth, in which there is life, I have given every green herb for food"; and it was so (Genesis 1:29–30).

From Genesis 1:29–30 we know that living things like animals and man were not eating meat originally. So meat-eaters today were all vegetarian *originally*, which indicates that death (bloodshed) was *not* part of the original creation. One would not expect a God of life to be a *god of death*. When we look at heaven in Revelation 21–22, there will be no death, pain, or suffering.

One might object and say, "But plants could have died!" But the person asking fails to realize that plants were not "alive" in the biblical sense of *nephesh chayyah* — only animals and man. Since plants are not alive by God's standard, then they can't die.

Plants were made for the purpose of food. They are like solar-powered, self-replicating, biological machines for the purpose of food, clothes, medicine, etc. So plants (microbes and cells too) are ruled out as an option of death before the Fall.[2] The Bible only describes humans and animals as living; and of course, man is distinguished from animals, as human life is made in the image of God.

If a Christian wants to side with the humanistic (e.g., atheistic) view of the world where death existed for millions of years and try to use the majority of the fossil layers as their evidence of slow gradual accumulation instead of a global Flood, they have major problems.[3]

2. Michael Todhunter, "Do Leaves Die?" September 6, 2006, http://www.answersingenesis. org/articles/am/v1/n2/do-leaves-die.

3. Bodie Hodge, "How Old Is the Earth?" May 30, 2007, AiG website, http://www. answersingenesis.org/articles/2007/05/30/how-old-is-earth.

The fossil layers contain examples of many animals that had eaten other animals and the remains are still found in stomach contents.[4] So this rules out many of the rock layers as being evidence of million of years, because the Lord declared that animals were originally vegetarian. The Flood of Noah's day is a much better explanation of the rock layers with examples of animals having eaten other animals, as such would have happened *after* sin.

Death is a punishment

> And the LORD God commanded the man, saying, "Of every tree of the garden you may freely eat; but of the tree of the knowledge of good and evil you shall not eat, for in the day that you eat of it you shall surely die" (Genesis 2:16–17).

God gave the command in Genesis 2:16–17 that sin would be punishable by death. This is significant when we look at the big picture of death. If death in *any* form was around prior to God's declaration in Genesis 1:31 that everything was "very good," then death would be very good too — hence it would not be a punishment at all! So death (and bloodshed, suffering, and disease) shouldn't be in the original perfect creation but only as a *punishment* for sin.

Some have pointed out that this passage is not referring to animal death. In one sense, we agree with them; this verse was not directed toward animals (more on this in a moment). But by the same logic, it was not directed toward Eve or to the rest of us (Adam's descendants), but Eve died and so do we! This passage is in reference to Adam's death, but as will be seen in a moment, this sin also affected Eve with death. Even sinful angels and Satan's sin is counted against them as eternal death in hell (e.g., Matthew 25:41,[5] 2 Peter 2:4,[6] Revelation 20:10,[7] 20:13–14[8]). This shows the all-encompassing effect of the sin-death relationship.

---

4. As an example see Ryan McClay, "Dino Dinner Hard to Swallow," Answers in Genesis website, January 21, 2005, http://www.answersingenesis.org/docs2005/0121dino_dinner.asp.
5. Then He will also say to those on the left hand, "Depart from Me, you cursed, into the everlasting fire prepared for the devil and his angels."
6. For if God did not spare the angels who sinned, but cast them down to hell and delivered them into chains of darkness, to be reserved for judgment.
7. The devil, who deceived them, was cast into the lake of fire and brimstone where the beast and the false prophet are. And they will be tormented day and night forever and ever.
8. The sea gave up the dead who were in it, and Death and Hades delivered up the dead who were in them. And they were judged, each one according to his works. Then Death and Hades were cast into the lake of fire. This is the second death.

ADAM KNEW WHAT 'DIE' MEANT

Some people have brought up the objection that if there was no death existing in the world, then how did Adam know what God meant in Genesis 2:17. God, the author of language, programmed Adam with language when He created him, as we know they conversed right from the start on day 6 (see Genesis 2). Since God makes things perfectly, Adam knew what death meant — even if he did not have *experiential* knowledge of it. Since God makes things perfectly, Adam knew what the word *death* meant in the language God had given him, and probably understood it better than any of us!

SIN BROUGHT ANIMAL DEATH

The first recorded death and passages referring to death as a reality came with sin in Genesis 3 when the serpent, Eve, and Adam all were disobedient to God. Please note that what happened is the first *hint* that things will die:

> So the LORD God said to the serpent: "Because you have done this, you are cursed more than all cattle, and more than every beast of the field; on your belly you shall go, and you shall eat dust all the days of your life (Genesis 3:14).

Genesis 3:14 indicates that animals, which were cursed along with the serpent, would no longer live forever but have a limited life (*all the days of your life*). This is the first hint of animal death, though this is not a "knock-down, drag-out" case but merely a hint. Since animals were cursed in this verse, it also affects them and they too will die. Though this particular verse doesn't rule out animal death prior to sin, its placement with sin and the Curse in Genesis 3 may very well be significant.

The first recorded death of animals was in Genesis 3:21, when God covered Adam and Eve with coats of *skins* to replace their fig leaf coverings they quickly assume would hide their nakedness.

> Also for Adam and his wife the LORD God made tunics of skin, and clothed them (Genesis 3:21).

Abel apparently mimicked something like this when he sacrificed from his flocks (fat portions) in Genesis 4:4 and Noah after the Flood in Genesis 8:20, and Abraham and the Israelites did this as well, giving sin offerings of lambs, doves, etc.

The Lord's sacrifice to make coats of skins for Adam and Eve

The punishment for sin was death, so something had to die. Rightly, Adam and Eve deserved to die, but we serve a God of grace, mercy, and love. And out of His love and His mercy, He basically gave us a "grace" period to repent.

Noah offering sacrifices

The Lord sacrificed animals to cover this sin. It was not enough to *take away* sin, but merely offered a temporary covering. This shows how much more valuable mankind is than animals (see also Matthew 6:26[9], 12:12[10]).

The punishment from an infinite God is an infinite punishment and animals are not infinite. They simply cannot take that punishment. We needed

---

9. Look at the birds of the air, for they neither sow nor reap nor gather into barns; yet your heavenly Father feeds them. Are you not of more value than they?

10. Of how much more value then is a man than a sheep? Therefore it is lawful to do good on the Sabbath.

a perfect and infinite sacrifice that could take the infinite punishment from an infinite God. Jesus Christ, the Son of God, who is infinite, could take that punishment. These animal sacrifices were foreshadowing Jesus Christ who was the ultimate, perfect, infinite sacrifice for our sins on the Cross. Hebrews reveals:

> And according to the law almost all things are purified with blood, and without shedding of blood there is no remission (Hebrews 9:22).

This is why Jesus had to die and this is why animals were sacrificed to cover sin. These passages make it clear that animal death has a relationship with *man's* sin. Consider the fact that animal death first came about *after* man's sin. It was a direct result of human sin. Also, it is the very basis and foundation of the gospel.

If there was millions of years of death and bloodshed of animals before sin, then what would the shedding of blood have to do with the remission of sin? It just doesn't work to try to fit millions of years of death and bloodshed before Adam sinned.

SIN BROUGHT HUMAN DEATH

This same type of proclamation that animals will ultimately die (*all the days of your life*) is mimicked in Genesis 3:17 where man would also die (*all the days of your life*). Like the animals, man would die fulfilling what was said in Genesis 2:17 (for in the day that you eat of it you shall *surely die*).

> Then to Adam He said, "Because you have heeded the voice of your wife, and have eaten from the tree of which I commanded you, saying, 'You shall not eat of it': Cursed is the ground for your sake; in toil you shall eat of it all the days of your life" (Genesis 3:17).

Some have stated that they believe this was only a *spiritual* death, but God made it clear in Genesis 3:19 by further describing it as "returning to dust" from which they came, which makes it clear it was not excluding a physical death.

> In the sweat of your face you shall eat bread till you return to the ground, for out of it you were taken; for dust you are, and to dust you shall return (Genesis 3:19).

Even Paul, when speaking of human death specifically says:

> Therefore, just as through one man sin entered the world, and death through sin, and thus death spread to all men, because all sinned (Romans 5:12).

> The last enemy that will be destroyed is death (1 Corinthians 15:26).

> Nevertheless death reigned from Adam to Moses, even over those who had not sinned according to the likeness of the transgression of Adam, who is a type of Him who was to come (Romans 5:14).

> For if by the one man's offense death reigned through the one, much more those who receive abundance of grace and of the gift of righteousness will reign in life through the One, Jesus Christ (Romans 5:17).

If the death God mentions is only spiritual, then why did Jesus have to die physically — or rise physically? If the Curse meant only spiritual death, then the gospel is undermined.

It is true that Adam and Eve didn't die the *exact* day they ate, as some seem to think Genesis 2:17 implies. The Hebrew is *die-die* (*muwth-muwth*), which is often translated as "surely die" or literally as "dying you shall die," which indicates the beginning of dying (i.e., an ingressive sense).

At that point, Adam and Eve began to die and would return to dust. If they were meant to have died right then, the text should have used *muwth* only once, as is used in the Hebrew meaning "dead, died, or die" and not "*beginning to* die" or "*surely* die."

DOes THe BIBLe TeacH DeaTH BeFore sIN?

The Bible tells us very clearly from many passages that there was no death before sin. In fact, there are *no Bible verses* indicating there was death prior to sin.

The only reason some people try to insert death before sin is to try to fit man's ideas of "millions of years" of death that is found in the fossil record into the Bible. But this makes a mockery of God's statement that everything was very good in Genesis 1:31.[11]

---

11. Then God saw everything that He had made, and indeed it was very good. So the evening and the morning were the sixth day.

Death before sin is a problem for a perfect creation at the end of day 6.

Death, animals eating other animals, thorns, cancer, tumors, and so on are not very good, and yet these are found in those fossil layers. But if one argues that these are part of a perfect world, then do they expect these things in heaven — which is a restoration that is to be a perfect new creation once again?

This leads to compromising what God plainly says to accommodate fallible man's ideas. Besides, the Scriptures reveal a global Flood in Genesis 6–8, *after sin*, which explains the vast majority of fossil layers. It is better to trust what God says:

> It is better to trust in the LORD than to put confidence in man (Psalm 118:8).

Keep in mind that having death before also undermines the very gospel where Jesus Christ stepped into history to conquer sin and death. In doing so, He had graciously offered the free gift of salvation to all who receive him.

TWO VIEWS OF DEATH

There are primarily two views of history (man's opinions/secular and God's view in the Bible) with two different authorities (man's fallible reason *apart* from God, and a perfect God) arguing over the past.

Biblical view of death

According to the Bible, a perfect God created a perfect creation and because of man's sin, death and suffering came into the world — death is an enemy. But through Christ we look forward to a time when there will be no more pain or death or suffering (Revelation 21:4). According to man's ideas about the past, death is actually the glorified hero in the story.

In a secular worldview, there has always been death and always will be. So when *Christians* try to incorporate secular history of millions of years into their theology, was there really change when Adam and Eve sinned? And what will heaven really be like then?

A secular view of death

Summary

In the fossil remains in the rock layers, there is evidence of death, suffering, thorns, carnivory, cancer, and other diseases like arthritis. So *all* old-earth worldviews have to then accept death, suffering, bloodshed, thorns, carnivory, and diseases like cancer before Adam's sin. Now after God created Adam, He said everything He made was "very good" (Genesis 1:31). This is confirmed as a *perfect* creation by the God of life in Deuteronomy 32:4 since every work of God is perfect.

But if one has accepted the millions-of-years idea to explain the fossil record, then millions of years of death, bloodshed, disease, thorns, suffering, and carnivory existed before man. But as the Bible makes clear, it was Adam's sin that caused death (Genesis 2:16–17, 3:19), suffering (e.g., Genesis 3:16–17), thorns, (Genesis 3:18) and the whole reason why we need a new heavens and a new earth (e.g., Isaiah 66:22;[12] 2 Peter 3:13;[13] Revelation 21:1[14]) — because what we have now are cursed and broken (Romans 8:22[15]).

Also, originally, the Bible makes it clear in Genesis 1:29–30[16] that man and animals were vegetarian — however, the fossil record has many evidences of animals eating animals. Genesis 1:30 is verified as a strictly vegetarian diet since man was not permitted to eat meat until after the Flood in Genesis 9:3,[17] which was directly contrasted to the command in Genesis 1:29.

To accept millions of years also means God called diseases like cancer (of which there is evidence in the fossil record) "very good." And because ". . . without shedding of blood there is no remission" (Hebrews 9:22[18]), then allowing the shedding of blood millions of years before sin would *undermine* the atonement. Really, believing in millions of years blames God for death and disease instead of blaming our sin from which Christ came to rescue us.

12. "For as the new heavens and the new earth which I will make shall remain before Me," declares the LORD, "so your descendants and your name remain.

13. Nevertheless, we, according to His promise, look for new heavens and a new earth in which righteousness dwells.

14. Now I saw a new heaven and a new earth, for the first heaven and the first earth had passed away. Also there was no more sea.

15. For we know that the whole creation groans and labors with birth pangs together until now.

16. And God said, "See, I have given you every herb that yields seed which is on the face of all the earth, and every tree whose fruit yields seed; to you it shall be for food. Also, to every beast of the earth, to every bird of the air, and to everything that creeps on the earth, in which there is life, I have given every green herb for food"; and it was so.

17. Every moving thing that lives shall be food for you. I have given you all things, even as the green herbs.

18. And according to the law almost all things are purified with blood, and without shedding of blood there is no remission.

One cannot deny biblically that there is a relationship between human sin and animal death. Just briefly look at the sacrifices of animals required for human sin throughout the Old Testament. This sacrifice began in the Garden of Eden (the first blood sacrifice as a covering for their sin, a picture of what was to come in the lamb of God who takes away the sin of the world), that points to Jesus Christ, the ultimate and final sacrifice:

> . . . for this He did once for all when He offered up Himself (Hebrews 7:27).

Our hope is that these Christians (who have bought into an old earth) will return to the plain teachings in the Bible and stop mixing God's Word with secular beliefs that clearly contradict God's revelation and undermine the gospel by blaming God for death instead of our sin.

12 | GLOBaL or LOCaL FLOOD?

Ken HaM and BODIe HODGe

IntroDuCTIOn

> The flood was indeed a river flood. . . . The language of Genesis allows for a regional flood. . . . The parts of modern Iraq which were occupied by the ancient Sumerians are extremely flat. The floodplain, surrounding the Tigris and the Euphrates rivers, covers over 50,000 square miles which slope toward the gulf at less than one foot per mile. . . . Drainage is extremely poor and flooding is quite common, even without large rainstorms during the summer river-level peak (when Noah's flood happened).[1]

A Christian who believes that Noah's Flood was local and did not cover the entire globe penned these words. In fact, the idea of a small regional flood in Noah's day is often promoted by Christians who mix their religion with "millions of years" of supposed naturalistic history!

As a reminder, you need to understand that the idea of millions of years comes from the idea that rock layers all over the world were laid down slowly over long ages without any major catastrophes. In other words, the idea of millions of years is predicated on the idea that there could NOT have been a global Flood. Otherwise, a global Flood would disrupt rock layers that exist and rearrange the sediment and lay down new rock layers!

---

1. Don Stoner, "The Historical Context for the Book of Genesis," Revision 2011-06-06, Part 3: Identifying Noah and the Great Flood, http://www.dstoner.net/Genesis_Context/Context.html#part3.

WHaT DoeS THe BIBLe Say?

Did Noah experience a local flood, which left only a few sediment layers, as floods do today? God's record is clear: the water covered the entire globe and killed all the animals on earth. Such unique conditions are the only consistent way to explain worldwide fossil-bearing layers thousands of feet deep.

Scripture is clear about the historic reality of a global Flood in Noah's day. Genesis 7:17–23 specifically says:

> Now the flood was on the earth forty days. The waters increased and lifted up the ark, and it rose high above the earth. The waters prevailed and greatly increased on the earth, and the ark moved about on the surface of the waters. And the waters prevailed exceedingly on the earth, and all the high hills under the whole heaven were covered. The waters prevailed fifteen cubits upward, and the mountains were covered. And all flesh died that moved on the earth: birds and cattle and beasts and every creeping thing that creeps on the earth, and every man. All in whose nostrils was the breath of the spirit of life, all that was on the dry land, died. So He destroyed all living things which were on the face of the ground: both man and cattle, creeping thing and bird of the air. They were destroyed from the earth. Only Noah and those who were with him in the ark remained alive (Genesis 7:17–23).

The Scripture is clear that "all the high hills under the whole heaven were covered" as "the waters prevailed fifteen cubits [that is about ~26 feet[2], or ~8 m] upward." All air-breathing land animals and people that were outside the ark that lived on the earth also died (Genesis 7:22–23).

Today, many people, including Christians, unfortunately do not accept the biblical account of a worldwide flood because they have been taught that most rocks and fossils were deposited over millions of years (and therefore not by a global Flood). Until the 1800s, most people from the Middle East to the Western World believed what the Bible records about creation and the global Flood. The secular idea of millions of years did not gain extensive

---

2. Using the long cubit of about 20.4 inches.

popularity until the 1830s, under the influence of a man named Charles Lyell — who opposed a global Flood!

Based on how slowly some rock layers seem to form today (assuming no catastrophes), Lyell rejected the Bible's claims and declared that the earth's many rock layers must have been laid down slowly over millions of years. But he never witnessed the actual formation of the earlier rocks to see whether a unique, one-time global Flood unlike anything we observe today could lay the majority of the rock layers with fossils.

Lyell's claim was based on his own preconceptions and belief in the religion of naturalism, not his observations. Lyell's idea took hold in Western universities and spread throughout the Western World.

As a response, many Christians simply tried to add this idea of long ages to the Bible. What these Christians should have done was stand on the authority of the Bible and defend the global Flood, which can easily account for the bulk of fossil-bearing rock layers we find all over the world. Naturally, we have had some rock layers since the time of the Flood with local catastrophes such as volcanoes or local floods. But the bulk of the rock layers with fossils came from the Flood of Noah.

Some Christians have tried to put millions of years of rock formation before the global Flood to explain the bulk of the rock layers that contain fossils. But the problem is that the Flood waters would have ripped up a number of these old rock layers and laid down new ones! So this compromise not only fails to explain the rock layers but also dishonors the clear claims of Scripture. The global Flood makes perfect sense, and it is foolish to stray from God's Word just because some men disagree.

Although there is tremendous physical evidence (fossil laden sedimentary strata over the earth) of a global flood, ultimately it is a matter of trust in a perfect God who created everything (Genesis 1:1[3]), knows everything (Colossians 2:3[4]), has always been there (Revelation 22:13[5]), and cannot lie (Titus 1:2[6]). The only alternative is to trust imperfect, fallible human beings who can only speculate on the past (see Romans 3:4[7]).

---

3. In the beginning God created the heavens and the earth.
4. In whom [Christ] are hidden all the treasures of wisdom and knowledge.
5. I am the Alpha and the Omega, the Beginning and the End, the First and the Last.
6. In hope of eternal life which God, who cannot lie, promised before time began.
7. Certainly not! Indeed, let God be true but every man a liar. As it is written: "That You may be justified in Your words, and may overcome when You are judged."

LOCAL FLOOD PROBLEMS

Additionally, there are many problems with the claim that Noah's Flood was local. For instance:

- Why did God tell Noah to build an ark? If the Flood had been only local, Noah and his family could have just moved to higher ground or over a local mountain range or hills to avoid the floodwaters.
- The wicked people that the Flood was intended to destroy could have escaped God's judgment in the same manner. They could have used small boats or floating debris to swim to the edge of the flood and survive.
- Why would Noah have to put birds on the ark when they could have flown over the hills to safe ground?
- Why would animals be required to be on the ark to keep their kinds alive on the earth (Genesis 7:2–3[8]), if representatives of their kinds existed all over the earth outside of the alleged local Flood area?
- Did God fail at His stated task where He said that He would destroy all land animals on the earth since the Flood was *local* (Genesis 6:17[9])?
- Why would a flood take place *over the course* of about a year if it were local?
- Why did Noah remain on the ark for about seven months after coming to rest from a little river flood? Does a local flood really have about five months of rising and five months of falling in a river valley? Such a flood would merely carve out a deep valley and wash Noah downstream to the ocean!
- How could the ark have landed in the mountains of Ararat far upstream (and up in the mountains above) of the alleged river valley when all flow is going to take the ark in the opposite direction?
- The Flood occurred about 1,656 years after creation. If all people outside the ark were judged and drowned in this little

---

8. You shall take with you seven each of every clean animal, a male and his female; two each of animals that are unclean, a male and his female; also seven each of birds of the air, male and female, to keep the species alive on the face of all the earth.

9. And behold, I Myself am bringing floodwaters on the earth, to destroy from under heaven all flesh in which is the breath of life; everything that is on the earth shall die.

local river flood (e.g., Genesis 7:23,[10] Matthew 24:39[11]) then they were all still living in this one little region on earth. Why didn't the Lord previously confuse their languages and scatter them for disobeying his command in Genesis 1 to be fruitful and multiply (Genesis 1:28[12])? It only took about 100 years or so after the Flood for God to judge mankind for not scattering at Babel.[13]

The proposal of a local Flood for Genesis 6–8 simply doesn't make sense of the context.

Rainbow Promise

Another problem presents itself. If the Flood were local, then God would be a liar, for God promised in Genesis 9:11[14] never to send a Flood like the one He just did to destroy the earth again. Yet the world has seen many local floods. Why the rainbow promise? The Bible says:

> Thus I establish My covenant with you: Never again shall all flesh be cut off by the waters of the flood; never again shall there be a flood to destroy the earth." And God said: "This is the sign of the covenant which I make between Me and you, and every living creature that is with you, for perpetual generations: I set My rainbow in the cloud, and it shall be for the sign of the covenant between Me and the earth. It shall be, when I bring a cloud over the earth, that the rainbow shall be seen in the cloud; and I will remember My covenant which is between Me and you and every living creature of all flesh; the waters shall never again become a flood to destroy all flesh. The rainbow shall be in the cloud, and I will look on it to remember the everlasting covenant between God and every living creature of all flesh that is on the earth." And God said to Noah,

---

10. So He destroyed all living things which were on the face of the ground: both man and cattle, creeping thing and bird of the air. They were destroyed from the earth. Only Noah and those who were with him in the ark remained alive.
11. And did not know until the flood came and took them all away, so also will the coming of the Son of Man be.
12. Then God blessed them, and God said to them, "Be fruitful and multiply; fill the earth and subdue it; have dominion over the fish of the sea, over the birds of the air, and over every living thing that moves on the earth."
13. Bodie Hodge, *Tower of Babel* (Green Forest, AR: Master Books, 2013), p. 37–42.
14. Thus I establish My covenant with you: Never again shall all flesh be cut off by the waters of the flood; never again shall there be a flood to destroy the earth.

"This is the sign of the covenant which I have established between
Me and all flesh that is on the earth" (Genesis 9:11–17).

This rules out the idea of a local flood. Some have commented that they
think rainbows didn't exist until this point in Genesis 9. However, the Bible
doesn't say this. Like bread and wine used in communion, so a rainbow
now takes on the meaning as designated by God. The main reason some
have suggested rainbows didn't exist was their assumption there was no rain
before the Flood. Let us discuss this idea, and where it came from.

Rain Before the Flood?

In Genesis 2, which is largely a breakdown of what occurred on day 6 of
creation, we read:

> This is the history of the heavens and the earth when they
> were created, in the day that the LORD God made the earth and
> the heavens, before any plant of the field was in the earth and
> before any herb of the field had grown. For the LORD God had
> not caused it to rain on the earth, and there was no man to till the
> ground; but a mist went up from the earth and watered the whole
> face of the ground (Genesis 2:4–6).

Where it states that "God had not caused it to rain on the earth" is projected
into the future until the time of the Flood. The Bible never mentions rain
from this point until the Flood. Is this warranted? Not necessarily.

The context of this passage is looking back over creation week, not pro-
jecting forward. The *field* crops had not grown yet (herbs and crops of the
field). Man did not exist yet either, so this is early on day 6. Though apparently God had planted the garden already, it just hadn't grown yet (Genesis
2:8[15]). That did not occur until after God made Adam and placed him in the
Garden (Genesis 2:9[16]). A mist had come up from the ground and watered
the face of the ground.

What we know is that this was the case when man was created. What
we don't know is whether or not the situation remained this way until the

---

15. The LORD God planted a garden eastward in Eden, and there He put the man whom He
    had formed.
16. And out of the ground the LORD God made every tree grow that is pleasant to the sight
    and good for food. The tree of life was also in the midst of the garden, and the tree of the
    knowledge of good and evil.

Flood. It would seem to defy the laws of physics that God Himself sustains. Dr. Tommy Mitchell sums this up nicely when he writes on the "no rain" subject as an argument we should avoid:

> The passage describes the environment before Adam was created. This mist may have been one of the primary methods that God used to hydrate the dry land He created on Day Three. Furthermore, while this mist was likely the watering source for that vegetation throughout the remainder of Creation Week, the text does not require it to be the only water source after Adam's creation.
>
> Some argue that this mist eliminated the need for rain until the time of the Flood. However, presence of the mist prior to Adam's creation does not preclude the existence of or the need for rain after he was created.
>
> Genesis 2:5–6 reveals that before the Sixth Day of Creation Week, God had watered the plants He made with a mist, but had not yet caused rain or created a man to till the ground. To demand that rain didn't happen until after the Flood from this passage has no more logical support than to claim, from the passage, that no one farmed until after the Flood."[17]

Enough said.

---

17. Tommy Mitchell, "There Was No Rain Before the Flood," October 19, 2010, https://answersingenesis.org/creationism/arguments-to-avoid/there-was-no-rain-before-the-flood/.

13 | THE RELIGIOUS ATTACK OF HUMANISM'S "MILLIONS OF YEARS" . . . IN MY ERA

BODIE HODGE

Growing up in the 80's and 90's, my state schooling constantly imposed the idea of millions of years on my impressionable mind. Little did I know that I was subtly being taught the religion of humanism.

Humanistic teachers, who taught evolution, millions of years, and big bang, had told me that there was a separation of religion from schools. They said that schools were neutral. But that was merely a lie, which was usually directed toward kids going to church, to make us think that what we were learning at school was perfectly compatible with any religion, including Christianity.

What most of these humanistic teachers don't tell you is that they are really attacking the Bible and want to influence you to start dismissing parts of the Bible (e.g., creation, belief in the biblical God, etc.). In other words, the humanistic teachers were fine with saying that you can believe [the humanistic elements] they were teaching and still be a "Christian," as long as you don't really believe what the Bible says.

Not all humanistic teachers were so subtle either. Some of the teachers I had openly attacked God and the Bible while promoting the religion of humanism. And let's not forget the handful of good Christian teachers who were stuck in the difficult position of being in an education system that is now set up to attack the Bible. They need our prayers by the way — they are like missionaries next to the humanists who now dominate our education system. But in retrospect, I was being deceived at my state schools not just regarding origins, but I also had humanistic morality imposed on me, humanistic views of sexuality, etc.

As I looked back, what these secular humanists really meant by separation of religion and state (so called 'separation of church and state'), was that they were trying to keep *Christianity* out of the classroom, while forcing their religion onto unsuspecting kids. It was a subtle attack on Christians, and many parents didn't know the wiser that they were sending their kids to be taught to be radical humanists!

The humanists are clever though. They understood that if you control the minds of the next generation, then you are discipling them to be the next generation of humanists. So they have crept in under the radar, if you will, to make it sound as though their religion is not a religion and then use the state (and your tax money) to fund their preaching projects in state schools. While cap-stoning what humanists were already doing in school, leading humanist John Dunphy stated in 1983:

> I am convinced that the battle for humankind's future must be waged and won in the public school classroom by teachers who correctly perceive their role as the proselytizers of a new faith: a religion of humanity that recognizes and respects the spark of what theologians call divinity in every human being. These teachers must embody the same selfless dedication as the most rabid fundamentalist preachers, for they will be ministers of another sort, utilizing a classroom instead of a pulpit to convey humanist values in whatever subject they teach, regardless of the educational level — preschool day care or large state university. The classroom must and will become an arena of conflict between the old and the new — the rotting corpse of Christianity, together with all its adjacent evils and misery, and the new faith of humanism.[1]

This quote came out when I was in grade school. I see reflections of this too. For example, I was in grade school when we were told we were no longer permitted to say the *Pledge of Allegiance* because it mentions God (thus, this promotes the anti-God religion of humanism). In our extracurricular activities like basketball and football, we used to pray to the Lord for safety for our team and the opposing team. I recall when the superintendent came out and suppressed this and said we are no longer allowed to

---

1. J. Dunphy, "A Religion for a New Age," *The Humanist*, Jan.–Feb. 1983, p. 23, 26; as cited by Wendell R. Bird, *Origin of the Species — Revisited*, Vol. II (New York, NY, Philosophical Library, c. 1989), p. 257.

pray — thus, our extracurricular activates were going to operate in accordance with humanism.

Many reading this may recall when prayer, the Bible, or creation was taken out of schools. More recently the *Ten Commandments* have been ripped out of public places and nativity scenes are being attacked and removed. But religion was not removed — merely replaced with the religion of humanism. We see the religion of humanism rampant like a disease in textbooks, state schools, museums, movies, law, and media, much of which is funded by taxes.

There is a concerted attack on Christian kids to try to subtly train them to be humanists! It is a government-funded program (i.e., state-funded schools, state-funded museums, etc.) to force this religion onto the youth. They tried to do it to me. This is nothing new — Hitler, prior to WWII did this with the kids in Germany, and raised himself an army of Nazis in one generation! Nazism is just one variant of humanism, just like atheism, evolutionism, agnosticism, and secularism. The Nazis and Hitler held firmly to humanism's tenants of naturalism, evolution, and millions of years.

Interestingly, education is *meaningless* in a humanistic worldview where everything is just rearranged chemicals doing what chemicals do! Consider that snails do not develop education systems to train in philosophy, science, history, literature, etc. Education is required by God's command to train (e.g., Exodus 18:20[2]; Proverbs 22:6[3]) and predicated on the fact that man is made in the image of a logical, knowledgeable God (Genesis 1:26–27[4]). In other words, education is a *Christian* institution that humanism infiltrates and tries to destroy. The humanists have been doing an effective job for a number of years at destroying education. We are seeing the fruits of it in our culture today.

My guess is that most Christian parents and grandparents in today's era do not realize that schools are openly teaching this religion, thinking that schools are *neutral*. But they are not. They teach philosophy from a secular humanistic perspective, they teach biology, earth science, history,

---

2. "And you shall teach them the statutes and the laws, and show them the way in which they must walk and the work they must do.

3. Train up a child in the way he should go, and when he is old he will not depart from it.

4. Then God said, "Let Us make man in Our image, according to Our likeness; let them have dominion over the fish of the sea, over the birds of the air, and over the cattle, over all the earth and over every creeping thing that creeps on the earth." So God created man in His own image; in the image of God He created him; male and female He created them.

sex education, and so on from a humanistic perspective. It was in my text-books as a kid and it is even more pronounced in the textbooks today!

If you have ever been taught big bang, steady states, abiogenesis (life accidentally came from matter/non-life), millions of years (no-global Flood), evolution, and the like, then you too were taught the religion of humanism!

Humanism teaches that man is the ultimate authority on all subjects (hence, God would *not* be seen as the ultimate authority). Humanism holds to a position of naturalism — that nature is all that exists. Hence, once again, God and the spiritual are not seen to exist. Humanism teaches things like evolution — that God had nothing to do with the creation of the kinds of life we find. Humanistic teachers and textbooks teach that life came from inanimate matter by accident — which is just another attack claiming God had nothing to do with life!

But I suggest one of the biggest attacks by humanists is the idea of "millions of years." Even many Christians in our generation have succumbed to this false tenet and stand with non-Christians to oppose Genesis! This may be one of the biggest problems within the Church today.

This religious idea of long ages was imposed on me from an early age in school from many different angles. I recall teacher after teacher discussing this alleged "truth" from grade school, then high school, to state university. As an example, one of my grade textbooks says:

> "that in the past 2 million years, many ice glaciers. . . ."[5]
> "About 200 million years ago. . . ."[6]
> "Over millions of years. . . ."[7]
> "Many millions of years later. . . ."[8]
> "For millions of years, most of earth. . . ."[9]
> "over millions of years, the parts of simple animals began to. . . ."[10]
> "about 500 million years ago."[11]
> "for a hundred million years."[12]

---

5. Albert Piltz and Roger Van Bever, *Discovering Science 5* (Columbus, OH: Charles E. Merrill Publishing Co., 1970), p. 205.
6. Ibid., p. 313.
7. Ibid., p. 313.
8. Ibid., p. 313.
9. Ibid., p. 314.
10. Ibid., p. 316.
11. Ibid., p. 317.
12. Ibid., p. 318.

"more than 500 million years."[13]
"had become extinct 70 million years ago."[14]
"lived on the earth fifty million years ago."[15]

This textbook also had subtle hints at long ages as well that simply permeate the mind of the undiscerning, which is what I was in those early formative years.

"Antarctic ice is more than 100,000 years old."[16]
"the last Ice Age began to melt away about 10,000 years ago."[17]
"After a long time, birds developed."[18]
"Some animals became extinct long before man lived on earth."[19]

Little did I know, or my parents know, that I was being educated in the religion of humanism, and specifically hit hard with *millions of years*, for 40 hours a week for most of my life by the time I was 18. Then I was grilled even harder with this concept at the university by the time I had finished with my master's degree at the age of 24!

Throughout my years I was indoctrinated to believe that it took millions of years to form oil (petroleum), coal, diamonds, precious gemstones, fossils, rock, petrified wood, canyons, etc. Knowing that this humanistic story of millions of years is just a false religion that had been imposed on me . . . *does* it take millions of years to form these things? Let's investigate and put this religious viewpoint to the test.

---

13. Ibid., p. 318.
14. Ibid., p. 319.
15. Ibid., p. 323.
16. Ibid., p. 206.
17. Ibid., p. 205.
18. Ibid., p. 322.
19. Ibid., p. 324.

14 | DOESN'T IT TAKE MILLIONS OF YEARS TO FORM ROCK AND ROCK LAYERS?

BODIE HODGE

I once had a student jump up and say, "But it takes millions of years to form rock." My response was, "What experiments have been run over the course of millions of years that proves it takes millions of years to form rock?"

There have never been any observations or experiments run over the course of millions of years. It is mere fantasy to think otherwise. Sadly, this student merely assumed what he had been indoctrinated with. He presumed that it took millions of years to form rock because that is what he had been inundated with and that we must have been "off of our rocker" to think otherwise. Naturally, I hadn't bought into his false religious belief on this issue.

It was he who arbitrarily had the false belief that something took millions of years to form. My response was to reveal that his belief was *mere opinion* (blind belief) that did not have any merit. His arbitrary opinion was just that . . . arbitrary and therefore fallacious.

Scientifically, we can prove that it doesn't take millions of years to form rock. The easiest example is concrete. Concrete can form in hours to days — we merely reproduce the chemical process to make certain rock (concretions). So it doesn't take millions of years to form rock, just the right conditions.

Following are a lot of examples of rapid rock. In 1975, a clock was found embedded in rock near the South Jetty at Westport, Washington.[1] This clock was not millions of years old! Another example is a recent marine spark plug encased in rock.[2]

---

1. The Clock in a Rock, *Creation*, 19, no 3 (June 1997), https://answersingenesis.org/geology/catastrophism/the-clock-in-the-rock/.
2. "Sparking Interest in Rapid Rocks," *Creation*, 21, no 4 (September 1999), https://answersingenesis.org/geology/geologic-time-scale/sparking-interest-in-rapid-rocks/.

Petrifying Well at Knaresborough

A ship's bell was encased in a natural marine concretion.[3] The bell came from a wooden ship named *Isabella Watson*. The ship sank in 1852 near Victoria, Australia. It is currently in the possession of the Maritime Archaeological Unit of Heritage Victoria.

In Spray Mine, which had been closed for 50 years, a hat that had been left had turned to stone.[4] This is the original *hard hat* I guess!

In the region of Yorkshire, England, there is a famous place that has attracted tourists since the 1600s. It is the famous Petrifying Well at Knaresborough and it is famous for converting teddy bears to stone in about three to five months![5]

When volcanoes go off, they can form rock quickly too. Even many items that were buried under the hot ash can petrify and turn to stone quickly. Mt. Tarawera blew its top in New Zealand in June of 1886 and killed over 150 people. After some excavation of one buried village called Te Wairoa, they found many items petrified, including a bowler hat, a ham, and a bag of flour.[6]

  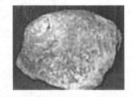

3. "Bell-ieve It: Rapid Rock Formation Rings True," *Creation*, vol. 20, no. 2, March 1998: 6, https://answersingenesis.org/geology/catastrophism/bell-ieve-it-rapid-rock-formation-rings-true/.

4. John Mackay, "Fossil Bolts and Fossil Hats," *Creation Ex Nihilo*, vol. 8, Nov., p. 10.

5. M. White, "The Amazing Stone Bears of Yorkshire," Answers in Genesis, June 1, 2002, http://www.answersingenesis.org/articles/cm/v24/n3/stone-bears.

6. Renton Maclachlan, "Tarawera's Night of Terror," *Creation*, vol. 18, no. 1, December 1995: 16–19, https://answersingenesis.org/geology/catastrophism/taraweras-night-of-terror/.

These few examples show proof that it doesn't take millions of years to form rock — just the right conditions.

Rock Layers - Do They Take Millions of Years to Accumulate?

Many of us have been taught that it takes millions of years of gradual accumulations to form the sedimentary rock layers. For example, we are told it took about 72–79 million years to lay down the Cretaceous rock layer. The secularists claim it was laid down from about 145 million years ago (give or take many millions of years) until about 66 million years ago. The Live Science website has more specific claims:

> The Cretaceous Period was the last and longest segment of the Mesozoic Era. It lasted approximately 79 million years, from the minor extinction event that closed the Jurassic Period about 145.5 million years ago to the Cretaceous-Paleogene (K-Pg) extinction event dated at 65.5 million years ago.[7]

Most of the rock layers that contain fossils are given huge amounts of time to accumulate. See the secular chart on the following page for the typical durations. To reiterate, this concept is called "uniformitarianism." In other words, the secularists assume the layers were formed *uniformly* over long, millions of years, ages. Because of this, they must reject that catastrophes occurred in the past, i.e., global Flood of Noah's day. This is where the geologic timescale (the chart above) came from — assuming that each layer required millions of years to form and that catastrophes didn't occur.

Mt. St. Helens Explosive Throwdown

The Mount St. Helens eruption (1980) laid down rock layers quickly — in a matter of hours and days. Some of these accumulated rock layers extended over 600 feet (~183 meters) in depth since the volcano exploded.[8] Differing types of sedimentary layers occurred sitting one on top of the other — some due to various types of flows (e.g., mudflows, hot or pyroclastic flows), others due to air fall, and so on. The point is that catastrophes can form rock layers quickly.

---

7. Mary Bagley, "Cretaceous Period: Animals, Plants & Extinction Event," Livescience.com, January 7, 2016, http://www.livescience.com/29231-cretaceous-period.html.

8. Dr. Steve Austin, "Why Is Mount St. Helens Important to the Origins Controversy?" *New Answers Book 3*, gen. ed., Ken Ham (Green Forest, AR: Master Books, 2010), https://answersingenesis.org/geology/mount-st-helens/why-is-mount-st-helens-important-to-the-origins-controversy/.

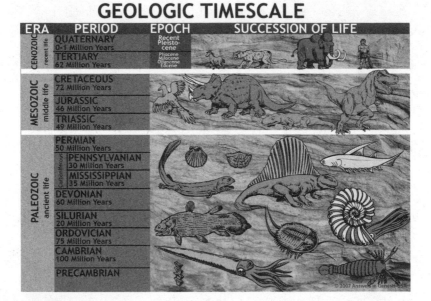

GEOLOGIC TIMESCALE

ERA	PERIOD	EPOCH	SUCCESSION OF LIFE
CENOZOIC recent life	QUATERNARY 0–1 Million Years	Recent Pleisto- cene	
	TERTIARY 62 Million Years	Pliocene Miocene Oligocene Eocene	
MESOZOIC middle life	CRETACEOUS 72 Million Years		
	JURASSIC 46 Million Years		
	TRIASSIC 49 Million Years		
PALEOZOIC ancient life	PERMIAN 50 Million Years		
	PENNSYLVANIAN 30 Million Years		
	MISSISSIPPIAN 35 Million Years		
	DEVONIAN 60 Million Years		
	SILURIAN 20 Million Years		
	ORDOVICIAN 75 Million Years		
	CAMBRIAN 100 Million Years		
	PRECAMBRIAN		

© 2007 Answers in Genesis USA

If this small catastrophic volcano did this in a short time, imagine what the catastrophic global Flood of Noah's day did all over the world.

Laminae Sediments (Varves) Quickly

Laminae (singular *lamina*) are basically fine layers of sedimentary rock — usually less than 1 cm (~4/10 inch). Researchers using laboratory tests have shown that many layers of lamina form quickly and at the same time in both air and water.[9] The phenomenon occurs in moments, not long periods of time.

Furthermore, these laminae are very similar to the tiny layers of sediment we see in nature. These tiny layers in nature, like lake deposits, are called "varves," and supposedly each one takes one year to form. I've always been stumped by the secular idea that every year at the same time, sedimentary deposits suddenly begin a *new* layer! One researcher, Mike Oard reports:

> A rhythmite is a repeating sequence of two or more lamina, which are thin layers. . . . Multiple *turbidites*, the deposits of fast-moving bottom flows of sediment, can form thick sequences of varve-like rhythmites quickly.[10]

9. Guy Berthault, "Experiments on Laminations of Sediments," April 1, 1988, https://answersingenesis.org/geology/sedimentation/experiments-on-lamination-of-sediments/.

10. Mike Oard, "Are There Half a Million Years in the Sediments of Lake Van?" *Answers in Depth*, Answers in Genesis, May 9, 2007, https://answersingenesis.org/geology/sedimentation/are-there-half-a-million-years-in-the-sediments-of-lake-van/.

In other words, currents moving downhill underwater carrying sediment make varves or laminae quickly. These types of examples can be observed with:

> . . . flowing sediment with different particle sizes, shapes, and densities; flooding into lakes; underwater slides; turbidity currents; snow-melt events; underflows from a muddy bottom layer; overflows from a muddy layer floating at the top of a lake; interflows from a muddy layer at intermediate depths; and multiple rapid blooms of microorganisms within one year.[11]

Varves do not require long periods of time. Multiple varve layers can occur quickly and have been observed.

Bent Rock Layers?

Doesn't rock break when it bends? Yes. Rock is a ceramic material and is brittle. So if you bend rocks it shatters (think of a glass or a ceramic plate being bent in half). And yet we find rock layers that have bent or folded layers.

These are often seen at the Grand Canyon. Perhaps the most popular is a

Carbon Canyon

sequence of sedimentary layers of the Tapeats Sandstone, which is a layer at the bottom of the Grand Canyon. Geologists have traced this 90-degree fold and the rock formation doesn't break or fracture! There are no signs of heat deformation either — so it is not metamorphic rock. The only signs of cracking are from drying, which is to be expected.[12]

The layers were still soft and pliable sediment when they were kinked into that angle during folding. *Then* they were solidified into solid rock. This means that each of those folded layers was laid down at the same time.

---

11. Ibid.
12. Andrew Snelling, "Rock Layers Folded, Not Fractured," *Answers Magazine*, April–June 2009, p. 80–83, https://answersingenesis.org/geology/rock-layers/rock-layers-folded-not-fractured/.

We also see this at another place in the Grand Canyon (many in fact). Another worth mentioning is Monument Fold. Rafters traveling down the Canyon come in close contact with this bent rock. It makes a "Z" shape.

Monument Fold

Other bent rock formations can be seen in various parts of the world. Here is one along a Pennsylvania highway in the Appalachian Mountains in the eastern United States.

You can see how this thrust came from below and the sediment simply

Appalachian Mountains

bent around it and then solidified into rock.

Polystrate Fossils

Another classic example of reducing the alleged long ages of rock layers comes from studying polystrate fossils. *Poly* means "many" and *strate* means "strata" or rock layers. So when we find fossils that extend through multiple rock layers, these are evidences that the rock layers are not as old as we have been led to believe.

Trees make great examples, even though there are others. Tree fossils often extend through several layers of rock. Are we to believe that the tree just sat there waiting for thousands and perhaps, millions of years to get covered up with sediment to transform into a fossil? Not at all. The tree would rot, decay, or otherwise disintegrate.

As we begin to conclude, it is obvious that rock layers are *not* evidence of millions of years. They can be made quickly in labs, we see it with catastrophes like a volcano, we observe it with flowing water that has sediment, and so forth. Bent rock layers and polystrate fossils also confirm rock layer formation to be rapid events.

A New Trend

So how does the world respond? An intriguing thing is happening in our culture right now. There is a shift going on.

Formerly, those who believed the rock layers were evidence of millions of years (uniformitarians) said the "millions of years" was to be counted *within* the rock layer. This idea was solidified in the minds of many scientists as a result of a lawyer, Charles Lyell, in the 1830s.

Lyell argued that rock layers were laid down slowly and gradually over millions of years. As a result, the secular idea is that the Cretaceous rock layer was supposedly laid down slowly and gradually over 72–79 million years — as well as all the dates on the popular geologic timescale.

This view has dominated since the mid-1800s *until recently* among the secularists. But all that is changing in our modern times. A secular scientist, Dr. Warren D. Allmon, says:

> Indeed geology appears at last to have outgrown Lyell. In an intellectual shift that may well rival that which accompanied the widespread acceptance of plate tectonics, the last 30 years have witnessed an increasing acceptance of rapid, rare, episodic, and "catastrophic" events.[13]

One cannot argue that catastrophes didn't occur in the past, because we see them all the time — like Mt. St. Helens, Hurricane Katrina, and so on. Therefore, many secularists have been shifting away from the idea that fossil layers were laid down slowly and gradually. They have been agreeing that catastrophes did occur in the past. They are now openly disagreeing with Lyell but still agree with the geological timescale and millions of years. So where do they put the "millions of years" if they don't put them where Lyell put them?

An Elephant in the Room

Let's just call out the *elephant in the room*. If the layers were not laid down slowly over millions of years (because the secularists now agree that

---

13. W. Allmon, "Post-Gradualism," review of *The New Catastrophism*, by Derek V. Ager (New York: Cambridge University Press, 1993); Science, vol. 262, October 1, 1993, p. 122.

catastrophes laid these fossil deposits down quickly), why do they still believe in the geological timescale and millions of years? Here is why.

Instead of the rock layers being where the millions of years were supposedly contained, they now say the millions of years is *in between* rapidly deposited layers. Thus, they claim that the space between the Jurassic rock layer and the Cretaceous is about 125 million years ago. Then there are a few "snapshots" of the Cretaceous over 72–79 million years due to a few catastrophes that laid down rock layers. Then, secularists claim the space between the Cretaceous and the Tertiary is 65 million years ago.

GEOLOGIC TIMESCALE

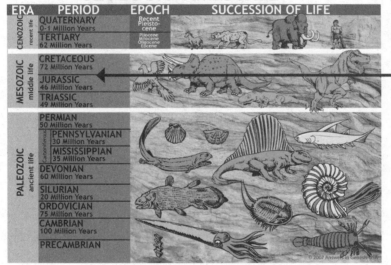

Alleged millions of years in between the rock layers

You might be thinking, "Hmm, that settles the issue of the elephant in the room." But it doesn't. It actually introduces a second elephant in the room. Here is why.

There is now *no evidence* for millions of years whatsoever. The evidence used to be the rock layers. However, the secularists are shifting to agree the rock layers are laid down quickly by catastrophes. So the secular view is that the imaginary space between the rock layers *is* the evidence for millions of years. Thus, they have no evidence for millions of years. Leaving open the idea of catastrophes that lays down sediment quickly destroys "millions of years."

15 | DOESN'T IT TAKE MILLIONS OF YEARS TO FORM CANYONS?

BODIE HODGE

INTRODUCTION

I still have my sixth grade textbook. It says:

> During millions of years, the Colorado River has worn away thousands of feet of rock and soil to form the Grand Canyon in Arizona.[1]

Other canyons supposedly formed over millions of years. Consider Copper Canyon in Mexico where the *USA Today* travel advisor to the canyon states:

> Copper Canyon's deep ravine was cut out of the mountainous region over the course of millions of years by the force of rushing water from six separate rivers.[2]

Or perhaps the beautiful Verdon Gorge (*Les Gorges du Verdon*) in France? This literally translates into *Grand Canyon* in English by the way, but is not to be confused with the Grand Canyon in the USA. The rafting site for Verdon Gorge casually states:

> From that point, we take some time to marvel at the work of millions of years of erosion on the impressive limestone cliffs surrounding us between the successive class II and III rapids.[3]

---

1. Albert Piltz and Roger Van Bever, *Discovering Science 5* (Columbus OH: Charles E. Merrill Publishing Co., 1970), p. 196.
2. Richard Kalinowski, "Mexico's Copper Canyon," accessed September 28, 2015, http://traveltips.usatoday.com/mexicos-copper-canyon-1388.html.
3. "Discovery of the Verdon," accessed September 28, 2015, http://www.rafting-verdon.com/gb/details-sheets-packages/Verdon-6-days-spring.html.

Hosts of references could be used of canyons all over the world that state that the canyons in question take millions of years of slow gradual erosion to carve them. Secularists have no scientific observations of its formation. They can't repeat it either. So they merely look at the rivers running through these canyons today (in the present) and *assume there are no significant catastrophes* in the past for millions of years and then draw the conclusion that these layers were slowly carved out over that time.

Did you catch that? You need to understand that for them to make such a statement, they are assuming that significant catastrophes, like major floods, didn't occur in the past! Sounds like a crazy assumption doesn't it? Well . . . it is. When a catastrophe occurs, things change quickly! We see major catastrophes all the time all over the world (tsunamis, earthquakes, floods, hurricanes, etc.). Why assume there weren't any in the past . . . for millions of years?

DO canyons really Take MILLIONS OF years TO Form?

Mt. St. Helens, a volcano in Washington State in the USA erupted in 1980 and it went off again in 1982. For once, scientists had the opportunity to see what a catastrophe could accomplish on a descent-sized scale! What was observed?

Drs. Steven A. Austin and John Morris pointed out:

> How long would it take to erode a 100-foot (30 meter) deep canyon, in hard basaltic rock? On Mount St. Helens, such a canyon was formed rapidly as rock avalanched from the crater followed by other episodic, catastrophic processes.[4]

The Little Grand Canyon

Drs. Austin and Morris also pointed out that the new drainage of the North Fork of the Toutle River occurred quickly too! Based on observations of the 1982 eruption, they write:

> In a single day, the new drainage channel of the North Fork of the Toutle River was established westward through the debris dam by a catastrophic mudflow! The Canyon produced by the mud has been called "The Little Grand Canyon" because it

---

4. John Morris and Steven A. Austin, *Footprints in Ash* (Green Forest, AR: Master Books, 2003), p. 70.

appears to be one-fortieth scale model of the Grand Canyon of Arizona.[5]

Interestingly, the topography of the Little Grand Canyon is very similar to the features we see at the Grand Canyon as well. It is more reasonable to believe that larger canyons like the Grand Canyon formed by similar (but bigger) processes as this catastrophic Little Grand Canyon. I find it fascinating that if someone had no idea that a catastrophe formed this large canyon, they might mistakenly assume it took long ages, perhaps millions of years, to form . . . especially if they assumed that catastrophes of this magnitude never occurred in the past.

Canyon Lake Gorge

In 2002, the Guadalupe River in Texas had extensive flooding. Water began pouring over Canyon Lake spillway (a reservoir) due to massive rain. In July of that year, it was estimated that about 70,000 cubic feet per second was exiting over the spillway, which was much more than the normal 350 cubic feet per second!

The Guadalupe River flood carved out a gorge about 1 mile (1.6 kilometers) in length. It was over 50 feet (15 meters) deep in places. Keep in mind this was carving through solid limestone! This rapid canyon exposed rock layers from the Flood of Noah's day while at the same time helping disprove this idea that it takes millions of years to form canyons! Researchers state:

> A narrow gorge is sometimes inferred to represent slow persistent erosion, whereas Canyon Lake Gorge was formed in a matter of days.[6]

The online encyclopedia, Wikipedia, has entries that tend to change rather often and is biased toward the religion of secularism. Even so, they write:

> Typically a steep-walled, narrow gorge is inferred to represent slow persistent erosion. But because many of the geological formations of Canyon Lake Gorge are virtually indistinguishable from other formations which have been attributed to long term (slower) processes, the data collected from Canyon Lake Gorge

5. Ibid., p. 75.
6. Michael P. Lamb and Mark A. Fonstad, "Rapid Formation of a Modern Bedrock Canyon by a Single Flood Event," *Nature Geoscience*, June 20, 2010, p. 4, DOI: 10.1038/NGEO894.

lends further credence to the hypothesis that some of the most spectacular canyons on Earth may have been carved rapidly during ancient megaflood events.[7]

Notice that the religion of secular humanism still reigns supreme in this quote. The encyclopedia refuses to give the possibility of a global Flood (Noah's Flood) being the triggering factor (as well as subsequent factors resulting from the Flood) for many of the great canyon's formations. Instead they appeal to "megafloods." But regardless, major floods and other catastrophes destroy the idea of millions of years and long ages.

These are not the only rapidly forming canyons. Providence Canyon in Georgia was a rapidly formed canyon now dubbed Georgia's "Little Grand Canyon."[8] Another in Walla Walla, Washington, formed in six days (Burlingame Canyon)![9] This list could continue! What we know from observation is that it doesn't take millions of years to form canyons, just the right catastrophic conditions!

7. Wikipedia, Entry: Canyon Lake Gorge, accessed September 28, 2015, https://en.wikipedia.org/wiki/Canyon_Lake_Gorge.
8. Rebecca Gibson, "Canyon Creation," September, 1, 2000, https://answersingenesis.org/geology/natural-features/canyon-creation/.
9. John Morris, "A Canyon in Six Days," September 1, 2002, https://answersingenesis.org/geology/natural-features/a-canyon-in-six-days/.

16 | AREN'T COAL AND OIL MILLIONS OF YEARS OLD?

BODIE HODGE

COAL

I grew up in Western Illinois. We used to have a lot of coal mines in our area. We even had a few lumps of coal that we would burn in our wood/coal stove in the farmhouse in which I grew up.

From time to time at school, we had videos shown in our classroom that taught that coal was a fossil fuel and took millions of years to form. This idea still persists today. As one example, the California Energy Commission writes:

> There are three major forms of fossil fuels: coal, oil and natural gas. All three were formed many hundreds of millions of years ago before the time of the dinosaurs — hence the name fossil fuels.[1]

The site continues:

> More and more rock piled on top of more rock, and it weighed more and more. It began to press down on the peat. The peat was squeezed and squeezed until the water came out of it and it eventually, over millions of years, it turned into coal, oil or petroleum, and natural gas.[2]

---

1. Energy Story, chapter 8: "Fossil Fuels — Coal, Oil and Natural Gas," California Energy Commission, 1994–2012, http://www.energyquest.ca.gov/story/chapter08.html.
2. Ibid.

Has the *California Energy Commission* actually repeated an experiment over the course of millions of years to prove that it takes millions of years to form coal (or these other things like oil)? No. Have they had any observations over millions of years to prove it takes millions of years to form coal? No. With this in mind, I want you to understand that this statement of theirs is not scientific, as science is based on observations and repeatability. This is their religious conviction that it takes millions of years to make things like coal and oil.

Does it really take millions of years to form coal? Based on research by geologist Dr. Steve Austin at Mt. St. Helens,[3] Dr. Gary Parker and his wife Mary write:

> In just minutes and months, Mount St. Helens and Spirit Lake produced a coal-like sediment pattern once thought to take millions of years to form.[4]

Furthermore, Argonne National Laboratory has proven that it doesn't take millions of years to form coal . . . but instead months.[5] They used wood, specifically lignin that makes up much of the wood, water, and clay that was acidic. Then they heated it to about 300°F (150°C) for about 1–9 months and it formed black coal. Since then, others have been able to use processes for the coalification of peat in short periods of time.[6]

So it doesn't take millions of years to form coal. This can be observed and repeated. So scientifically, we know that it doesn't take millions of years to form coal.

C14 IN COAL (SEMI-TECHNICAL)

But there is more. An interesting thing about coal is that is it is made of *carbon*. If coal layers are supposed to be millions of years old, then there

---

3. For more, see John Morris and Steven A. Austin, *Footprints in the Ash* (Green Forest, AR: Master Books, 2003), p. 78–89.
4. Gary and Mary Parker, *The Fossil Book* (Green Forest, AR: Master Books), p. 15.
5. R. Hayatsu, R.L. McBeth, R.G. Scott, R.E. Botto, R.E. Winans, *Organic Geochemistry*, vol. 6 (1984), p. 463–471.
6. W.H. Orem, S.G. Neuzil, H.E. Lerch, and C.B. Cecil, "Experimental Early-stage Coalification of a Peat Sample and a Peatified Wood Sample from Indonesia," *Organic Geochemistry* 24(2):111–125, 1996; A.D. Cohen and A.M. Bailey, "Petrographic Changes Induced by Artificial Coalification of Peat: Comparison of Two Planar Facies (Rhizophora and Cladium) from the Everglades-Mangrove Complex of Florida and a Domed Facies (Cyrilla) from the Okefenokee Swamp of Georgia," *International Journal of Coal Geology* 34:163–194, 1997; S. Yao, C. Xue, W. Hu, J. Cao, C. Zhang, "A Comparative Study of Experimental Maturation of Peat, Brown Coal and Subbituminous Coal: Implications for Coalification," *International Journal of Coal Geology* 66:108–118, 2006.

should be no carbon-14 (^{14}C) left in it — ^{14}C can only give dates of thousands of years, not millions of years, otherwise it should all be decayed away. Now as a caveat, ^{14}C dates have hosts of problems such as living creatures that date to outrageously old dates. For example, we find incorrect dates for:

- Living mollusks supposedly 23,000 years old[7]
- Living snails were supposedly 27,000 years old[8]
- A freshly killed seal was supposedly 1,300 years old[9]
- Dinosaur bones with ^{14}C[10]

People may offer excuses for these, but the fact is that they came out with inaccurate dates. If we can't trust ^{14}C dating on dates we know, how can we trust it on dates we don't know? That would be illogical. The measured half-life of ^{14}C is 5,730 years in a laboratory under certain conditions, though this has never been fully observed and there may be things that affect the rate of decay even more than we already know. But for the sake of argument, let's assume this half-life is accurate for now.

Based on the half-life of ^{14}C, that means we should have no ^{14}C in any sample that is about 50,000–100,000 years (theoretically). Geophysicist Dr. John Baumgardner has a listing of 90 samples from secular literature of things *supposedly older than 100,000 years old in the secular reasoning*, and yet they have measurable ^{14}C in them![11] This means these things cannot be that old!

In fact, anything that is supposed to be a million years or more should have no ^{14}C. In other words, coal, which is supposed to be many millions of years old, should have no ^{14}C in it whatsoever. And yet, we find ^{14}C all over in it![12] We find C14 in things supposedly millions and billions of years old such as:

7. *Science*, vol. 141 (1963), p. 634–637.
8. *Science*, vol. 224, (1984), p. 58–61.
9. *Antarctic Journal*, vol. 6 (Sept.–Oct. 1971), p. 211.
10. Brian Thomas, "Carbon-14 Found in Dinosaur Fossils," ICR, July 6, 2015, http://www. icr.org/article/carbon-14-found-dinosaur-fossils/.
11. L. Vardiman, A.A. Snelling, and E.F. Chaffin (eds.), *Radioisotopes and the Age of the Earth, Vol. 2: Results of a Young-earth Creationist Research Initiative* (El Cajon, CA: Institute for Creation Research and Chino Valley, AZ: Creation Research Society, 2005), p. 596–597.
12. Ibid., p. 587–630.

- Diamonds[13]
- Meteorites[14]
- Coal[15]

Yes, even coal is replete with ^{14}C, so it *cannot* be millions of years old.

OIL/PETROLEUM

What about oil or petroleum? The California Energy Commission also included petroleum/oil items as millions of years old too. Even the Live Science website says of oil:

> Nature has been transmuting dead life into black gold for millions of years using little more than heat, pressure and time, scientists tell us.[16]

Sinclair Oil Corporation even utilizes an Apatosaurus on their emblem, relating the idea that the oil was supposedly from millions of years ago.

Sinclair Oil's advertising writers struggled with this question in 1930. They needed a vehicle for their message. At that time, Sinclair's oils and lubricants came from Pennsylvania crude oil more than 270 million years old. Those oils perked and mellowed in the ground when dinosaurs wandered the

---

13. Ibid., p. 609–614.
14. Many meteorites contain Cosmogenic Carbon 14, which means they really can't be millions or billions of years old (some via internal sampling). The secularists assume that the C-14 became part of them after entering the atmosphere and remaining on the ground and try to use this for terrestrial dates. How does a meteorite take in C-14; they are not plants and animals that utilize this as part of their diet. For example see: A. Snelling, "Radioisotope Dating of Meteorites: I. The Allende CV3 Carbonaceous Chrondrite," *Answers Research Journal*, vol. 7, 2014, p. 103–145, https://cdn-assets.answersingenesis.org/doc/articles/pdf-versions/radioisotope_dating_Allende.pdf. See also Pillinger et al, "The Meteorite from Lake House," 74th Annual Meteoritical Society Meeting, 2011, http://www.lpi.usra.edu/meetings/metsoc2011/pdf/5326.pdf.
15. L. Vardiman, A.A. Snelling, and E.F. Chaffin (eds.), *Radioisotopes and the Age of the Earth, Vol. 2: Results of a Young-earth Creationist Research Initiative* (El Cajon, CA: Institute for Creation Research and Chino Valley, AZ: Creation Research Society, 2005), p. 587–630.
16. K. Than, "The Mysterious Origin and Supply of Oil," Live Science, October 10, 2005, http://www.livescience.com/9404-mysterious-origin-supply-oil.html.

earth. So Sinclair's ad writers developed a campaign using about a dozen different dinosaurs: the tyrannosaurus rex, triceratops and the apatosaurus (brontosaurus) were but a few.[17]

The sauropod (Apatosaurus) won out and so millions of people have seen this emblem all over the USA since the 1930s.

But does oil/petroleum take millions of years to form? Not at all. Animal wastes are also being used to make oil. Geologist Dr. Andrew Snelling writes:

> Turkey and pig slaughterhouse wastes are daily trucked into the world's first biorefinery, a thermal conversion processing plant in Carthage, Missouri. On peak production days, 500 barrels of high-quality fuel oil better than crude oil are made from 270 tons of turkey guts and 20 tons of pig fat.[18]

Oil can be made from brown coal in a matter of days too. Dr. Snelling continues:

> Thus, for example, it has been demonstrated in the laboratory that moderate heating of the brown coals of the Gippsland Basin of Victoria, Australia, to simulate their rapid deeper burial,

17. Christopher Bennett, "Why Do Sinclair Gas Stations Use a Dinosaur in Their Logo?" *Winona Daily News*, March 15, 2007, http://www.winonadailynews.com/news/why-do-sinclair-gas-stations-use-a-dinosaur-in-their/article_566e7613-d6f3-5f68-bdc5-9f90ade1b29a.html.
18. Dr. Andrew Snelling, "The Origin of Oil," Answers 2, no. 1, p. 74–77, http://www.answersingenesis.org/articles/am/v2/n1/origin-of-oil.

will generate crude oil and natural gas similar to that found in reservoir rocks offshore in only 2–5 days.[19]

Algae can also be made into oil . . . but in minutes. Researcher Brian Thomas reports:

> Researchers at the Pacific Northwest National Laboratory (PNNL) in Washington State have pioneered a new technology that makes diesel fuel from algae — and their cutting-edge machine produces the fuel in just minutes. . . . Simply heat pea-green algal soup to 662°F (350°C) at 3,000 psi for almost 60 minutes.[20]

But now it is quicker than that! The same lab has been able to make crude oil from algae in 30 minutes. The news report said:

> Scientists at the Pacific Northwest National Laboratory are claiming success in perfecting a method that can transform a pea-soupy solution of algae into crude oil by pressure cooking it for about 30 minutes. The process, called hydrothermal liquefaction, also works on other streams of organic matter, such as municipal sewage.[21]

Even sewage sludge is being used to make oil (diesel grade fuel) in Australia.[22] Perhaps it is time to cast this false religious idea that it takes millions of years to form *oil and flush it down the toilet!* Okay, so that was "tongue in cheek" humor. But seriously, this idea of oil taking millions of years to form is false — and industry is not wasting time in capitalizing on the truth.

---

19. Ibid.
20. B. Thomas, "One-Hour Oil Production," ICR, January 13, 2014, https://www.icr.org/article/7874/.
21. Christopher Helman, Green Oil: Scientists Turn Algae Into Petroleum In 30 Minutes, Forbes.com, 12/23/2013, http://www.forbes.com/sites/christopherhelman/2013/12/23/green-oil-scientists-turn-algae-into-petroleum-in-30-minutes/.
22. Australian Stock Exchange Release, Environmental Solutions International Ltd, Osborne Park, Western Australia, Oct. 25, 1996. Media Statement, Minister for Water Resources, Western Australia, October 25, 1996.

17 | WHAT ABOUT STALAGMITES AND STALACTITES – DO THEY TAKE MILLIONS OF YEARS?

BODIE HODGE

A WARM INTRODUCTION TO THE SUBJECT

Being that I was originally from Illinois, I often ventured across the border to Missouri and went caving. One of my favorite trips was exploring random caves while on a float trip down the Meramec River. There were hosts of caves to explore. I even visited the famous Meramec Caverns, which is beautiful.

Of course, for anyone who likes caves, remember one simple thing. Do not enter a warm cave. Let me repeat this . . . do not enter a warm cave. While on this float trip in the 1990s, a group of us (toward the end of our trip) floated our canoe into what looked like a watery entrance of a cave. And of course . . . our flashlights had finally stopped working. So we went in based on the vague light entering the cave's entrance. The canoe finally struck ground and we meandered on strange damp ground in that *warm* cave. In fact — the ground *crunched*.

We realized we needed light since things could not be discerned at all at this depth of the cave. So one of my buddies pulled out a handy lighter that had miraculously not gotten wet. We ignited it. We found ourselves surrounded by more spiders, more strange insects, and snakes than I had ever seen in one condensed spot in my entire life. We shrieked, the lighter went out, and we were all darting for the water in what seemed like dense darkness. And we didn't care if we made it in the canoe, we just wanted out.

I think this was a natural reaction to the creatures that were now crawling on us. And I'm pretty sure I stepped on at least two snakes trying to exit that cave before I jumped in the water and began dragging the canoe toward the cave's entrance with the two gents in tow!

Needless to say, we were all a little hesitant to EVER enter another cave. That was until we inquired and a cave guide at Meramec Caverns told us to be careful entering a *warm* cave. Ahhh, *cold* . . . that was the key to a good cave adventure — it keeps out the creepy crawlies! Since that time, I have been in many caves in several states, but I always take note of the temperature the moment that I take that first step into one.

NOW TO THE *Hardened* QUESTION

So how many times have I entered a cave and a guide has told me that things like stalactites and stalagmites were millions of years old? It has been too many to count. For the reader, stalactites are the formations on top (think of it like this: they hold on to the roof of the cave *tight* being sta-lag-*tites*). The formations that form on the bottom of the cave and work their way up are called stalagmites. Now there are other formations, like a column (when a stalagtite and stalagmite grow together) or straws or flowstone, and so on. All cave formations are basically summed up in the technical term *speleothem*.

But does it take millions of years to form things like stalactites and stalagmites? Knowing that all cave formations have occurred since the time of the Flood (in some cases as resultant actions of the end stages of the Flood) then they cannot be millions of years old.

Let's look at this a little closer. A cave specialist reported an instance in which it only took days for a stalactite to grow several inches. The article reads:

> Jerry Trout (cave specialist with the Forest Service) says that through photo monitoring, he has watched a stalactite grow several inches in a matter of days.[1]

In Jenolan Caves in Australia, a bottle was left in the cave in early 1950s. The bottle is coated in a layer of calcite and continues to get thicker. It is already a bottle stalagmite![2]

---

1. Marilyn Taylor, "Descent," *Arizona Highways*, January 1993, p. 11.
2. Editors, "Bottle Stalagmite," Answers in Genesis, March 1, 1995, originally published in *Creation*, vol. 17, no. 2, March 1995:6, https://answersingenesis.org/geology/caves/bottle-stalagmite/.

Cave geologist, Dr. Emil Silvestru comments:

> In the Cripple Creek Gold Mine in Colorado, stalagmites and stalactites over a meter long have grown in less than 100 years![3]

I have personally had the opportunity to see a stalagmite that had formed rapidly. I was touring Cosmic Caverns in northern Arkansas with my family, and draping over our footpath was a huge stalagmite. The guide told us to step around it and as I did, the guide made a comment about how that large stalagmite formed the previous year due to excessive rainstorms (in 2011). So I stopped and took a picture.

In a general sense, a cave can be active (called a *live* cave) or inactive (called a *relict* cave). Active means they have water action that transports minerals, and we see some growth of certain features in the cave (some have a little action, some have more). Inactive (relict) is a dry cave that has little to no growth as the water table is likely below the cave or is diverted from passing through the cave. It may be in an arid region with little to no rain to seep down through it. All *inactive* caves that have cave features were at one time *active* caves and have since "dried" out.

This particular cave in Arkansas obviously saw an increase in water to move mineral due to heavy rains that year that affected the cave and made it more active to grow that stalagmite. But with all this, it doesn't take millions of years to form stalactites and stalagmites.

---

3. Emil Silvestru, *The Cave Book* (Green Forest, AR: Master Books, 2008), p. 46.

18 | DOESN'T IT TAKE MILLIONS OF YEARS TO FORM PRECIOUS GEMS?

BODIE HODGE

DIAMONDS

Gemstones are often touted as being *millions* of years old, and in some cases *billions* of years old — diamonds for example. But do they really take this long to form? *Physics.org* seems to think so. They write:

> In addition, the scientists show that diamonds take millions of years to grow. Moreover, diamonds are often half as old as the Earth.[1]

Of course, no scientist has ever *shown* this to be the case over the course of millions and billions of years! The article continues:

> The investigated diamonds are from Yakutia in Russia and show that in this region they formed in two important periods in the past: 1 billion years ago and 2 billion years ago. Many individual diamonds record growth in both periods proving for the first time that diamonds take millions of years to form.[2]

Do diamonds really take millions of years to form? Two companies, Apollo Diamond Incorporated in Massachusetts and Gemesis Corporation in Florida, are manufacturing diamonds![3] They use two different methods, no less.

---

1. "Diamonds Grow Like Trees, but Over Millions of Years," Physics.org, September 16, 2013, http://phys.org/news/2013-09-diamonds-trees-millions-years.html.
2. Ibid.
3. Greg Hunter and Andrew Paparella, "Lab-Made Diamonds Just Like Natural Ones," September 9, 2015, ABC News Internet Ventures, produced for *Good Morning America*, http://abcnews.go.com/GMA/story?id=124787.

The article reports:

> The new manmade diamonds from Apollo Diamond are cre-
> ated in a few days by a machine in an industrial park near Boston
> through a process called chemical vapor deposition.[4]
>
> At Gemesis, which is based in Sarasota, Fla., synthetic di-
> amonds are created through a high-pressure, high-temperature
> technique that mimics the geologic conditions under which natu-
> ral diamonds are formed. In a capsule placed under high tempera-
> ture and pressure, graphite — a form of carbon — breaks down
> into atoms and travels through a metal solvent to bond to a tiny
> diamond seed, crystallizing layer by layer. Three or four days later,
> the stone that is formed is then removed from the chamber and
> cut and polished into a synthetic diamond.[5]

In both cases, the methods make diamonds *in days*. The article says of the
manufactured diamonds:

> "They are real," said Linares. "They meet every measure of be-
> ing diamond. From the aesthetic point of view, from the scientific
> point of view, they are diamonds and so therefore they have all the
> properties of diamond.[6]

But there is more . . . you can now take the remains of your cremated loved
one and have their remaining carbon pressed into a diamond! Companies
like *LifeGem* or *Algordanza* are currently doing this. The whole process only
takes months. Writing about *Algordanza's* work, Rae Ellen Bichell comments:

> Swiss company Algordanza takes cremated human remains
> and — under high heat and pressure that mimic conditions deep
> within the Earth — compress them into diamonds. . . . Each year,
> the remains of between 800 and 900 people enter the facility.
> About three months later, they exit as diamonds, to be kept in a
> box or turned into jewelry.[7]

---

4. Ibid.
5. Ibid.
6. Ibid.
7. Rae Ellen Bichell, "From Ashes To Ashes To Diamonds: A Way To Treasure The Dead,"
   NPR, January 19, 2014, http://www.npr.org/2014/01/19/263128098/swiss-company-
   compresses-cremation-ashes-into-diamonds.

There are also companies (like *DNA-2Diamonds* or *Pet-Gems*) that specialize in turning your beloved pet's ashes or hair into diamonds. The point is, it doesn't take millions or billions of years to form diamonds, but rather days and weeks.

other gemstones

Opals were once thought to take millions of years to form. In discussions with people over the years, I've heard them drop the date to as low as 30,000 years, but I've heard nothing lower than that. But the norm is to teach millions of years. One gemologist writes in an article called, "The Truth About Opals":

> Like most precious gemstones, opals take millions of years to form. . . . Over millions of years, these silica layers accumulate, forming beautiful polychromatic opal deposits for lucky miners to discover.[8]

Again, this is not the case. Researcher Len Cram has figured out how to make opal! He does it in a matter of weeks. Dr. Andrew Snelling writes:

> A committed Christian, Len [Cram] has discovered the secret that has enabled him to actually "grow" opals in glass jars stored in his wooden shed laboratory, and the process takes only a matter of weeks![9]

When it comes to gemstones (like rubies, topaz, garnet, cubic zirconia, emeralds, etc.), most can easily be made in a laboratory. It is such a thriving business now that much jewelry actually utilizes these newly made gems. They are called "synthetic" gemstones and can be found at jewelry shops across many parts of the world.

---

8. K. Jetter, GIA graduate gemologist and accredited jewelry designer, "The Truth About Opals," originally published in *Elite Traveler*, Santa Fe, New Mexico, http://www.katherinejetter.com/history-of-opals.

9. Dr. Andrew Snelling, "Creating Opals," *Creation ex nihilo* 17, no. 1, Dec. 1994: 14–17.

In fact, this process is nothing new. *Flame fusion* is a process used in the late 1800s and early 1900s to grow rubies. These types of rubies (called "Verneuil Rubies") are named for one of the scientists who improved the method.[10] Germany was growing emeralds in the 1930s by a *flux-grown* method.[11]

Gemstones are often produced naturally and quickly too when a volcano erupts. This is due to the rapid heat and pressure. At Mount St. Helens, which blew its top in 1980 and went off again in 1982, a magnificent array of gemstones was produced! The Mount St. Helens Gift shop website openly states:

> Volcanoes are an incubator for many of the World's treasures. Other gems commonly associated with volcanic origins include Emerald, Diamond, Garnet, Peridot, and Topaz.[12]

The *GemSelect* website also confirms the origin of most gemstones in *igneous* rock layers (think volcanic). Their site says:

> The long list of gemstones formed from igneous rock include the chrysoberyl group, all quartz (including amethyst, citrine and ametrine), beryl (emerald, morganite and aquamarine), garnet, moonstone, apatite, diamond, spinel, tanzanite, tourmaline, topaz and zircon.[13]

Dr. Andrew Snelling researched the idea of rapid diamond production in the earth in which diamonds were then transported to the surface with magmas to form the famous Argyle diamond deposit in Australia. Interestingly, the Aborigines witnessed this volcanic event in years past (showing it is recent) and this account passed down through the tribe. Dr. Snelling concludes:

> The diamond crystals themselves are thus carried rapidly from their place of formation deep in the earth into these pipes,

10. Editors, "Synthetic and Artificial Gemstone Growth Methods: In-Depth Treatment Information," Jewelry Television online, July 2012, http://www.jtv.com/library/synthetic-artificial-gemstone-methods.html.
11. Ibid.
12. Editors, Mount St. Helens Gift Shop Website, http://www.mt-st-helens.com/obsidianite.html, downloaded April 7, 2014.
13. Editors, "How Gemstones Are Formed," GemSelect, accessed August 18, 2015, http://www.gemselect.com/other-info/gemstone-formation.php.

where we find them today along with the shattered remains of the magmas that brought them up to the earth's surface.

This evidence for the rapid formation of diamond deposits confirms that there are extremely rapid and catastrophic geological processes which evolutionary geologists have been forced to concede do occur. Furthermore, the eyewitness testimony from the Australian Aborigines, distorted by verbal transmission and the 'mists of time', undoubtedly points to their having seen the explosive eruption that produced the Argyle diamond deposit, which places its formation therefore in the very recent post-Flood period.[14]

So it doesn't take millions of years to form gemstones including diamonds. Even natural diamonds can be formed quickly by the heat and pressures in the earth and quickly formed and deposited by volcanic eruptions.

14. Andrew Snelling, "Diamonds — Evidence of Explosive Geological Processes," *Creation*, vol. 16, no. 1, December 1993: 42–45, https://answersingenesis.org/geology/rocks-and-minerals/diamonds-evidence-of-explosive-geological-processes/.

19 | ISN'T PETRIFIED WOOD MILLIONS OF YEARS OLD?

BODIE HODGE

INTRODUCTION

The Live Science website proclaims:

> Petrified wood forms when fallen trees get washed down a river and buried under layers of mud, ash from volcanoes and other materials. Sealed beneath this muck deprives the rotting wood from oxygen — the necessary ingredient for decay. As the wood's organic tissues slowly break down, the resulting voids in the tree are filled with minerals such as silica — the stuff of rocks. Over millions of years, these minerals crystallize within the wood's cellular structure forming the stone-like material known as petrified wood.[1]

Does it really take millions of years to form petrified wood? Once again, keep in mind this has never been observed or repeated over the course of millions of years, so it is really just a religious belief about the past. What do we really observe?

RAPID PETRIFIED WOOD

Researchers have proven it doesn't take millions of years to form petrified wood. In 1986, Hamilton Hicks received his patent for developing a process

---

1. Michelle Bryner, "How Long Does It Take to Make Petrified Wood?" Live Science website, November 20, 2012, http://www.livescience.com/32316-how-long-does-it-take-to-make-petrified-wood.html.

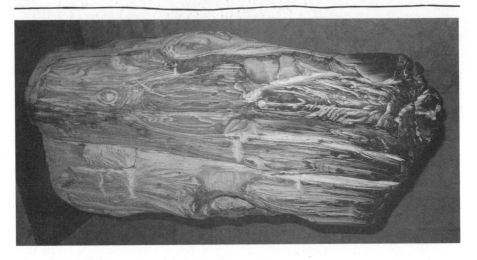

to petrify wood quickly with a mineral and acid-rich solution.[2] The solution is applied to wood and the patent states:

> When applied to wood or wood cellulose products, the observable action is hardening, density increase and apparent petrification similar to that occurring in naturally petrified wood.[3]

This solution is similar to what is found naturally and Hicks' patent points out:

> It is possible to use natural or volcanic mineral water into which the commercial sodium silicate solution (water glass) is dissolved, or to artificially mineralize water, by mixing it with mineral clay or gypsum, for example.[4]

In other words, this type of solution could be produced naturally, such as utilizing volcanic mineral water. It is interesting that most natural petrified wood is found associated with volcanic rock layers (i.e., which was occurring during and after the Flood). These are ideal conditions to produce petrified wood quickly.

This process is now used to manufacture petrified wood, and even you can be a recipient of it. You can go to your local home store or flooring store and order some petrified wood flooring too if you want to renovate your floors!

---

2. Hamilton Hicks, Sodium silicate composition, United States Patent Number 4,612,050, September 16,1986, http://www.google.com/patents/US4612050.

3. Ibid.

4. Ibid.

In the article "Petrified Wood in Days," we read about petrified wood experiments by Yongsoon Shin, at Pacific Northwest National Laboratory (PNNL). The researchers state:

> Back at PNNL, they gave a 1 centimeter cube of wood a two-day acid bath, soaked it in a silica solution for two more (for best results, repeat this step up to three times), air-dried it, popped it into an argon-filled furnace gradually cranked up to 1,400 degrees centigrade to cook for two hours, then let cool in argon to room temperature. Presto. Instant petrified wood, the silica taking up permanent residence with the carbon left in the cellulose to form a new silicon carbide, or SiC, ceramic.[5]

Yes this is hot — 1,400 degrees! I've had people point out that temperatures that hot are not likely in the natural world. So they assumed that making petrified wood via this route would be impossible. But this is not necessarily the case. Recall, most petrified wood is found associated with volcanic rock layers where it does get around these temperatures and even hotter! Certain magma has been calculated to be around 1,560 degrees centigrade (e.g., komatiite melts) at eruption![6]

There are also examples of petrified wood occurring as a mere product of nature — even without the heat! As an example, Dr. Andrew Snelling recounts:

> From the other side of the world comes a report of the chapel of Santa Maria of Health (Santa Maria de Salute), built in 1630 in Venice, Italy, to celebrate the end of The Plague. Because Venice is built on water saturated clay and sand, the chapel was constructed on 180,000 wooden pilings to reinforce the foundations. Even though the chapel is a massive stone block structure, it has remained firm since its construction. How have the wooden pilings lasted over 360 years? They have petrified! The chapel now rests on "stone" pilings![7]

5. Editors, "Instant Petrified Wood," Physics.org, January 25, 2005, http://phys.org/news/2005-01-petrified-wood-days.html.

6. For example, see E.G. Nisbet, M.J. Cheadle, N.T. Arndt, and M.J. Bickle, "Constraining the Potential Temperature of the Archaean Mantle: A Review of the Evidence from Komatiites," *Elsevier* journal, vol. 30, Issues 3–4, September 1993, p. 291–307, http://www.sciencedirect.com/science/article/pii/002449379390042B.

7. Andrew Snelling, " 'Instant' Petrified Wood," *Creation*, vol. 17, no. 4, September 1995, p. 38-40, online September 1, 1995, https://answersingenesis.org/fossils/how-are-fossils-formed/instant-petrified-wood/.

These few examples discussed[8] prove it doesn't take the *alleged* millions of years to form petrified wood. Volcanic activity from the Flood and its aftermath (especially the mountain-building phase of the Flood) as well as naturally occurring mineral waters in certain places can cause the petrified wood we find without the appeal to *millions of years.*

---

8. For more examples, please see the previous reference by Dr. Andrew Snelling and his excellent research into this subject.

20 | DOESN'T IT TAKE MILLIONS OF YEARS TO FORM FOSSILS?

KEN HAM AND BODIE HODGE

Much of the world has been inundated to believe that fossils are preserved remains of creatures that often lived *millions or billions of years* ago. While fossils *are* preserved remains or impressions, they *are not* millions of years old. Millions of years are not required for fossil formation.

Nevertheless, we are often led to believe that long ages are a prerequisite for fossil formation. The *Oxford University Museum of Natural History* (OUMNH) writes:

> An animal dies and its body sinks to the sea floor. . . . The skeleton continues to be buried as sediment is added to the surface of the sea floor. As the sea floor sinks, pressure increases in the lower layers of sediment and it turns it into hard rock.[1]

Just so we are clear, we don't observe fossils forming at the bottom of lakes and ocean floors. But as the evolutionary story unfolds, this bone is finally buried and the bone is left in a mold (British spelling is "mould") within the new rock layers. OUMNH continues:

> Water rich in minerals enters the mould, and fills the cavity. The minerals deposited in the mould form a cast of the mould. . . . Millions of years later, the rock surrounding the skeleton rises to the Earth's surface (this happens during mountain building, earthquakes and other earth processes). The rock is worn away

---

1. Oxford University Museum of Natural History, The Learning Zone, "How Do Fossils Form?" 2006, http://www.oum.ox.ac.uk/thezone/fossils/intro/form.htm.

by wind and rain, and the fossil is now exposed, waiting to be found![2]

You see how "millions of years" are thrust into the discussion of fossil formation. We see this elsewhere too. For example, in *A Guide to Dinosaurs* (which is geared toward the youth), they use a dinosaur instead of a fish as their example of the formation of fossils. They write:

> Below the surface of a lake a dead dinosaur's flesh rots away or is eaten by aquatic creatures. Layers of silt build up over the dinosaur's bones and prevent them from being washed away. Weighted down by sediment, the dinosaur bones are slowly replaced by minerals. Millions of years later, seismic disturbances bring the fossilized bones to the surface.[3]

They just had to insert "millions of years." Once again, though, we do not see fossils forming slowly at the bottom of lakebeds.

HOW TO MaKe a FOSSIL

Fossils do not require long ages to form. In fact, they *must* form quickly, otherwise the organism's softer tissues and even bones suffer decay (shells or teeth enamel naturally take longer to disintegrate). The photo is of a bone left to the elements in just a short time (note the deterioration).

Fossils can be made in labs and it is done quickly. Wood fossils can be made *in days* in the lab.[4] Turning hard material (e.g., bones) into fossils is easy in a lab setting, but in 1993, scientists were even able to make fossils from *soft* animal tissues! *New York Times'* Science Watch reports:

2. Ibid.
3. Christopher Brochu et al, *A Guide to Dinosaurs* (San Francisco, CA: Fog City Press, 1997–2004), p. 19.
4. Geoff Brumflel, "Furnace Creates Instant Fossils," Nature.com, January 28, 2005, http://www.nature.com/news/2005/050128/full/news050124-14.html.

Scientists have for the first time produced fossils of soft animal tissues in a laboratory. In the process they discovered that most of the phosphate required for the fossilization of small animal carcasses comes from within the animal itself.[5]

Notice that the creature already provided the necessary chemicals to fossilize itself. This makes sense since many of the fossils we find were buried quickly and left to themselves. As expected, the lab fossils are actually better specimen than natural ones and only takes weeks to months to form.

Fossil formation is actually a rapid event and many today, even secularists, are finally conceding this. It requires rapid burial to seal out the oxygen (so it doesn't entirely decay away). Then mineral-rich water takes out the organic material and replaces it with minerals like limestone, etc.

It is a rapid event as witnessed by the fact that we even find fossils that preserved soft tissue — like the case of massive numbers of jellyfish being fossilized. Jellyfish decay quickly, and yet their fragile tissue was rapidly fossilized before disintegration. Dr. Gary Parker writes:

Jellyfish often wash ashore, but in a matter of hours they have turned into nondescript "blobs" (although watch out — the stinging cells continue to work for quite a while!). To preserve the markings and detail of the Ediacara jellyfish, the organisms seem to have landed on a wet sand that acted as a natural cement. The sand turned to sandstone before the jellyfish had time to rot, preserving the jellyfish's markings, somewhat as you can preserve your handprint if you push it into cement during that brief time when it's neither too wet nor too dry. Indeed, the evolutionist who discovered the Ediacara jellyfish said the fossils must have formed in less than 24 hours. He didn't mean one jellyfish in 24 hours; he meant millions of jellyfish and other forms had fossilized throughout the entire Ediacara formation, which stretches about 300 miles or 500 km from South Australia into the Northern Territory, in less than 24 hours! In short, floods form fossils fast![6]

5. "Man-Made Fossils," *New York Times*, Science Watch, March 9, 1993, http://www.nytimes.com/1993/03/09/science/science-watch-man-made-fossils.html.
6. Gary Parker, *Creation Facts of Life*, Chapter 3: "How Fast," January 1, 1994, https://answersingenesis.org/fossils/how-are-fossils-formed/how-fast/.

Another reason we know that fossils can be made quickly is . . . the rapid number of fakes hitting the market! Let's not forget the famous faked fossil Archaeorapter that was found to be a fraud and published in the *National Geographic* in the year 2000. The problem of faked fossils is all too common and now researchers are turning to CT Scans, x-rays, and other techniques to spot faked and manipulated fossils. The *Scientific American* states:

> Another much more serious problem, however, is posed by forged, faked and manipulated specimens — such as *National Geographic*'s Archaeoraptor — which are becoming increasingly common.[7]

> The problem of faked fossils in China is serious and growing.[8]

> An investigative report published in *Science* in 2010 revealed that as many as 80 percent of marine reptile fossils on display in Chinese museums had been altered or manipulated.[9]

People are getting better at making fake fossils, which is why technical papers are now being written on how to spot the fakes! But being frank, if a poor person who has little concern for God and His Law can fake or manipulate a fossil to sell and make incredible money — they are going to try it.

CONDITIONS DURING FLOOD FOR FOSSILIZATION

The conditions during the Flood were ideal for fossil formation. Even though many things surely rotted and decayed, many other specimens were rapidly buried and fossilized. Genesis 6:13 points out:

> And God said to Noah, "The end of all flesh has come before Me, for the earth is filled with violence through them; and behold, I will destroy them with the earth.

The Flood was not merely a mass of water; but a collection of mud/sediment (earth) that was utilized to destroy the pre-Flood world for their sin. So we

---

7. John Pickert, How Fake Fossils Pervert Paleontology [excerpt], *Scientific American*, November 15, 2014, http://www.scientificamerican.com/article/how-fake-fossils-pervert-paleontology-excerpt/.
8. Ibid.
9. Ibid.

expect fossils and we even expect a general trend of order. Some of these factors include elevation, sorting power of water, and buoyancy.

Obviously, things living at a lower level have a better chance of being buried and fossilized, hence why about 95 percent of fossil layers consist of marine organisms.[10] There is also the natural sorting power of water that separates creatures' burial in the Flood.

Another factor is that reptiles and amphibians tend to sink, so they are more likely to be fossilized than other creatures like mammals. It also makes sense why mammals and birds are less likely to be fossilized since they are lighter (more buoyant, less dense) and many tend to float. Thus, they would be better candidates for rotting and decaying. Of course, there are exceptions to this but we would expect a general trend in the fossil layers.[11]

Where Did the Organic Material Go That Was Originally Part of the Creatures That Were Fossilized?

Most oil deposits that we have are a result of the Flood. There may be other factors (e.g., oil production from bacteria), but most of it came from the Flood and the conditions thereof. Think about the fossils of marine organisms, plants and trees, algae, land creatures, etc. When they fossilize, their organic material is removed by water and replaced by minerals (e.g., limestone) to turn it into rock. Where does all that organic material go?

It seeps down with the water into pockets in the earth. Then it separates from the water into pools or deposits. What remains is primarily a mixture of hydrocarbons, gases, and water. We call this " crude oil."

Rapid Fossils

There are hosts of examples of rapid fossils. Let's entertain a few shall we?

There is a fossil at the Creation Museum of a horseshoe crab that was walking (footprints fossilized too) and then it was stopped and fossilized dead in its tracks.

10. Andrew Snelling, "Where Are All the Human Fossils?" *Creation* 14(1):28–33, December 1991; John Morris, *The Young Earth* (Green Forest, AR: Master Books, 2002), p. 71.

11. For more on the order of fossils see Andrew Snelling, "Doesn't the Order of Fossils in the Rock Record Favor Long Ages?" in Ken Ham, gen. ed., *The New Answers Book 2* (Green Forest, AR: Master Books, 2008), p. 341–354, https://answersingenesis.org/fossils/fossil-record/doesnt-order-of-fossils-in-rock-favor-long-ages/.

Horseshoe
crab fossil

A marine reptile called an ichthyosaur was buried and fossilized so fast
that it didn't finish the birthing process.

This fish
didn't get an
opportunity to
finish its dinner
(on display at
the Creation
Museum).

Dozens of fragile closed
shells that were buried
rapidly and fossilized
before they could open

The sample of dozens of fragile closed shells that were buried rapidly and fossilized before they could open, which is what shellfish typically do, are in the Andes Mountains of Peru above Cusco, which is over two miles high. A local guide took us to the site. We left the fossils in the care of a local church in Cusco.

A group of turtles were buried and fossilized so fast that all nine pairs were still stuck in the process of mating.[12] Being critical of the report's slow gradual explanation of fossil formation, these turtle pairs are better explained by catastrophe and rapid events. This happens often, showing the speed at which burial and fossilization took place.

Picture of mating turtles, taken at Genesis Expo and Fossil Shop in England

These few examples should whet your appetite for the immense numbers of fossils that display rapid burial and fossilization.

THORN FOSSILS . . . AND THEIR SIGNIFICANCE

One type of fossil needs to be mentioned that has incredible theological significance. It is thorn fossils. We find a number of these in the fossil record like *Sawdonia* — which has nasty, vicious thorns. Others like *Psilophyton crenulatum* are found in rock layers that the secular world considers to be 350–400 million years old (Devonian rock layer).[13]

Reading the Bible, we find that thorns did not exist until the curse after Adam and Eve sinned, which was a matter of a few thousand of years ago (Genesis 3:18[14]). So how can these thorns be millions of years old (which many Christians sadly teach)? They cannot! As an example, Devonian rock is not millions of years old, but rock formed *during* the Flood of Noah's day a few thousand years ago. Having thorns buried in Flood sediment, which occurred after Adam sinned, makes perfect sense.

---

12. Brian Switek, "Sex Locked in Stone," *Nature*, 20, June 2012, http://www.nature.com/news/sex-locked-in-stone-1.10850.
13. Wilson N. Stewart and Gar W. Rothwell, *Paleobotany and the Evolution of Plants* (Cambridge, UK: Cambridge University Press, 1993), p. 172–176.
14. Both thorns and thistles it shall bring forth for you, and you shall eat the herb of the field.

Let's evaluate this from a big picture theological angle. First, Genesis 1:29–30[15] teaches that man and animals were originally vegetarian (before Adam's sin). How do we know this for sure? Humans weren't told they could eat meat until after the Flood in Genesis 9:3.[16] This later verse makes it clear that mankind was originally vegetarian, but this changed after the Flood. Verse 30 of Genesis 1 (about animals' diet) is worded in the same basic way as verse 29 (man's diet), so it confirms that originally the animals were vegetarian too.

Second, at the end of the creation week, God described everything He had made as "very good" (Genesis 1:31[17]). Third, Genesis 3 makes it clear that the animals (v. 14[18]) and the ground (v. 17[19]) were cursed. And verse 18 makes it clear that thorns came into existence after sin and the Curse: "Both thorns and thistles it [the ground] shall bring forth for you."

Recall that the idea that things have been around for millions of years came from the belief that the fossil record was laid down slowly over millions of years, long before man's existence. So when Christians accept millions of years, they must also accept that the fossil layers were laid down before Adam — before the first human sin.

Yet the fossil record contains fossil thorns — claimed by evolutionists to be hundreds of millions of years old. How could that be if thorns came *after* Adam's sin?

Coupled with this, the fossil record also contains lots of examples of animals that ate other animals — bones in their stomachs, teeth marks on bones, and so on. But according to the Bible, animals were vegetarian before sin. Furthermore, the fossil record contains well-documented examples of diseases, such as brain tumors, cancer, and arthritis. But if these existed before man, then God called such diseases "very good."

---

15. And God said, "See, I have given you every herb that yields seed which is on the face of all the earth, and every tree whose fruit yields seed; to you it shall be for food. Also, to every beast of the earth, to every bird of the air, and to everything that creeps on the earth, in which there is life, I have given every green herb for food"; and it was so.

16. Every moving thing that lives shall be food for you. I have given you all things, even as the green herbs.

17. Then God saw everything that He had made, and indeed it was very good. So the evening and the morning were the sixth day.

18. So the LORD God said to the serpent: "Because you have done this, you are cursed more than all cattle, and more than every beast of the field; on your belly you shall go, and you shall eat dust all the days of your life."

19. Then to Adam He said, "Because you have heeded the voice of your wife, and have eaten from the tree of which I commanded you, saying, 'You shall not eat of it': Cursed is the ground for your sake; in toil you shall eat of it all the days of your life."

Taking all this into consideration, it seems obvious that bloodshed, death of animals and man, disease, suffering, and thorns came *after* sin. So the fossil record had to be laid down after sin, too. Noah's Flood would easily account for the majority of the fossils.

But what does this have to do with a gospel issue? The Bible calls death an "enemy" (1 Corinthians 15:26[20]). When God clothed Adam and Eve with coats of skins (Genesis 3:21[21]), this was the first death witnessed in Scripture — the death and bloodshed of an animal (a direct result of human sin!).

Elsewhere in Scripture we learn that without the shedding of blood there is no remission of sins (Hebrews 9:22[22]), and the life of the flesh is in the blood (Leviticus 17:11[23]). Because Adam sinned, a payment for sin was needed. Because sin's penalty was death, then death and bloodshed were needed to atone for sin. So Genesis 3:21 would describe the first blood sacrifice as a penalty for sin — looking forward to the One who would die "once for all" (Hebrews 10:10–14[24]).

An Indirect Salvation Issue

Many Christians believe in millions of years and are truly born again. Their belief in millions of years doesn't affect their salvation. But what does it do? It affects how *other* people, such as their children or others they teach, view Scripture.

Their example can be a stumbling block to others. For instance, telling young people they can reinterpret Genesis to fit in millions of years sets a deadly example: they can start outside Scripture and add ideas into Scripture.

We suggest that such people can, over time, get the idea that the Bible is not God's infallible Word. This creates doubt in God's Word — and doubt often leads to unbelief. Eventually they can reject Scripture altogether. Since

---

20. The last enemy that will be destroyed is death.
21. Also for Adam and his wife the Lord God made tunics of skin, and clothed them.
22. And according to the law almost all things are purified with blood, and without shedding of blood there is no remission.
23. For the life of the flesh is in the blood, and I have given it to you upon the altar to make atonement for your souls; for it is the blood that makes atonement for the soul.
24. By that will we have been sanctified through the offering of the body of Jesus Christ once for all. And every priest stands ministering daily and offering repeatedly the same sacrifices, which can never take away sins. But this Man, after He had offered one sacrifice for sins forever, sat down at the right hand of God, from that time waiting till His enemies are made His footstool. For by one offering He has perfected forever those who are being sanctified.

the gospel comes from a book they don't trust or believe is true, they can easily reject the gospel itself.

So the age of the earth and universe is not a salvation issue *per se* — somebody can be saved even without believing what the Bible says on this issue. But it is a salvation issue indirectly. Christians who compromise on millions of years can encourage *others* toward unbelief concerning God's Word and the gospel.

The Israelites sacrificed animals over and over again, as a ceremonial covering for sin. But Hebrews 10:4[25] tells us that the blood of bulls and goats can't take away our sin — we are not physically related to animals. We needed a perfect human sacrifice. So all this animal sacrifice was looking forward to the One called the Messiah (Jesus Christ).

Now if there was death and bloodshed of animals before sin, then this undermines the atonement. Also, if there were death, disease, bloodshed, and suffering before sin, then such would be God's fault — not our fault! Why would God require death as a sacrifice for sin if He were the one responsible for death and bloodshed, having created the world with these bad things in place?

One of today's most-asked questions is how Christians can believe in a loving God with so much death and suffering in the world. The correct answer is that God's just Curse because of Adam's sin resulted in this death and suffering. *We* are to blame. God is not an unloving or incompetent Creator of a "very bad" world. He had a loving plan from eternity to rescue people from sin and its consequence of eternal separation from God in hell.

So to believe in millions of years is a gospel issue. This belief ultimately impugns the character of the Creator and Savior and undermines the foundation of the soul-saving gospel.

---

25. For it is not possible that the blood of bulls and goats could take away sins.

DOES IT TAKE LONG AGES TO GROW CORAL, LAY DOWN ICE LAYERS (CORES), AND GROW TREE RINGS?

BODIE HODGE

CORAL

The National Oceanic and Atmospheric Administration states:

> How old are today's reefs? The geological record indicates that ancestors of modern coral reef ecosystems were formed at least 240 million years ago. The coral reefs existing today began growing as early as 50 million years ago. Most established coral reefs are between 5,000 and 10,000 years old.[1]

Bill Nye, in the famous debate with Ken Ham in February of 2013, also concurred when discussing zooxanthellae coral. Nye says:

> And when you look at it closely you can see that they live their entire lives, they lived typically 20 years, sometimes more than that if the water conditions are correct. And so we are standing on millions of layers of ancient life.[2]

To the untrained eye, one might think Bill Nye just presented a devastating argument. But this is a fallacious means of arguing. Nye is assuming naturalism to try to prove naturalism. He has assumed there were no catastrophes in the past and that rates and processes have always been identical (this is called "uniformitarianism" and is based on naturalism) to make the claims

---

1. "From Polyp to Colony: Coral Reefs," NOAA Coral Reef Conservation Program, Nation Ocean Service, September 3, 2005, http://coralreef.noaa.gov/aboutcorals/coral101/polypcolony/.
2. http://www.youngearth.org/index.php/archives/rmcf-articles/item/21-transcript-of-ken-ham-vs-bill-nye-debate.

at hand. Then he proceeds to use this to definitively state the naturalistic position of millions of years. This fallacy is called *affirming the consequent* and is arguably the most common fallacy that evolutionists commit. Nye has proven nothing, but has merely assumed what he is trying to prove and thus is being arbitrary and self-refuting.

But does it take long ages for coral growth and accumulation? Dr. John Whitmore, a geologist and professor at Cedarville University, writes (with his references included):

> Corals which build coral reefs have been reported to grow as much as 99 to 432 mm per year.[3] Large coral accumulations have been found on sunken World War II ships only after several decades.[4] *Acropora* colonies have reached 60–80 cm in diameter in just 4.5 years in some experimental rehabilitation studies.[5] At the highest known growth rates, the Eniwetok Atoll (the thickest known reef at 1400 m) would have taken about 3,240 years to rise from the ocean floor.[6]

Dr. Whitmore goes on to point out that it doesn't require long ages to form coral reefs but thousands of years given the right conditions and starting point. This makes sense in light of a global Flood that "reset" things in the oceans as a new starting point to grow coral reefs on all sorts of underwater features such as volcanic platforms, chalk beds, and so forth.

Ice Cores

Speaking of Bill Nye, he also used ice cores in an effort to discredit the idea of a global Flood. Ice cores are cores of ice that have been drilled out of ice sheets such as those on Greenland or Antarctica. These compacted ice layers came from previous storms of ice and snow to build them up.

Nye points out there are some cores with upwards of 680,000 layers that are to be assumed in them — and he purports that it took long ages to form them. Now we agree there are certainly a lot of these ice layers. Of course,

---

3. A.A. Roth, *Origins* (Hagerstown, MD: Review and Herald Publishing Association, 1998), p. 237.

4. S.A. Earle, "Life springs from death in Truk Lagoon," *National Geographic* 149(5):578–603, 1976.

5. H.E. Fox, "Rapid Coral Growth on Reef Rehabilitation Treatments in Komodo National Park, Indonesia," *Coral Reefs* 24:263, 2005.

6. John Whitmore, "Aren't Millions of Years Required for Geological Processes?" in *The New Answers Book 2*, Ken Ham, gen. ed. (Green Forest, AR: Master Books, 2008), p. 240–241.

the layers toward the bottom — due to compression — have molecular diffusion (where multiple layers fuse together). Thus, they have to be *estimated* as to how many layers might have been there (it is true that there is long age assumption here too, of which one needs to be careful). But generally, we agree that there are a lot of ice layers. But remember — the ice layers don't come with labels on them telling us their age!

Nye makes an interpretation of these observable *and* estimated ice layers. He says:

> And we find certain of these cylinders to have 680,000 layers.
> 680,000 snow winter-summer cycles.[7]

Nye assumed these layers were divided by winter-summer cycles. Apparently, there miraculously becomes an observable division between ice layers, where all the ice and snow from storms in one year get compacted into one single layer and all the ice and snow from storms the next year get compacted into the next layer, and so on!

I have personally seen multiple ice layers in *one winter* in Kentucky! It was simply several ice storms and snow storms that piled one on top of the other. Sometimes it was merely due to various phases within the same storm (such as ice-snow-ice in the same storm). The lower layers sometimes became more compact with the layers on top of it — and yet this was merely *one winter* in Kentucky.

Many people around the world could concur that multiple storms will produce multiple layers of snow and ice and can and have observed this every winter. In places like Kentucky, these ice layers melt off each year, but in places where ice sheets are growing (some places in Antarctica and Greenland, for example), they do not melt off but continue to accumulate.

The point is that multiple storms can be observed to produce multiple ice layers. So why assume each of these layers are winter-summer cycles? That would go against scientific observation to say the least. Such abundant ice layers are not dependent upon a winter-summer cycle. Bill Nye has made a fallible assumption — one that does not fit with what we observe.

But let's discuss this further. Dr. Larry Vardiman (PhD in atmospheric science from Colorado State University), while working with the Institute for Creation Research, and Mike Oard, an expert meteorologist (M.Sc.

---

7. http://www.youngearth.org/index.php/archives/rmcf-articles/item/21-transcript-of-ken-ham-vs-bill-nye-debate.

in Atmospheric science from the University of Washington) and board member of the Creation Research Society and former National Weather Service meteorologist, are both weather scientists who have dealt with this issue extensively. Neither would yield to the ice cores as being evidence for long ages or winter-summer cycles.

Dr. Vardiman has pointed out that WWII planes that were buried just 50 years before in Greenland, were already under 250 feet of ice when found![8] This is not 250 ice layers, but 250 *feet* of minuscule ice layers! Dr. Vardiman points out that if uniformitarian rates were to be assumed from this data alone, it would take less than 1,000 years to form the entire Greenland ice sheet! Dr. Vardiman did further calculations and found that a few thousands years were all that would be required for the entire sheet.[9]

Mr. Oard has also addressed the ice cores in great detail from a technical perspective, addressing oxygen content which is to be expected since climates and atmospheric changes do occur and have occurred since the time of the Flood.[10] Such things are actually perfectly expected in a biblical creationist's framework.

Tree Rings: Bristlecone Pines

Bill Nye also brought up bristlecone pines in the debate and arbitrarily asserts that some of them are over 6,000 years old in an effort to discredit the age of the earth based on God's Word. And to back this up, Nye made another arbitrary assertion that a tree (Old Tjikko) is specifically 9,550 years old. That tree is a Norway spruce, not a bristlecone pine, and its age is based on carbon dating, not tree rings.

Please note that when skeptics, like Nye or others, make a claim like this without proving it (i.e., "just take my word for it"), it is arbitrary. An arbitrary claim is simply that, *arbitrary*, and carries no weight in an argument or debate.

Let me explain where the so-called dates for these trees come from. They come from tree rings. In simple form, people add up tree rings (this involves

8. Editors, "Deep Layers," Answers in Genesis, October 26, 2002, https://answersingenesis. org/evidence-against-evolution/deep-layers/.

9. Larry Vardiman, Ph.D., "Ice Cores and the Age of the Earth," *Acts & Facts* 21 (4) 1992, http://www.icr.org/article/ice-cores-age-earth/.

10. Michael Oard, "Do Greenland Ice Cores Show over One Hundred Thousand Years of Annual Layers?" December 1, 2001, http://www.answersingenesis.org/articles/tj/v15/n3/ greenland.

assumptions too), as there can be thousands of them. Then one has to try to cross match them with others to determine a supposed unbroken chronology. Of course, there is a degree of guesswork here.

So what is the big deal? Simple: there is the assumption that each tree ring is a yearly cycle and that it would be impossible to have more than one per year. It would be like every March 1st, all these trees decide to make a new ring.

But the answer is rather easy: the tree rings are actually from *growth* cycles, not necessarily from *yearly* cycles. Many types of trees are observed to have multiple growth cycles even in one year with favorable conditions. So, depending on previous wet-dry cycles (or otherwise good or bad growth periods within a year) there could be multiple growth cycles, thus multiple rings.[11]

Bristlecone pines are no exception. The ones that tend to have more rings and live longer are those in arid, higher altitudes where little rain occurs each year. Let me explain; in the dry arid areas, growth stops until the next rain or watering, then the tree can again begin to grow. But when it becomes dry and arid again, it ceases growing once more.

So growth is dependent upon getting water, not a calendar date (yearly). Having great numbers of rings simply means greater numbers of growth cycles in the past. To say that each ring is a yearly ring would require skeptics to prove that each year in the past, there was only one rainfall per year — a truly bold and unprovable assumption.

The point to take here is that when someone says the Bristlecone Pines are of a certain age, it is *not* due to direct observation, but by interpretation based on un-provable assumptions. Mark Matthews, writing about Bristlecone Pines, says:

> Perhaps the best evidence that some BCPs can grow multiple rings per year is the fact that it has already been demonstrated. Lammerts, a creationist, induced multiple ring growth in sapling BCPs by simply simulating a two-week drought.[12] Some dismiss this evidence, saying that while multiplicity has been demonstrated in young BCPs, it hasn't been demonstrated in mature BCPs and

11. Mark Matthews, "Evidence for Multiple Ring Growth Per Year in Bristlecone Pines," *Journal of Creation* 20(3):95–103, December 2006.
12. W.E. Lammerts, "Are the Bristle-cone Pine Trees Really So Old?" *Creation Research Society Quarterly* 20(2):108–115, 1983.

therefore may not occur in mature BCPs.[13] While this hypothesis could be true, surely the burden of proof should be on those who propose that what happens in immature trees doesn't happen in mature trees.

An expert in the genus *Pinus* didn't seem to have any problem believing that White Mountain BCPs grew multiple rings per year. In his book, *The Genus Pinus*, Nicholas Mirov states, "Apparently a semblance of annual rings is formed after every rather infrequent cloudburst."[14] If an expert like Mirov readily accepted multiplicity in these BCPs, then perhaps the doubters of this notion should at least give the evidence a serious examination.[15]

The Bristlecone Pines, with the dry climate as it is today, doesn't afford multiple tree rings readily, but to assume the climate has always been identical to today is without warrant, even by the long ager's standard.

In short, trees with high numbers of tree rings are not a problem with an age of the earth about 6,000 years and Flood about 4,350 years ago. It is merely arbitrary to say they took long ages.

---

13. V.C. LaMarche Jr. and T.P. Harlan, "Accuracy of Tree Ring Dating of Bristlecone Pine for Calibration of the Radiocarbon Time Scale," *Journal of Geophysical Research* 78(36):8849–8858, 1973.

14. Ibid.

15. Matthews, "Evidence for Multiple Ring Growth Per Year in Bristlecone Pines."

22 | WAS THERE AN ICE AGE THAT FOLLOWED THE FLOOD?

KEN HAM AND BODIE HODGE

INTRODUCTION

Creationists and evolutionists essentially agree there was an ice age. Creationists argue there was one major Ice Age that followed the Flood of Noah. In the secular world, they believe in a multitude of ice ages going back for what seems like an eternity. As a point of clarification, when creationists typically discuss the post-Flood Ice Age, it is denoted in caps, whereas the supposed secular ice ages are not capped to distinguish which is being discussed.

Creationists hold to an Ice Age that was triggered by the Flood. The Flood occurred about 2348 B.C., which is about 4,300 years ago.[1] The secularists' most recent ice age was supposedly about 10,000 years ago (by their dating system).

HOW DOES AN ICE AGE OCCUR?

An ice age does not occur by simply making the earth cold. If the earth became cold, you would have a cold earth, not an ice age.

Instead, an ice age occurs when you have warm oceans to get extra evaporation and thus, extra-accumulated snowfall in winter, *and* cool summers so that the accumulated snow and ice does not get a chance to melt off. Then the following winter, additional accumulation piles on and it builds up into an ice age. Warm oceans and cool summers are the primary reason for an ice age, even though other factors are involved.

---

1. According to Ussher's date.

HOW DID THE FLOOD TRIGGER THE ICE AGE?

Warm Oceans

The Flood would generate immense amounts of heat as evidenced from its onset with the springs of the great deep bursting forth. Continental movements would generate heat; volcanic activity occurring while mountain building was occurring generates heat; and so forth. The point is that it heats the ocean water significantly. Naturally, the ocean would have more evaporation, subsequently causing immense fog, excessive clouds, and storms with more rain, ice, and snowfall than what we get currently.

Cool Summers

What about cooler summers? The Flood explains this as well. But first, a little volcano knowledge is required.

For 200 years, we have known how volcanoes affect our climate. When a volcano erupts, it sends ash particles and dioxides (such as sulfur dioxide) into the atmosphere. If the eruption is powerful enough, it sends these things to the upper atmosphere (stratosphere).

When these sub-microscopic items get to that height it is difficult for them to wash out. It takes a long time. So they linger and cause all sorts of problem for the climate, simply because they reflect sunlight back to space causing the temperature of the globe to cool.

As an example, Mount St. Helens, a relatively small volcano, caused a drop of 0.1 degree Celsius in global temperature.[2] Remember that Mount St. Helens was a small volcano acting alone, so we didn't expect much of a change; but notice that the global temperature went down for a short time.

Larger volcanoes of the past have had much more damaging effects. Some have dropped the global temperature by 1 degree Celsius (e.g., El Chichon), which is quite significant![3] Mt. Tambora blasted in 1815 and caused summer to cease in the Northern Hemisphere in 1816. It is called "the year without a summer," and it was estimated to drop the global temperature by 3 degrees Celsius![4]

---

2. Jack Williams, "The Epic Volcano Eruption That Led to the 'Year Without a Summer,' " *The Washington Post*, April 24, 2015, https://www.washingtonpost.com/news/capital-weather-gang/wp/2015/04/24/the-epic-volcano-eruption-that-led-to-the-year-without-a-summer/.

3. Ibid. Keep in mind that those arguing for a global warming and climate change see only tenths of a degree change, which is quite common in fluctuations that usually match the suns output — but consider a tenth of degree versus an entire degree with this volcano!

4. Ibid.

As you can see, volcanoes that send particles and dioxides into the upper atmosphere can cause severe weather problems — specifically causing summers to be cooler. Most volcanoes we have in modern times are acting alone.

But consider the mountain-building period of the Flood of Noah's day (e.g., Genesis 8:4,[5] Psalm 104:8–9,[6] etc.) involving immense volcanic activity *acting in conjunction* for more than half of the year and surely some volcanic activity that was post-Flood too — which would extend the effects. The point is that immense amounts of fine ash and dioxides were put in the upper atmosphere to linger for hundreds and hundreds of years.

The result was a lot of reflected sunlight and cooler summers back to back for extended amounts of time. Initially, you get accumulation at the poles, and then it extends downward from the North Pole and upward from the South Pole. Then you get more that pile on top of each other and compacts lower layers into ice layers (some layers even combine with each other when the ice gets deep enough and this is called *molecular diffusion*). Some of these ice layers glaciate. Some glaciers move horizontally or downhill as a result of the weight of the ice above them.

Warm oceans and cool summers are the key to the Ice Age.

When did the Ice Age peak and retreat?

Creationists believe the Flood triggered the Ice Age. But that doesn't mean the Ice Age was in full effect immediately. It took time to accumulate up to a maximum (called maximum glaciation). Then, it took time to wane.

Surely, there were some minor fluctuations during the Ice Age where increases and decreases in ice occurred. During the Ice Age, there were times when it advanced and retreated even though the general trend was a growing ice extent. Conversely, there were times when ice sheets were growing when the general trend was reducing.

Even in later times, these fluctuations are felt. For example, there is the Little Ice Age where growth of glaciers was occurring in medieval times. This brings us to two important questions: When did the Ice Age peak? And when did it end (finish its retreat)?

---

5. Then the ark rested in the seventh month, the seventeenth day of the month, on the mountains of Ararat.
6. The mountains rose; the valleys sank down to the place which You established for them. You set a boundary that they may not pass over, so that they will not return to cover the earth (NASB).

Frankly, the Bible doesn't tell us. Thus, creation scientists construct various scientific models to try to answer the question. Naturally, not all models agree with each other.

When did the Ice Age end? Some might argue that it never really ended, since we still have glaciers and ice sheets today (even the Greenland and Antarctic ice sheets are still growing — others are waning!).

This answer doesn't really help us much, so let's refine the question. When did the retreat of the Ice Age finally get to a point of approximate equilibrium? In other words, when did the ice and snow melt off to a point that it remains relatively stable (not growing and not reducing much). This depends on when the peak of the Ice Age was, and so it brings us back to the first question.

Some weather experts (Dr. Jake Hebert,[7] Dr. Larry Vardiman,[8] and retired meteorologist Mike Oard[9]) working with weather data have independently suggested a build up and peak of about 500 years after the Flood, with about 200 or so years for the ice to melt off and retreat to equilibrium.

A competing model by geologist Dr. Andrew Snelling and writer/editor Mike Matthews, based on radiometric dating, have suggested a peak about 250 years after the Flood and about 100 years after that to equalize.[10] Either way, it is a matter of hundreds of years after the Flood. Keep in mind that models are not absolute and are subject to change.

One thing we would like to see an expert research in more detail is based on observations we see today. Some ice sheets are growing while others are retreating. Is it possible that the ice was growing and retreating in different areas, causing some areas to be affected by the Ice Age at one time and other areas affected by it later? After all, what we see in the rock record is an overall ice extent, but did this peak occur *all at once* in the past? Perhaps future research would be helpful.

7. Jake Hebert, "Ice Cores, Seafloor Sediments, and the Age of the Earth," Part 2, *Acts & Facts* 43 (7), 2014, http://www.icr.org/article/8181.
8. See Larry Vardiman, "An Analytical Young-Earth Flow Model of the Ice Sheet Formation During the 'Ice-Age,'" in *Proceedings of the Third International Conference on Creationism*, Robert Walsh, ed. (Pittsburg, PA: Creation Science Fellowship, Inc., 1994), p. 561–568; Larry Vardiman, "Ice Cores and the Age of the Earth," *Acts & Facts* 21 (4), 1992, http://www.icr.org/article/ice-cores-age-earth/.
9. Mike Oard, *An Ice Age Caused by the Genesis Flood* (El Cajon, CA: Institute for Creation Research, 1990), p. 23–38.
10. Andrew Snelling and Mike Matthews, "When was the Ice Age in Biblical History?" *Answers* magazine, vol. 8 no. 2, April–June, 2013, p. 46–52.

23 | DO WE FIND HUMAN FOSSILS WITH DINOSAUR FOSSILS?

KEN HAM *AND* BODIE HODGE

HUMANS AND DINOSAUR FOSSILS TOGETHER: THE MISCONCEPTION

Land animals (which includes dinosaurs) and man were made on day 6 of the creation week. So we lived at the same time.

Often, people believe that if human bones aren't found with dinosaur bones, then they *didn't* live together. This is a false assumption. If human bones aren't found buried directly with dinosaur bones, it simply means they weren't buried together during the Flood.

As the floodwaters advanced during the global Flood, humans would have fled to higher ground, swam, or held on to floating debris for as long as possible. Also, human corpses tend to bloat and therefore float on the water's surface. Hence, it makes sense that very few, if any, humans would be buried by sediment. Instead, they would have rotted and decayed without fossilization.

It is expected that marine creatures and plants were the first things buried and fossilized, since they are at a lower elevation and couldn't escape the sediment and water. When we look at the fossil record, statistically we find:

> 95% of all fossils were marine organisms.
>
> 95% of the remaining 5% were algae, plants/trees.
>
> 95% of the remaining 0.25% were invertebrates, including insects.
>
> The remaining 0.0125% were vertebrates, mostly fish.[1]

---

1. John Morris, *The Young Earth* (Green Forest, AR: Master Books, 2002), p. 70; Andrew Snelling, "Where Are All the Human Fossils?" *Creation* 14(1):28–33, December 1991.

So we shouldn't expect to find many human fossils at all. There is still the possibility of finding human fossils in the lower levels of Flood sediments, but the creation/Flood model doesn't require it.

Remember, we don't find human bones buried with coelacanths either, but we live together today. (Coelacanths are a type of fish, which scientists claimed to have gone extinct millions of years ago but have recently been found alive.) Some were even enjoying them for dinner!

Pre-FLOOD POPULATION

Estimates for the pre-Flood population are based on very little information since Genesis 1 doesn't give extensive family size and growth information. We know that Noah was in the tenth generation of his line and it was about 1,650 years after creation. Genesis also indicates that in Noah's lineage children were being born when their fathers were between the ages of 65 (Enoch to Methuselah) to well over 500 (Noah to his three sons).

How many generations were there in other lineages? We don't know. We know the line from Adam to Noah was living upward of 900 years, but we can't be certain everyone lived this long. How often and how many children were born? We don't know. What were the death rates? We don't know.

Despite this lack of information, some estimates have been done. Tom Pickett gives a range of about 5 to 17 billion people.[2] This is based on various population growth rates and generations of 16–22 prior to the Flood. Dr. John Gill, the famous Baptist expositor, in the 1700s was also open to 11 billion people or higher.[3]

Recall that Noah was only in the tenth generation, so this may be well beyond the higher end of the population maximum. The late Henry Morris had conservative estimates as low as 235 million people. He also calculated rates based on modern population growth, giving about 3 billion people.[4]

John Morris reports estimates that there were about 350 million people pre-Flood.[5] Based on these estimates, pre-Flood populations may have ranged from the low hundreds of millions to 17 billion people. Considering that the

---

2. Tom Pickett, "Population of the PreFlood World," http://www.ldolphin.org/pickett.html, accessed 8/21/2006.
3. John Gill, *Exposition of Genesis*, notes on Genesis 7:21, 1748–1763, http://www.studylight.org/commentary/genesis/7-21.html#geb.
4. Henry Morris, *Biblical Cosmology and Modern Science* (Grand Rapids, MI: Baker Book House, 1970), p. 77–78.
5. John Morris, *The Young Earth* (Green Forest, AR: Master Books, 2002), 11th printing, p. 71.

world was violent (Genesis 6:11–13[6]) and wicked (Genesis 6:5[7]) to such a horrible extreme before the Flood for 120 years, how many people were left at the onset of the Flood? In other words, if the entire world consisted of murderers, then the world's population could be cut in half in one day! It is possible that the population was much lower than we might think. (See chapter 39 for a more detailed discussion of the pre-Flood population.)

Were All Humans Fossilized?

During the 2004 tsunami in Southeast Asia, the Associated Press reported that although many humans were killed during the catastrophe, surprisingly very few livestock animals were killed.[8] Based on this evidence, it is possible that land animals may have had a better chance of survival as the Flood began to devastate and overtake the coastlines than humans did. Initially, people swept out to sea would not be candidates for fossilization. Additionally, inland people could try to flee to higher ground, float, or latch onto debris, reducing their probability of fossilization too.

As sad as it was, the tsunami of 2004 was a good example of the destructiveness of water — even though it was a relatively small flood. According to the United Nation's Office of the Special Envoy for Tsunami Recovery, nearly 43,000 of the approximate 230,000 people that died, were never found — and we know exactly where they were lost — but definitely *not* fossilized.[9]

Were All Humans Evenly Distributed in the Flood Sediment?

We know humans have a tendency to live in groups like towns, villages, and cities. People were probably not evenly distributed before the Flood. Before the Flood, a city was recorded in Genesis 4:17.[10] In accordance with this,

---

6. The earth also was corrupt before God, and the earth was filled with violence. So God looked upon the earth, and indeed it was corrupt; for all flesh had corrupted their way on the earth. And God said to Noah, "The end of all flesh has come before Me, for the earth is filled with violence through them; and behold, I will destroy them with the earth. (Scripture in this chapter is from the New King James Version of the Bible unless otherwise noted.)

7. Then the LORD saw that the wickedness of man was great in the earth, and that every intent of the thoughts of his heart was only evil continually.

8. Gemunu Amarasinghe, "Tsunami Kills Few Animals in Sri Lanka," Associated Press, December 30, 2004, http://www.livescience.com/animalworld/tsunami_wildlife_041230. html, accessed 8/25/2006.

9. "The Human Toll," http://www.tsunamispecialenvoy.org/country/humantoll.asp, accessed June 6, 2006.

10. And Cain knew his wife, and she conceived and bore Enoch. And he built a city, and called the name of the city after the name of his son — Enoch.

most of the population today lives within 100 miles of the coastline. One report says:

> Already nearly two-thirds of humanity — some 3.6 billion people — crowd along a coastline, or live within 150 kilometers of one.[11]

This is further confirmation that the pre-Flood civilizations probably were not evenly distributed either. If man wasn't evenly distributed, then the likelihood of man being evenly distributed ·in Flood sediment becomes extremely remote.

How Much Flood Sediment Is There?

John Woodmorappe's studies indicate that there are about 700 million cubic kilometers, which translates to about 168 million cubic miles of Flood sediment.[12] Dr. John Morris states that there is about 350 million cubic miles of Flood sediment.[13] However, this number may be high since the total volume of water on the earth is estimated at about 332.5 million cubic miles according to the U.S. Geological Survey.[14]

So, a small human population and massive amounts of sediment are two prominent factors why we haven't found human fossils in Flood sediments. It also may simply be that we haven't found the sediment where humans were living and were buried.

Let's Think about the Question

Again, people mistakenly believe that if human bones aren't found with dinosaur bones, then they didn't live together. Let's think about it this way instead: if human bones aren't found buried with dinosaur bones, it simply means they weren't *buried* together.

A great example is that of the coelacanth. Coelacanth fossils are found in layers below dinosaurs.[15] It was thought the Coelacanth became

11. "Coastal Policy," http://coastalpolicy.blogspot.com/2005_02_01_archive.html.
12. John Woodmorappe, *Studies in Flood Geology* (Dallas, TX: Institute for Creation Research, 1999), p. 59. This number actually comes from *International Geology Review* 24(11) 1982, A.B. Ronov, "The Earth's Sedimentary Shell," p. 1321–1339.
13. Morris, *The Young Earth*, p. 71.
14. "The World's Water," U.S. Geological Survey, http://ga.water.usgs.gov/edu/earthwherewater.html.
15. Lynn Dicks, "The Creatures Time Forgot," *New Scientist*, October 23, 1999; 164: (2209) p. 36–39.

extinct about 70 million years ago (by secular reckoning) because their fossils are not found after this time. However, in 1938 living populations were found in the Indian Ocean![16]

Humans are not buried with crocodiles, but we live together. Humans are not buried with ginkgo trees but exist at the same time. The list can go on! This shows that the fossil record is not complete, not necessarily that things did or did not co-exist.

If human and dinosaur bones are found in the same geologic layers in the future, it would be consistent with the biblical view. In fact, it would be more of a problem for those who accept the geologic layers as evidence for millions of years. If the fossil layers really represented millions of years, then finding a human and dinosaur fossilized in the same layers would cause problems because in the old-earth view, man wasn't supposed to be that old, or dinosaurs that young.

As biblical creationists, we don't *require* that human and dinosaur fossils have to be found buried together. Whether they are found together or not does not affect the biblical view.

16. Rebecca Driver, "Sea Monsters . . . More Than a Legend?" *Creation* magazine 19(4):38–42, September 1997, http://www.answersingenesis.org/creation/v19/i4/seamonsters.asp.

24 | WAS THERE ORIGINALLY ONE CONTINENT?

BODIE HODGE

INTRODUCTION

> Then God said, "Let the waters under the heavens be gathered together into one place, and let the dry land appear"; and it was so. And God called the dry land Earth, and the gathering together of the waters He called Seas. And God saw that it was good (Genesis 1:9–10).

Most creationists believe there was one continent originally, in light of these verses. However, we need to be careful because the text doesn't specifically say this. It says the *waters* (under the heaven) were gathered into one place.

At this point of gathering with the land appearing, one could rightfully assume the earth has taken its familiar shape of a sphere, leaving open the option that this watery mass may *not* have been a sphere beforehand (perhaps close though). From children's books to scientific models, we assume the earth was a nearly perfect sphere of water initially, but that is an assumption.

Keep in mind these initial created waters had no *specific* form according to Genesis 1:2,[1] merely a surface. The waters were since separated (Genesis 1:6-7[2]). The portion of waters below the heavens were then gathered together into our seas.

---

1. The earth was formless and void, and darkness was over the surface of the deep, and the Spirit of God was moving over the surface of the waters (NASB).
2. Then God said, "Let there be an expanse in the midst of the waters, and let it separate the waters from the waters." God made the expanse, and separated the waters which were below the expanse from the waters which were above the expanse; and it was so (NASB).

Consider God's poetic description of the gathering of the waters into a "heap" or a "storehouse" as in Psalm 33:6–9:

> By the word of the LORD the heavens were made, and all the host of them by the breath of His mouth. He gathers the waters of the sea together as a heap; He lays up the deep in storehouses. Let all the earth fear the LORD; let all the inhabitants of the world stand in awe of Him. For He spoke, and it was done; He commanded, and it stood fast.

So the gathering stage may have been more significant than we have often been led to think. However, we would not be adamant about this interpretation, but leave it open.

Pangaea and Rodinia?

Regarding the continent though, it is possible to have more than one continent with a situation where waters are still in one place. Even so, some have proposed an initial supercontinent that looked like Pangaea going back to a creationist, Antonio Snider, in the 1800s.[3] In this model, Pangaea breaks apart into the continents we have today during a catastrophic breakup during the Flood.

Others, including some creationists, have models with a supercontinent that looks like Rodinia[4] (one of the alleged supercontinent reconstructions that secularists have *prior* to Pangaea based on radiometric dating[5]). The creationist form of the model has Rodinia breaking up during the Flood, coming back together as Pangaea, and then breaking up again late in the Flood.[6]

Still others have left open the option that we simply do not know the size or shape of an original continent(s) especially in light of a global Flood that destroyed the surface of the earth (Genesis 6–8; 2 Peter 3:5–6[7]). These potential models play off the fact that so much happened in the Flood that it may be too difficult to reconstruct what the original earth looked like (e.g.,

---

3. A. Snider, *Le Création et ses Mystères Devoilés* (Paris, France: Franck and Dentu, 1859).
4. *Rodinia* is the Russian word for "The Motherland."
5. More specifically, it is based on radiometric dates of A-type granites and radiometric dates of fold mountains called orogenic belts.
6. Andrew Snelling, "Noah's Lost World," https://answersingenesis.org/geology/plate-tectonics/noahs-lost-world/.
7. For this they willfully forget: that by the word of God the heavens were of old, and the earth standing out of water and in the water, by which the world that then existed perished, being flooded with water.

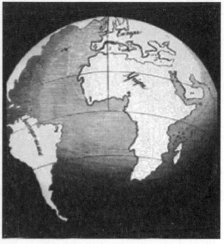

Maps made in 1858 by geographer Antonio Snider, showing his version of how the American and African continents may have once fit together, then later separated.

could it have origically been something half way between Pangaea and what we have today for example).

One continent is a possibility and makes sense, but keep in mind this is not exactly what the text says, so it would be wise not to attack those who are open to more than one, though most agree that it was the Flood of Noah's day

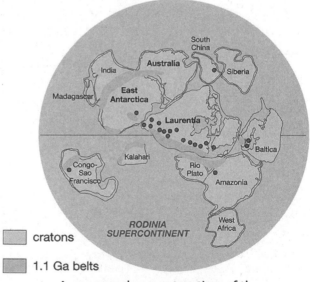

A proposed reconstruction of the supercontinent Rodinia

that broke apart what was originally made to what we have today.

About the breakup to what we have today, the text of Scripture gives us some clues. By the 150th day of the Flood, the mountains of Ararat existed

(Genesis 7:24–8:4[8]). These mountains (as well as the others in the Alpide stretch of mountain ranges that go from Europe to Asia) appear to have been built by the continental collisions of the Arabian, African, Indian, and Eurasian plates. Thus, continental movement for these mountains and plates may well have been largely stopped by the 150th day.[9]

This makes sense as the primary mechanisms for the Flood (*springs of the great deep and windows of heaven*) were stopped on the 150th day as well. Thus, it triggered the waters to now be in a recessional stage as the valleys go down (e.g., ocean basins etc.). This is subsequent to the mountains rising, which had already been occurring up to the 150th day (e.g., mountain ranges and continent extending above the waters) at this stage of the Flood (Psalm 104:6–9[10]).

At creation, was the land *under* the surface of the waters or was it made uniquely on day 3?

There are two models/positions on this.

1. The first is that the land was under the surface of the water the whole time (from Genesis 1:1) and the water was moved out of the way as the land raised through the waters and then the land dried out to become dry.

2. The earth was pure water on day 1. Then the waters were separated and those below were gathered into one place (on day 2) and then the dry land was made separately and uniquely (being that it is creation week) or that some of the water transformed into dry land directly.

---

8. And the waters prevailed on the earth one hundred and fifty days. Then God remembered Noah, and every living thing, and all the animals that were with him in the ark. And God made a wind to pass over the earth, and the waters subsided. The fountains of the deep and the windows of heaven were also stopped, and the rain from heaven was restrained. And the waters receded continually from the earth. At the end of the hundred and fifty days the waters decreased. Then the ark rested in the seventh month, the seventeenth day of the month, on the mountains of Ararat.

9. Naturally this causes a problem for the *Rodinia-to-Pangaea-to-today* scenario. If Rodinia breaks into Pangaea and late in the Flood Pangaea is still under water and needs to break apart into what we have today, then the mountains of Ararat should not have existed so early in the Flood on the 150th day of the Flood.

10. You covered it with the deep as with a garment; the waters were standing above the mountains. At Your rebuke they fled, at the sound of Your thunder they hurried away. The mountains rose; the valleys sank down to the place which You established for them. You set a boundary that they may not pass over, so that they will not return to cover the earth (NASB).

If the waters were truly void as Genesis 1:2[11] says, then the idea of a land mass in the midst from the very beginning, may not be the best solution — especially if the midst of the water was where the point of water separation was to occur on day 2! It makes more sense that the land was made later *on* day 3 out of water. This comes from 2 Peter 3:5–6[12] that says the earth was formed "out of water and by water" and these waters were used later in the Flood!

But one point can be made: the land was dry, *not wet,* when it appeared. This was so important that God stated it multiple times, in Genesis 1:9[13] and 1:10[14] as well as Psalm 95:5.[15] This is a good argument for a supernatural fiat of the appearance of the land, not a wet sedimentary flow on day 3 that was naturally pushed up through the waters and later became dry, unless God supernaturally dried it. But this is another assumption that would be required that is not in the text. Again, that would be wetland that *became* dry.

When the land appeared in Genesis 1 on day 3, the land that was being separated from the water was *dry*, not wet. The text in Genesis says that the waters were gathered into one place (i.e., in heaps and storehouses) *and then* the dry land appeared. It says nothing of water running off of the land as it rises; otherwise, "wet" land would have appeared and then *become dry*. The response from God, "and it was so" seems to refute the idea that it was wet, and then became dry.

But really, all we can be certain about is that the *dry land appeared on day 3*. And keep in mind that models are not Scripture and subject to change.

---

11. The earth was without form, and void; and darkness was on the face of the deep. And the Spirit of God was hovering over the face of the waters.
12. For this they willfully forget: that by the word of God the heavens were of old, and the earth standing out of water and in the water, by which the world that then existed perished, being flooded with water.
13. Then God said, "Let the waters under the heavens be gathered together into one place, and let the dry land appear"; and it was so.
14. And God called the dry land Earth, and the gathering together of the waters He called Seas. And God saw that it was good.
15. The sea is His, for He made it; and His hands formed the dry land.

25 | HOW LONG DID IT TAKE FOR NOAH TO BUILD THE ARK?

BODIE HODGE

Let's dispel something up front. Some confuse God's statement in Genesis 6:3 as describing the time it took Noah to build the ark. It states:

> And the Lord said, "My Spirit shall not strive with man forever, for he is indeed flesh; yet his days shall be one hundred and twenty years."

However, these 120 years are a countdown to the Flood.[1] In other words, mankind's violence had reached its peak and God declared that 120 years was the "drop dead" date for mankind who is a mortal being (Genesis 6:3–7[2]). From a quick look, these 120 years would seem to be the absolute maximum for the time given to build the ark, but the Scriptures reveal much more, allowing us to be more accurate.

---

1. Some have also described this as the longevity of mankind. For a number of generations after the Flood, people lived to be much older than this (e.g., Isaac lived to 180 years), so it is not referring to longevity.
2. And the Lord said, "My Spirit shall not strive with man forever, for he is indeed flesh; yet his days shall be one hundred and twenty years." There were giants on the earth in those days, and also afterward, when the sons of God came in to the daughters of men and they bore children to them. Those were the mighty men who were of old, men of renown. Then the Lord saw that the wickedness of man was great in the earth, and that every intent of the thoughts of his heart was only evil continually. And the Lord was sorry that He had made man on the earth, and He was grieved in His heart. So the Lord said, "I will destroy man whom I have created from the face of the earth, both man and beast, creeping thing and birds of the air, for I am sorry that I have made them."

For example, Noah was 500 years old when Japheth, the first of his sons, was born (Genesis 5:32[3]). And yet Noah's second son, Shem, had his first son two years after the Flood, when he was 100 (Genesis 11:10[4]).[5] This means that Shem was 98 years old when the Flood came and it also means that Shem was born when Noah was 502 years old. So for Noah to begin having children at 500 means that Japheth was indeed the older brother, as per Genesis 10:21,[6] being born when Noah was 500. Ham is mentioned as the youngest of Noah (Genesis 9:24[7]).

When God finally gave Noah instructions to build the ark, it was not at the beginning of the 120-year countdown. God told Noah that he, his wife, and his three sons and their wives (Genesis 6:15–18[8])[9] would go aboard the ark at this same time.

Deducing that Shem was born 98 years before the Flood, it could be no more than this. But even more so, Ham hadn't been born yet! If we were to assume the same time between Ham and Shem as between Japheth and Shem, then Ham could have been born around 96 years before the Flood.

Although the Bible is silent on the exact timing, it is reasonable to assume that some time elapsed for the three sons to grow up and find wives. I would be most comfortable giving a tentative range of anywhere from 20 to 40 years, making Ham no less than 16 at his marriage.

So if we think about this logically and tabulate it, we would end up with a tentative range of about 55 to 75 years for a reasonable *maximum* time to build the ark (see table). Of course, it could be less than this depending on the ages of Noah's sons when they took wives.

---

3. And Noah was five hundred years old, and Noah begot Shem, Ham, and Japheth.
4. This is the genealogy of Shem: Shem was one hundred years old, and begot Arphaxad two years after the flood.
5. Shem is often listed first (e.g., Genesis 6:10, 7:13) due to *importance*, much as Abraham is listed first; yet, Shem was not the oldest. From the lineage of Shem and Abraham came Christ.
6. And children were born also to Shem, the father of all the children of Eber, the brother of Japheth the elder.
7. So Noah awoke from his wine, and knew what his younger son had done to him.
8. And this is how you shall make it: The length of the ark shall be three hundred cubits, its width fifty cubits, and its height thirty cubits. You shall make a window for the ark, and you shall finish it to a cubit from above; and set the door of the ark in its side. You shall make it with lower, second, and third decks. And behold, I Myself am bringing floodwaters on the earth, to destroy from under heaven all flesh in which is the breath of life; everything that is on the earth shall die. But I will establish My covenant with you; and you shall go into the ark — you, your sons, your wife, and your sons' wives with you.
9. *Youngest* is used in ESV, NAS, and other translations for the word qatan, which means small, young, or insignificant.

Years until the Flood	Event	Bible reference
120	Countdown to the Flood begins	Genesis 6:3
100	Noah had Japheth, the first of his sons, when he was 500 years old	Genesis 5:32[1], 10:21[2]
98	Noah had Shem who was 100 two years after the Flood	Genesis 11:10[3]
? Perhaps 95 or 96, the same time between Japheth and Shem	Ham was the youngest one born to Noah and was aboard the ark, so he was born prior to the Flood	Genesis 9:24[4]; Genesis 7:13[5]
? Perhaps 20-40 years for all of the sons to be raised and find a wife	Each son was old enough to be married before construction on the ark began	Genesis 6:18[6]
~ 55–75 years (estimate)	Noah was told to build the ark, for he, his wife, his sons, and his sons' wives would be aboard the ark	Genesis 6:18[7]
Ark Completed		
?	Gather food and put it aboard the ark	Genesis 6:21[8]
7 days	Loading the ark	Genesis 7:2-3[9]
0	Noah was 600 when the floodwaters came on the earth.	Genesis 7:6[10]

Footnotes for Table

1. And Noah was five hundred years old, and Noah begot Shem, Ham, and Japheth.
2. And children were born also to Shem, the father of all the children of Eber, the brother of Japheth the elder.
3. This is the genealogy of Shem: Shem was one hundred years old, and begot Arphaxad two years after the flood.
4. So Noah awoke from his wine, and knew what his younger son had done to him.
5. On the very same day Noah and Noah's sons, Shem, Ham, and Japheth, and Noah's wife and the three wives of his sons with them, entered the ark.
6. But I will establish My covenant with you; and you shall go into the ark — you, your sons, your wife, and your sons' wives with you.
7. Ibid.
8. And you shall take for yourself of all food that is eaten, and you shall gather it to yourself; and it shall be food for you and for them.
9. You shall take with you seven each of every clean animal, a male and his female; two each of animals that are unclean, a male and his female; also seven each of birds of the air, male and female, to keep the species alive on the face of all the earth.
10. Noah was six hundred years old when the floodwaters were on the earth.

Keep in mind that Noah may have researched the subject for years or worked to get funds/supplies to build the ark. Hosts of things could have occurred prior to Noah and his family "breaking ground" on the ark.

We know that the ark was completed prior to loading the animals that the Lord brought to Noah (Genesis 6:22–7:4[10]) and that they had to take time to gather food and store it aboard the ark (Genesis 6:21[11]). So carefully considering the text, we can conclude that the construction of the ark did not involve the 120 years mentioned in Genesis 6:3 but 75 years at the most.

---

10. Thus Noah did; according to all that God commanded him, so he did. Then the LORD said to Noah, "Come into the ark, you and all your household, because I have seen that you are righteous before Me in this generation. You shall take with you seven each of every clean animal, a male and his female; two each of animals that are unclean, a male and his female; also seven each of birds of the air, male and female, to keep the species alive on the face of all the earth. For after seven more days I will cause it to rain on the earth forty days and forty nights, and I will destroy from the face of the earth all living things that I have made.

11. And you shall take for yourself of all food that is eaten, and you shall gather it to yourself; and it shall be food for you and for them.

26 | TIMELINE OF THE FLOOD

BODIE HODGE

What was the duration of the Flood you might ask? The Bible gives us the answer. It was from the 2nd month, the 17th day of the month, of Noah's 600th year until the next year (Noah's 601st year) on the 2nd month, the 27th day of the month. So it was one year and 10 days, by Noah's calendar year. So how many total days was that? That will depend on what calendar Noah was using!

WHAT CALENDAR?

Obviously, Noah was not using our modern Gregorian calendar that came into effect in its present form in A.D. 1582. No one used the 365-day year until the Egyptians, according to ancient historian Herodotus [in book 2, line 4]. Prior to this, the Egyptians used a 360-day calendar with an intercalary month thrown in from time to time to bring it back to where it should be.

The Egyptians were descendants of Noah's grandson Mizraim, so this was well after the Flood.[1] Most early ancient calendars used a 360-day year with an intercalary month every few years — from Egypt to the Mayans.[2] This may have been a carryover from Noah through Babel.

It is possible that the Flood account used the calendar that Moses was accustomed to since he was the one who gave us the inspired text of Genesis (likely from pre-existing texts and by the power of the Holy

---

1. Bodie Hodge, *The Tower of Babel* (Green Forest, AR: Master Books, 2013), p. 122–124.
2. James Ussher, *The Annals of the World, The Epistle to the Reader, 1656*, translated by Larry and Marion Pierce (Green Forest, AR: Master Books, 2003), p. 9.

Spirit).[3] If so, that would mean that the dates had to be translated from Noah's system of timekeeping to the one Moses and the Israelites used before the captivity — which was a Canaanite calendar. It makes sense that they used a Canaanite calendar, as it was surely a carryover from the sojourn of his ancestors Abraham, Isaac, and Israel in Canaan, though Moses was surely familiar with the ancient Egyptian calendar that had 360 days too, since he was educated in Egypt's elite royal house.

Much later, the Israelites adopted the Babylonian calendar upon their captivity beginning with Nebuchadnezzar (e.g., the month of *Tammuz* is in the Jewish calendar is named for the Babylonian "god" Tammuz). The Canaanite month names used in Scripture prior to the captivity (with their roughly corresponding Babylonian names) are:

- *Abib* (Exodus 13:4,[4] 23:1,5[5] 34:18,[6] and Deuteronomy 16:1[7]) was later called *Nisan*, 30 days
- *Ziv* (1 Kings 6:1,[8] 6:37,[9] 29 days) was later called *Iyyar*
- *Ethanim* (1 Kings 8:2,[10] 30 days) which was later called *Tishri*
- *Bul* (1 Kings 6:38,[11] usually 29 days) which was later called *Marcheshvan* or simply *Cheshvan* or *Heshvan*

If we look at the text of Scripture, the Flood account in Genesis 6–8 never uses month names that Moses and other Israelites used later (Canaanite or Babylonian names). Instead, Moses chose *not* to insert names from the Canaanite

---

3. Terry Mortenson and Bodie Hodge, "Did Moses Write Genesis?" in *How Do We Know the Bible Is True?* Volume 1, Ken Ham and Bodie Hodge, gen. eds. (Green Forest, AR: Master Books, 2011), p. 85–102.
4. On this day you are going out, in the month Abib.
5. You shall keep the Feast of Unleavened Bread (you shall eat unleavened bread seven days, as I commanded you, at the time appointed in the month of Abib, for in it you came out of Egypt; none shall appear before Me empty).
6. The Feast of Unleavened Bread you shall keep. Seven days you shall eat unleavened bread, as I commanded you, in the appointed time of the month of Abib; for in the month of Abib you came out from Egypt.
7. Observe the month of Abib, and keep the Passover to the LORD your God, for in the month of Abib the LORD your God brought you out of Egypt by night.
8. And it came to pass in the four hundred and eightieth year after the children of Israel had come out of the land of Egypt, in the fourth year of Solomon's reign over Israel, in the month of Ziv, which is the second month, that he began to build the house of the LORD.
9. In the fourth year the foundation of the house of the LORD was laid, in the month of Ziv.
10. Therefore all the men of Israel assembled with King Solomon at the feast in the month of Ethanim, which is the seventh month.
11. And in the eleventh year, in the month of Bul, which is the eighth month, the house was finished in all its details and according to all its plans. So he was seven years in building it.

calendar but left them numbered (first month, second month, etc.). Since the dates are referenced to Noah's age, it makes the most sense that Moses kept the dating system that was utilized on the ark while penning Genesis 7–8.

Keep in mind that the later Israelite calendar (i.e., the Babylonian calendar) was lunar.[12] The months alternated with 29 or 30 days. In the Bible, we find that 150 days was equivalent to 5 months based on the context in the Flood account (Genesis 7:24–8:4[13]). This would yield month-lengths of 30 days each, not 29 and 30 days alternating for 5 months (as in a lunar calendar).

So with this in mind, it makes the most sense to stick with the common 360-day calendar that many ancients used that had 30-day months. James Ussher states in *The Epistle to the Reader* of his treatise *The Annals of the World*:

> Moreover, we find that the years of our forefathers, the years of the ancient Egyptians and Hebrews, were the same length as the Julian year. It consisted of twelve months containing thirty days each. (It cannot be proven that the Hebrews used lunar months before the Babylonian captivity.) Five days were added after the twelfth month each year. Every four years, six days were added after the twelfth month. {*Diod. Sic., l. 1. c. 50. s. 2. 1:177} {*Strabo, l. 17. c. 1. s. 46. 8:125} {*Strabo, l. 17. c. 1. s. 29. 8:85} {*Herodotus, l. 2. c. 4. 1:279} {#Ge 7:11,24 8:3-5,13,14}.[14]

Furthermore, applying any lunar calendar to the duration of the onset of the Flood until the date that the ark struck the mountains of Ararat (the 2nd month, 17th day of the month to the 7th month, 17th day of the month) would have the ark landing in the mountains of Ararat two to three days *before* the waters receded, subsided, and the rain and great deep

---

12. My friend and astronomer Dr. Danny Faulkner prefers the lunar calendar to be applied to the Flood account, though I respectfully disagree. But nonetheless, I encourage him in his research. See: Danny Faulkner, How Long Did the Flood Last?, *Answers Research Journal*, 8 (2015):253–259, May 13, 2015, https://answersingenesis.org/the-flood/how-long-did-the-flood-last/.

13. And the waters prevailed on the earth one hundred and fifty days. Then God remembered Noah, and every living thing, and all the animals that were with him in the ark. And God made a wind to pass over the earth, and the waters subsided. The fountains of the deep and the windows of heaven were also stopped, and the rain from heaven was restrained. And the waters receded continually from the earth. At the end of the hundred and fifty days the waters decreased. Then the ark rested in the seventh month, the seventeenth day of the month, on the mountains of Ararat.

14. James Ussher, *The Annals of the World*, revised and updated by Larry and Marion Pierce (Green Forest, AR: Master Books, 2003), p. 9.

were restrained (the Flood mechanisms). Based on the context and theological issues, I humbly suggest that the best calendar to use is the 360-day calendar, which was often used in the Bible.[15]

TIMELINE OF THE FLOOD

The following tentative table utilizes a 360-day calendar as most ancient calendars had in the Middle East (and elsewhere). This understanding of the Flood is assumed to *exclude* an intercalary month.

An examination of the Flood account in Genesis 6–8 gives some time-related milestones that form the overall structure in the progression of the yearlong global Flood. Table 1 briefly summarizes these milestones that can help us understand some of the geologic details of the Flood.

Table 1: Timeline of Flood Duration

Timeline (days)	Duration	Month/Day	Description	Bible reference*
0	Initial reference point	600th year of Noah's life: 2nd month, 17th day of the month	The fountains of the great deep broke apart and the windows of heaven were opened; it began to rain. This happened on the 17th day of the 2nd month. Noah actually entered the ark seven days prior to this.	Genesis 7:11
40	40 days and nights	3rd month, 27th day of the month	Rain fell for 40 days then it covered the earth's highest places (at that time) by over ~20 feet (15 cubits) and began the stage of Flooding until the next milestone.** At this time, the ark was lifted up.	Genesis 7:11–12 Genesis 7:17–20
150	150 days (including the initial 40 days)	7th month, 17th day of the month	The water rose to its highest level (covering the whole earth) sometime between the 40th and 150th day, and the end of these 150 days was the 17th day of the 7th month. The ark rested on the mountains of Ararat. On the 150th day, the springs of the great deep were shut off, and the rain from above ceased, and the water began continually receding.	Genesis 7:24–8:5

---

15. For examples, the Persians still used a 360-day calendar as witnessed in Esther 1:4 where a 180 days equated with a half year feast; John used 3 and half years as 42 months with 1260 days, which uses a 360-day calendar (Revelation 11:2-3, 12: 6, 13:5-7), etc.

150 + 74 = 224	74 days	10th month, 1st day of the month	The tops of the mountains became visible on the tenth month, first day.	Genesis 8:5
224 + 40 = 264	40 days	11th month, 11th day	After 40 more days, Noah sent out a raven.	Genesis 8:6
264 + 7 = 271	7 days	11th month, 18th day of the month	The dove was sent out seven days after the raven. It had no resting place and returned to Noah.	Genesis 8:6–12
271 + 7 = 278	7 days	11th month, 25th day of the month	After seven more days, Noah sent out the dove again. It returned again, but this time with an olive leaf in its beak.	Genesis 8:10–11
278 + 7 = 285	7 days	12th month, 2nd day of the month	After seven more days, Noah sent out the dove again, and it did not return.	Genesis 8:12
314	29 days	601st year of Noah's life: 1st month, 1st day of the month	Noah removed the cover of the ark on the first day of the first month. The *surface* of the earth was dried up and Noah could verify this to the extent of what he could see.	Genesis 8:13
370 (371 if counting the first day and last day as full days)	56 days	2nd month, 27th day of the month	The *earth* was dry and God commanded Noah's family and the animals to come out of the ark. From the first day of the year during the daylight portion there were 29.5 more days left in the month plus 26.5 more days left in the second month until the exit.	Genesis 8:14–17 Genesis 7:11

* References not listed in the footnotes for the table — see chapter 2 for the text of the Flood account.

** Some argue from the Hebrew that the ark officially rose off the surface on the 40th day, e.g., William D. Barrick and Roger Sigler, "Hebrew and Geologic Analysis of the Chronology and Parallelism of the Flood: Implications for the Interpretations of the Geologic Record," in *Proceedings of the Fifth International Conference on Creationism*, ed. Robert L. Ivey Jr., (Pittsburg, PA: Creation Science Fellowship, 2003), p. 397–408.

Because the biblical account is a reliable record of earth history, it is to be expected that these milestones would be significant in correlating the prominent geological features preserved in the rock record. For example, we are told that the onset of the Flood was triggered by the breaking up of the fountains of "the great deep."

This would imply a violent beginning to the Flood, as springs or fountains of water burst forth to spew vast quantities of water and perhaps other material onto the surface from deeper inside the earth. Furthermore, because this subterranean water and other materials bursting forth is mentioned *first* in Genesis 7:11[16] and 8:2,[17] this may suggest that the majority of the water for the Flood came from that source and perhaps helped to supply the waters that are referred to as falling through "the windows of heaven."[18]

The springs of the great deep were likely the trigger that ultimately resulted in continental scale breaking up of the earth's crust. The bursting forth of subterranean waters would probably produce tsunamis (granting the ocean depth was sufficient) and would therefore seem to also imply that the Flood began with catastrophic means. Thus, this description of the onset of the Flood provides clues as to where we should look in the geologic record for the pre-Flood/Flood boundary.

Of course the issue of pre-Flood sedimentation needs to be discussed. Rivers, such as Hiddekel, Gihon, Tigris, and Euphrates, would have been carrying some sediment for about 1,650 years. It is also possible for other smaller catastrophes to have occurred during this time — e.g., volcanoes. So the question really becomes, were these sediments disturbed and/or redistributed during the Flood or were they buried *in situ*?

Another milestone with geological implications is day 150. At this stage of the Flood we are told that the ark came to rest in the mountains of Ararat. This implies that modern mountain building, at least in what we now call the Middle East, had begun (see also Psalm 104:8–9).[19]

---

16. In the six hundredth year of Noah's life, in the second month, the seventeenth day of the month, on that day all the fountains of the great deep were broken up, and the windows of heaven were opened.
17. The fountains of the deep and the windows of heaven were also stopped, and the rain from heaven was restrained.
18. A.A. Snelling, "A Catastrophic Breakup: A Scientific Look at Catastrophic Plate Tectonics," *Answers*, 2:2 (2007), p. 44–48.
19. Psalm 104 begins with a reference to the events of creation week and goes on to mention ships (vs. 26) and Lebanon (vs. 16), which are near the time of the Psalmist. So logically, other events in history since creation, such as the Flood, should be expected within the Psalm as it continues. It should be obvious that vs. 6–9 are referring to the Flood since verse 9 specifically says the water will not *return* to cover the earth, which refers to God's post-Flood declarations in Genesis 9:11, 15 and Isaiah 54:9. Had verses 6–9 been referring to creation week, then God would have erred since water did return to cover the earth during the Flood. For these and other reasons, Psalms 104:8a should be rendered from Hebrew into English as: "The mountains rose and valleys sank down . . .", which several translations

Furthermore, if our current understanding of mountain building is correct, for the mountains of Ararat to have been formed requires the Eurasian Plate, African Plate, and Arabian Plate to be colliding with one another (perhaps with some contribution from movement of the Indian Plate).

The biblical account also indicates that on day 150 the springs of the great deep were stopped and the windows of heaven were closed, so from then on the waters began to steadily recede. We might therefore expect to see in the geologic record evidence of a transition perhaps from larger scale sediment layers to smaller scale geologic effects as well as higher concentration of basin, abyssal plain, and continental shelf sedimentation.

Yet another milestone is day 314 (see Table 1). By this time during the Flood event the biblical account indicates that the water had receded from off the continental land surfaces sufficiently for the surface of the landscape to essentially be dry, at least in the areas as far as Noah could observe.

Then finally, by day 370 the earth's continental land surfaces were dry from the Flood waters. Thus, it can be noted that the recessional stage of the Flood (when the waters were receding) lasted about five and half months, while the Flood's inundatory stage (when the waters were rising) lasted exactly five months. The recessional stage lasted almost the same length of time as it took for the water to overtake the earth globally. The Flood event finished with another two months needed to complete the drying process.

After the Flood ended on day 370 (with the proclamation for Noah to exit the ark), it would seem that the hydrological cycle had already been re-established with renewed regularity, as indicated by the rain clouds through which Noah saw the rainbow and the set times for seed time and harvest in accordance with the seasonal cycle of rain (Genesis 8:22,[20] 9:12–17). Other milestones throughout the Flood account could of course be highlighted, but these are ones that are most related to geological and weather processes and should suffice for this brief tentative overview.

---

have concluded (e.g., Latin Vulgate A.D. 405, Geneva Bible A.D. 1599, Tyndale/Coverdale A.D. 1535, New American Standard A.D. 1971 and 1995, English Standard Version A.D. 2001, Holman Christian Standard Bible A.D. 2004, etc.).

20. While the earth remains, seedtime and harvest, cold and heat, winter and summer, and day and night shall not cease.

27 | WHERE IS THE FLOOD ROCK?

KEN HAM AND BODIE HODGE

The answer to this is simple; and yet I'm surprised so many people miss it. The flood rock is all over the world, sometimes miles deep. It is the majority of the fossil layers in the "backyard" of most people reading this. These fossil layers can be found in most parts of the world (e.g., some have been scraped off by glaciers since the Flood, etc.). Many basins and mountains consist of them (e.g., the Appalachian mountains). Naturally, we have had some layering and erosion since the time of the Flood and that brings us to a debate.

One of the most hotly debated subjects in creationist literature is the placement of what is Flood rock and what is post-Flood rock. Of course, the debate breaks into a boil in some technical conferences, especially when interpreting what is found in various rock layers toward the top of the fossil sediments. You need to understand that creationists generally agree upon the majority of the fossil layers (e.g., the pre-Flood boundary, the Ice Age rock being Pleistocene, etc.), but it is those pesky layers on which creationists don't agree surrounding the post-Flood boundary that causes the controversy.

Furthermore, there are implications depending on where the post-Flood boundary is.[1] In some creationists' eyes, particular fossil deposits or rock layers could be seen as Flood rock, while others have it as post-Flood rock. The difference here is immense . . . while some say the animal remains found in those fossil layers are from the Flood, others would have to find migration routes from the ark to these deposits very soon after the Flood.

---

1. Layers discussed here will be layers that encompass the Flood and post-Flood, not pre-Flood layering unless noted.

As this simple example reveals, the technical differences can be large and creationists can be very intense about this subject. As a preface before we get into the post-Flood boundary discussion, let's first review the relevant biblical passages, geological layers, and the pre-Flood boundary so we can properly understand the debate at hand.

A FEW MILESTONES

Many of the milestones in the previous chapter are significant to geological features. For example, the onset of the Flood was triggered by the springs of the great deep bursting forth. In light of this, we would expect a violent beginning to the Flood (bursting forth).

We would also expect that most of the water coming from springs as "water bursting forth" would *help supply* the waters that are classified as the windows of heaven. The bursting forth would likely begin a series of rapid catastrophic events that lead to massive sedimentation as well as continental scale break up. This particular milestone will play a roll when looking at the pre-Flood boundary.

Another milestone in geology is day 150. This is when the ark strikes the mountains of Ararat. This shows that mountain building, at least involving plates that collide in the Middle East, had begun. For the mountains of Ararat to have been formed requires that the Eurasian Plate, Arabian Plate, and African Plate (perhaps with some influence of a few other continental plates) have come together. On day 150, the Bible also reveals that the waters sub-sided, then the rain stopped, the waters then begin to steadily recede, the springs of the great deep are stopped, the windows of heaven stopped, and therefore, should transition to smaller scale effects, as opposed to continental scale layers.

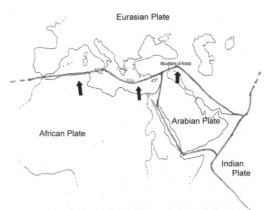

Another milestone is day 314. The water from the earth had receded in order for the surface of the earth to be dry

Plate movement resulted in the formation of the mountains of Ararat.
(Drawing: Bodie Hodge)

(see also Psalm 104:8–10[2]) in Noah's view. And finally by day 370, the earth was completely dry, likely including the muddy areas that would have still persisted under the surface on day 314. But if we take note, the recessional stage of the Flood took about 5½ months, and the Flood's inundatory stage was exactly 5 months. So the recession stage took nearly the same time as it took for the water to prevail on the earth. Then there was another couple of months to complete the drying process.

After day 370, it seems the hydrological cycle was then more uniform with regularity (Genesis 8:22,[3] Genesis 9:12–14[4]) with the coming of clouds (Noah saw the rainbow which require droplets of moisture) and set times for seedtime and harvest (which require rain). Of course, other milestones throughout the Flood account can be found but this should suffice for a brief overview.

Geological Layers

The geological layers are generally stacked in a vertical column in books and articles that looks similar to the chart.

Even though most of these layers are exposed at various places around the earth, they are often stacked, because these layers have a general trend to be found on top of another layer when they are found together, though this is not always the case. For example, when one finds Cambrian layers, they are normally above Pre-Cambrian layers; Ordovician layers are generally above Cambrian layers; and so on. Though there are some exceptions, this is the *general* trend.

The names of the geological layers[5] were usually given based on a name of the area or something similar where they were found. For example, the Devonian layer was named for Devonshire (Devon), England. Cambrian

---

2. The mountains rose; the valleys sank down To the place which You established for them. You set a boundary that they may not pass over, So that they will not return to cover the earth. He sends forth springs in the valleys; They flow between the mountains. (NASB).
3. While the earth remains, seedtime and harvest, cold and heat, winter and summer, and day and night shall not cease.
4. And God said: "This is the sign of the covenant which I make between Me and you, and every living creature that is with you, for perpetual generations: I set My rainbow in the cloud, and it shall be for the sign of the covenant between Me and the earth. It shall be, when I bring a cloud over the earth, that the rainbow shall be seen in the cloud.
5. The classification of geological layers was often done by determining what fossils it contains. Logically, this can be very confusing and lead to some vicious circular arguments, but for the sake of what has been classified, we will continue to use the names for those layers.

was named for Cambria, the Latin name for Wales. Ordovician and Silurian were named for Ordices and Silures, early peoples in Britain and Wales, respectively. Permian was named for the Perm district in Russian and so on.[6]

So the names of the actual layers have very little to do with long ages; however, other names have been given to groups of these layers that have long-age implications. These are:

Recent
Pleistocene
Pliocene
Miocene
Oligocene
Eocene
Paleocene
Cretaceous
Jurassic
Triassic
Permian
Pennsylvanian
Mississippian
Devonian
Silurian
Ordovician
Cambrian
Precambrian

Eons
1. Era
2. Period
3. Epoch

Some of the names under these subcategories have been changing and continue to change, such as "Tertiary" or "Quaternary," which are viewed as out-of-date technical names, though they are still commonly used. The layers themselves would be better understood as depths, but more precisely as rock layers that contain particular sediment type and/or particular fossils, not necessarily representations of millions of years.

For the most part, both creationists and evolutionists generally agree that layers below another layer are older and the layers above are younger. However, we disagree by orders of magnitude. Typically for creationists, the deeper the Flood layers the earlier it was laid down during the Flood year, not millions of years of separation.

THE PRE-FLOOD BOUNDARY

With very few exceptions, creationists agree that the Flood in Genesis 6–8 explains the vast majority of rock layers that contain fossils on earth. Naturally, smaller rock layer units have formed since the time of the Flood, such as volcanoes and other local catastrophes (e.g., the Mount St. Helens sediment). Even so, most creationists have a general agreement about the placement of the pre-Flood boundary. This boundary is between the Pre-Cambrian and Cambrian layers. Of course, there are again exceptions,

---

6. "Table of Geological Periods," Information Please® Database, Pearson Education, Inc., 2007, http://www.infoplease.com/ipa/A0001822.html, accessed 12/18/2008.

depending on some specific places being studied.

When looking at the Tapeats Sandstone (the lowest sedimentary layer from the Flood in the Grand Canyon), it sits immediately above the Great Unconformity, which is the boundary where the Flood layers begin. Below the Tapeats are inverse rock layers that contain virtually no fossils. It makes sense that these lower non-fossiliferous layers were inverted at the onset of the Flood and then flood layers began to accumulate above it.

In fact, the vast rock layers of the Flood that encompass large areas, even entire continents, began to form at this time. This is what would be expected from a global scale Flood.

The Great Unconformity in the Grand Canyon reveals the beginning of the Flood layers with a Cambrian layer (Tapeats Sandstone) sitting immediately above Precambrian rock (Vishnu Schist) — quarter for scale

POST-FLOOD BOUNDARY CONTROVERSY

If only the post-Flood boundary could have been determined so easily! With the Flood's steady decline from day 150 until day 314, and then further drying out until day 370, it can be a disaster trying to figure out what aspects of geology occurred during and after the Flood, particularly the end stages of the event. But even then we need a definitive point in the Flood account in Genesis to determine what the end of the Flood is. Most would recognize that when the Lord called Noah off the ark (day 370), then that is the official end of the Flood.

Based on mapping and boreholes of the geological layers, some appear to stretch across continents, or at least a vast majority of a continent. Most creationists recognize these as Flood layers. These dominate layers from the Cambrian to the end of the Cretaceous where it strikes the Tertiary sediment (Paleocene, Eocene, Oligocene, Miocene, and Pliocene). This is also known as the K/T boundary because the German for Cretaceous is Kreide, hence Kreide-Tertiary or K/T. After that, we begin to see smaller regional scale deposits (though still quite voluminous). From here, the situation gets difficult.

For example, during the slow recessional stage there would be sedimentary runoff that settled in some areas, breached dams that could burst, settling in stagnant areas, volcanoes that would go off during mountain building, mountain building that *caused* further sedimentation, and so on. Regional effects would surely begin during the recessional stage.

But also, *after* the recessional stage of the Flood, there could be sedimentary runoff that settled in some areas due to breached dams that burst, volcanoes that went off, and so on. A lot was happening from the moment the ark struck the mountains of Ararat and when Noah was called off the ark. This dangerous time is likely the reason that Noah wasn't called off the ark sooner!

Further regional affects could surely take place after the Flood as well (in fact, we see regional residual affects today). In the post-Flood era, there could be settling sediments, plate movement, drying effects, warm oceans causing rough weather, volcanic activity that is still proceeding, breached dams of water being released. But for the most part, the world was safe enough for Noah and his family to disembark and the Lord to give the declaration for them to be fruitful and fill the earth.

But here is the question . . . how can we be certain if one of these breached dams, volcanoes, or other regional effects happened prior to day 370 or soon after? This is where the debate heats up and why creationists tend to disagree with each other so much!

Technical articles (too many to cite) propose different positions of the post-Flood boundary in various places around the world and based on various aspects. Depending on which deposit, some say the boundary is as far down as the end of the Cretaceous (some even place it a little farther down *in* the Cretaceous layers, below the K/T boundary).[7] Others place it as high as the middle of the Pleistocene in some areas. Still others have it in other places (mostly in between). The various placements of the post-Flood

7. There are some holding to a Anglo-European model who try to place the post-Flood boundary at Pre-Cambrian and Cambrian boundary and claim all the sedimentation above that point has accumulated since then. However, most creationists rightly reject this, but that is not for discussion in this chapter.

boundary are *scientific* models, which are built on theological models, which are built on biblical models, which are taken from the text of Scripture.

So what does this really mean with regard to biblical authority? It means scientific models are not absolute and debate is *encouraged* on the subject in an *iron sharpening iron* (Proverbs 27:17) fashion. For creationists, scientific models are about debate and questioning, and in the future can change or be discarded. If one or both of the most popular placements of the Flood boundary are one day discarded, it in no way affects the truth of Scripture, which is absolute. This short article on the subject is not meant to be a treatise to battle for one or the other, but to educate on the views and the implications of the views.

Where Is the Post-Flood Boundary?

In the *flood* of creationist literature thereof, we find that for a hundred years most look in their backyard to try to determine the post-Flood boundary. Let me put it like this: Australian geologists tend to look at Australian geology, Americans tend to look at American geology, and Europeans tend to look at European geology. Naturally, there are exceptions to this.

But researchers tend to look at the size of the rock layers and the extent, and try to determine if they are large enough layers to identify as being from the Flood, or if they are more regional then they may be post-Flood. They look at the fossils in the layers and try to determine if they would be from the Flood or post-Flood (i.e., if kangaroos are found in the tertiary rock layers in Australia, then it seems likely these are post-Flood rock layers, as kangaroos migrated to Australia after the Flood to where they live today).[8]

In short, researchers look at the geology on various continents, and based on man-made criteria, they arbitrarily try to determine if it is from the Flood. For example, one such paper was published that did this very thing, but using suites of criteria.[9] But is this the best method?

---

8. Others, however, object and point out that there is a 16.7% change of any animal kind repopulating and thriving in the same continental area where they lived pre-Flood. This comes from the odds of them returning to that particular continent out of six continents after the Flood. So this is expected for some creatures anyway.

9. John Whitmore and Paul Garner, "Using Suites of Criteria to Recognize Pre-Flood, Flood and Post-Flood Strata in the Rock Record with Application to Wyoming (USA)," Andrew Snelling, editor, *Proceedings of the Sixth International Conference on Creationism* (Pittsburg, PA: Creation Science Fellowship, Inc. and Dallas TX: Institute for Creation Research, 2008), p. 425–448.

Let's start with the Bible. We know that the mountains of Ararat were formed in the Flood, by the 150th day. The water receded and never returned to overtake them. So of what are the mountains of Ararat made? This should give us a clue as to what was made *well before* the end of the Flood; in fact, we would know what was formed by 150th day of the Flood (less than half-way through the Flood).

Two different geologists (who simply do not have a hand in this debate since they are secular), who were searching for oil deposits, have mapped the regions that include the mountains of Ararat and beyond extensively.[10] What we find are layers intrinsic to the formation of the mountains of Ararat (Armenia and Anatolia regions) that include:

1. Permian
2. Lower-Middle Triassic
3. Middle Triassic-Middle Cretaceous
4. Paleocene-Lower Eocene
5. Lower Eocene
6. Middle Eocene
7. Middle-Upper Miocene

For much of this, the Eocene and Miocene rock layers are *inverted* and pushing up the Cretaceous and Triassic rock layers. In other words, without the Eocene and Miocene rock layers, the mountains of Ararat cannot exist!

What can we glean from this? It means that Miocene and Eocene rock layers existed by day 150 in the mountains of Ararat. These layers are tertiary sediments much higher than the K/T boundary. What we can know is that these Eocene and Miocene rock layers were formed prior to the post-Flood period. Does this mean that other Miocene and Eocene and other tertiary sediments (outside the mountains of Ararat) are also Flood deposits? It is possible. But I will leave the researchers to debate this further.

---

10. Y. Yilmaz, "Alochthonous Terranes in the Tethyan Middle East: Anatolia and the Surrounding Regions," *Philosophical Transactions of the Royal Society*, London, A 331, 611–624 (1990); G.C. Schmidt, "A Review of Permian and Mesozoic Formations Exposed Near the Turkey/Iraq Border at Harbol," Mobil Exploration Mediterranean, Inc. Ankara, MTA *Bulletin of the Mineral Research and Exploration Institute*, no. 62, 1964, p. 103–119.

conclusion

So where should new creationists sit on this issue?

	Recent	Regional Layers
	Pleistocene (Ice Age)	
End of the Flood?	Pliocene	
↕	Miocene (Mts. of Ararat)	
	Oligocene	
	Eocene (Mts. of Ararat)	
	Paleocene	
End of the Flood?	Cretaceous (Mts. of Ararat)	Worldwide Layers
	Jurassic	
	Triassic (Mts. of Ararat)	
	Permian (Mts. of Ararat)	
	Pennsylvanian	
	Mississippian	
	Devonian	
	Silurian	
	Ordovician	
Beginning of the Flood	Cambrian	
	Precambrian	Pre-Flood Layers

We should keep in mind that scientific models that deal with the placement of the post-Flood boundary are good but not perfect, as the Scriptures are. Also, we need to keep in mind that there is a friendly debate in this area and there are implications. Answers in Genesis has tended to hold to a higher placement of the post-Flood boundary from the K/T boundary (end of the Cretaceous) or above but also recognizes there is a debate going on.

As for the details, we want to encourage both sides to have a kind debate as they hash out various regional formations to determine if they are Flood (day 150–day 370) or post-Flood deposits, but we think the biblical clue gives us a brilliant foundation by which future research is to be developed.

Noah's Ark

28 | WHAT ABOUT THE SIZE OF NOAH'S ARK?

BODIE HODGE

> If you are wise, you are wise for yourself, and if you scoff, you
> will bear it alone (Proverbs 9:12).

People often scoff at Noah's ark, saying it was not big enough to hold the animals. Others scoff at the ark because they say it was too big and thus couldn't be seaworthy! Did you realize that scoffers scoff for the sake of scoffing sometimes? Let's look at the size of Noah's ark, and leave the scoffers to bear it alone.

ARK SIZE

God tells us the dimensions of Noah's ark:

> And this is how you shall make it: The length of the ark shall
> be three hundred cubits, its width fifty cubits, and its height thirty
> cubits (Genesis 6:15).

Unlike the measure of cubits, we either use a metric (e.g., *decimal* based like centimeters, meters, kilometers, liters) or English/Imperial/US Customary system of units (e.g., often *fraction* based like inches, feet, miles, gallons). So while the Bible tells us that the length of Noah's ark was 300 cubits, its width 50 cubits, and its height 30 cubits, we must first ask, "How long is a cubit?"

The answer, however, is not so precise, because ancient people groups assigned different lengths to the term "cubit" (Hebrew word אמה [*ammah*]), the primary unit of measure in the Old Testament. This unit of measure was also used for the ark of the covenant (Exodus 25:10[1]), the Altar (Exodus 38:1[2]), Goliath (1 Samuel 17:4[3]), and Solomon's Temple (1 Kings 6:2[4])?

The length of a cubit was based on the distance from the elbow to the fingertips, so it varied between different ancient groups of people. Here are some samples from Egypt, Babylon, and ancient Israel:

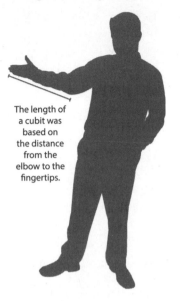

The length of a cubit was based on the distance from the elbow to the fingertips.

Culture	Inches (Centimeters)
Hebrew (short)	17.5 (44.5)
Egyptian	17.6 (44.7)
Common (short)	18 (45.7)
Babylonian (long)	19.8 (50.3)
Hebrew or royal (long)	20.4 (51.8)
Egyptian (long)	20.6 (52.3)

When Noah came off the ark, naturally it was his cubit measurement that existed — the one he had used to construct the ark. Unfortunately, the exact length of this cubit is unknown. After the nations were divided years later at the Tower of Babel, different cultures (people groups) adopted different sized cubits. So it requires some logical guesswork (based on historical research) to reconstruct the most likely length of the original cubit.

Since the Babel dispersion was so soon after the Flood, it is reasonable to assume that builders of that time were still using the cubit that Noah used. Moreover, we would expect that the people who settled near Babel would have retained or remained close to the original cubit. Yet cubits from that region (the ancient Near East) are generally either a common (short) or a long cubit. Which one is most likely to have come from Noah?

---

1. And they shall make an ark of acacia wood; two and a half cubits shall be its length, a cubit and a half its width, and a cubit and a half its height.
2. He made the altar of burnt offering of acacia wood; five cubits was its length and five cubits its width — it was square — and its height was three cubits.
3. And a champion went out from the camp of the Philistines, named Goliath, from Gath, whose height was six cubits and a span.
4. Now the house which King Solomon built for the LORD, its length was sixty cubits, its width twenty, and its height thirty cubits.

In large-scale construction projects, ancient civilizations typically used the long cubit (about 19.8–20.6 inches [52 cm]). The Bible offers some input in 2 Chronicles 3:3,[5] which reveals that Solomon used an older (long) cubit in construction of the Temple.

Most archaeological finds in Israel are not as ancient as Solomon. More modern finds consistently reveal the use of a short cubit, such as confirmed by archaeologists while measuring Hezekiah's tunnel. However, in Ezekiel's vision, an angel used "a cubit plus a handbreadth," an unmistakable definition for the long cubit (Ezekiel 43:13[6]). The long cubit appears to be God's preferred standard of measurement. Perhaps this matter did not escape Solomon's notice either.

The original cubit length is uncertain. It was most likely one of the long cubits (about 19.8–20.6 inches). If so, the ark was actually bigger than the size described in most books today (prior to the opening of the Ark Encounter), which usually use the short cubit of 18 inches.

Using the short cubit (18 inches), Noah's ark would have been about:

- 450 feet (137 meters) by 75 feet (22.9 meters) by 45 feet (13.7 meters)

Short cubit ark put to a box shape

Whereas using the long cubit of about 20.4 inches, Noah's ark would have been about:

---

5. This is the foundation which Solomon laid for building the house of God: The length was sixty cubits (by cubits according to the former measure) and the width twenty cubits.
6. These are the measurements of the altar in cubits (the cubit is one cubit and a handbreadth): the base one cubit high and one cubit wide, with a rim all around its edge of one span. This is the height of the altar.

- 510 feet (155 meters) long by 85 feet (25.9 meters) by 51 feet (15.5 meters)

51 feet

85 feet

510 Feet

Long cubit ark put to ship shape

Again, the long (older) cubit is to be preferred, so Noah's vessel was likely about this length, give or take a little. Also take note that these dimensions for length and width are to be measured from the water level, which is called the "draft level."[7]

COULD a WOODEN SHIP THIS BIG BE POSSIBLE?

Many scoffers have attacked the fact that a wooden ship with the dimensions of Noah's ark (which was 300 cubits long; that is about 450 feet or 510 feet, depending on the short or long cubit) could survive the Flood.[8]

For example, Bill Nye, a skeptic, compared the ark to a wooden ship called the *Wyoming*, which was one of the biggest wooden sailing ships built with 1800s technology.

The *Wyoming* was a sailing ship, not a floater like Noah's ark. Interestingly, it was about the same length of Noah's ark if you use the short cubit (18-inch cubit as opposed to the 20.4-inch cubit). It was 450 feet long if you count the jib-boom. Bill Nye pointed out that the *Wyoming* was not a

---

7. Draft is simply where the water level is on the outside of a ship, based on how heavy it is.
8. T. Chaffey, "Bill Nye the Straw Man Guy and Noah's Ark," Answers in Genesis, http://www.answersingenesis.org/articles/2014/02/28/bill-nye-straw-man-guy-noahs-ark.

great seaworthy vessel and it twisted and sank, killing all 14 on board. Ergo, Noah's ark was basically "an impossibility."

We beg to differ. The *Wyoming* was a great example to show that the ark was indeed possible. Besides, using one example of a wooden ship (when there is much historic information about massive wooden ships built in the past) to claim Noah's ark couldn't have been built to survive the Flood is a very poor argument indeed.

The *Wyoming* was used and sailed for *14 years* before she sank. Noah's ark only needed a maximum of about 110 days of floating time.[9] Second, the *Wyoming* used 1800s technology, and by then mankind had lost a great deal of technology about boat building. Ark researcher and mechanical engineer Tim Lovett writes:

> Ancient shipbuilders usually began with a shell of planks (strakes) and then built internal framing (ribs) to fit inside. This is the complete reverse of the familiar European method where planking was added to the frame. In shell-first construction, the planks must be attached to each other somehow. Some used overlapping (clinker) planks that were dowelled or nailed, while others used rope to sew the planks together. The ancient Greeks used a sophisticated system where the planks were interlocked with thousands of precise mortise and tenon joints. The resulting hull was strong enough to ram another ship, yet light enough to be hauled onto a beach by the crew.[10]

It makes sense that this ancient technology was passed down through the Flood to the coastline/maritime peoples (Genesis 10:5[11]) and had been lost by the Age of Exploration. Lovett writes:

> At first, historians dismissed ancient Greek claims that the *Tessarakonteres* was 425 feet (130 m) long. But as more information was learned, the reputation of these early shipbuilders grew markedly. One of the greatest challenges to the construction of large

---

9. B. Hodge, "Biblical Overview of the Flood Timeline," Answers in Genesis, http://www. answersingenesis.org/articles/2010/08/23/overview-flood-timeline; Also, see chapter 26 in this book.

10. T. Lovett with B. Hodge, "What Did Noah's Ark Look Like?" in K. Ham, gen. ed., *The New Answers Book 3* (Green Forest, AR: Master Books, 2010), p. 17–28.

11. From these the coastland peoples of the Gentiles were separated into their lands, everyone according to his language, according to his families, into their nations.

wooden ships is finding a way to lay planks around the outside in a way that will ensure little or no leaking, which is caused when there is too much movement between the planks. Apparently, the Greeks had access to an extraordinary method of planking that was lost for centuries, and only recently brought to light by marine archaeology.[12]

Larry Pierce (translator of James Ussher's *Annals of the World*) discusses several ancient wooden ships of antiquity that have been recorded in ancient history.[13] One of these ships was the *Leontifera*, and based on its description of rowers, the ship was about 400–500 feet long (120–150 meters). Those mentioned by Pierce were:

- *Leontifera* (warship): ~400–500 feet (~120–150 meters)
- Ships of Demetrius: ~400 feet (~120 meters)
- Ptolemy Philopator's warship: 420 feet (130)

Unlike Noah's ark, which was a floater, these ships required extra space just to man oars, sails, and the like. These sizes show that ancients possessed the brilliant capability to build large wooden ships that were known to ram other ships in war and stay afloat. That technology had all been lost throughout the ages.

WaS NOaH UnSKILLeD aT SHIP BUILDInG?

There is the claim that Noah and his family were unskilled at shipbuilding and so the feat of building the ark of such a size would be impossible. The Bible reveals that Noah had 500 years under his belt before he was given the instruction to build the ark. Unlike shipbuilders in the ancient world (post-Flood) or even up through the Age of Exploration (~A.D. 1900), few would have a resume such as Noah had!

Noah also had 50–75 years (estimate) to research and build the ark.[14] I trust that few people in the past 3,000 years would ask someone to build them a ship and give them upward of 75 years to do it! The point is, if Noah

---

12. Tim Lovett, "Thinking Outside the Box," Answers in Genesis, https://answersingenesis. org/noahs-ark/thinking-outside-the-box/.
13. Larry Pierce, "The Large Ships of Antiquity," Answers in Genesis, https://answersingenesis. org/noahs-ark/the-large-ships-of-antiquity/.
14. B. Hodge, "How Long Did It Take for Noah to Build the Ark?" http://www.answersingenesis. org/articles/2010/06/01/long-to-build-the-ark; also see chapter 25 in this book.

wasn't an expert already, then he could easily have had the time to become one. It is the same with his family.

Second, how does anyone know that God didn't give Noah specific instruction on how to build it? The Bible simply doesn't say, but this is a possibility. The Bible tells us that God gave him the dimensions and what wood to use (as well as a few other specifics). It would be outrageous to believe that an all-knowing God wouldn't know how to design an ark to survive a Flood.

Next, it is possible that Noah had help. He could easily have contracted with people that may have been experts on certain things. Furthermore, other family and friends could have been helping until they died, such as Methuselah, Lamech, or others (Genesis 5:30,[15] 6:11[16]). There could have been righteous people helping until they were killed or died.

What we know was that Noah (with his family) was all that was left to be saved by God at the time of the Flood. But Noah knew this. He was comforted in knowing that his family would not be killed and would be aboard the ark as the Lord revealed this to him well in advance (Genesis 6:18[17]).

---

15. After he begot Noah, Lamech lived five hundred and ninety-five years, and had sons and daughters.
16. The earth also was corrupt before God, and the earth was filled with violence.
17. But I will establish My covenant with you; and you shall go into the ark — you, your sons, your wife, and your sons' wives with you.

29 | WHAT WAS THE SHAPE OF NOAH'S ARK?

BODIE HODGE

INTRODUCTION

Many readers have surely seen a multitude of images of Noah's ark. In the last chapter, we just saw two. Sadly, many are quite fanciful, unrealistic, and even laughable, in their proportions. We often call these "bathtub arks" because they look like an overloaded bathtub with today's animals (and usually with giraffes sticking out through the chimney).

Figure 1: False arks *do* play a role.

We suggest these types of "mythical arks" are actually quite dangerous. Many kids are raised with them. Although they look cute, it sends a subtle and false message that Noah's ark was not a real ship and certainly couldn't fit all the animals needed on board.

Even atheists proclaimed that the idea of the ark being a mythological account was the first step in their move to the religion of atheism: "I remember the moment in 1995 that I realized that the story of Noah's ark was just an ancient hand-me-down ridiculous mythological tale." Interestingly, the comment was accompanied by an unrealistic Noah's ark image (see figure 1).[1]

---

1. Linda LaScola, "Leaving Religion: Like Crumbling Jenga Blocks," http://www.patheos. com/blogs/rationaldoubt/2015/09/leaving-religion-in-stages-like-crumbling-jenga-blocks/.

Ancient Arks

At Answer in Genesis, we received a letter from Harlan and Stacy Hutchins with a printed image of an engraving done in London in 1760 by a man named P. Simms. Mr. Hutchins came across this engraving while working as an antique map and print dealer.

At first glance, you would recognize the antiquity of such an image. But it is what was *on* the image that got me excited! It was a treasure indeed — an engraving of Noah's ark.

What Makes This Ark Unique?

This ark was not like the common inaccurate bathtub arks that "float" around in today's culture. Instead, Simms took the time to think about Noah's ark, its dimensions, and its construction. A copy of the image can be seen on the following page, along with detailed portions.

The first thing you will notice is that Simms' ark is much closer to the biblical proportions that were given: 300 by 50 by 30 cubits (Genesis 6:15). Mr. Simms simply squares them off.

I'm surprised many illustrators and researchers today have failed to attain this basic information, considering it is given in the Scriptures. Instead, they proceed to depict bathtub or otherwise inaccurate arks.[2]

Another feature you will notice is that Simms' ark clearly has three decks, as revealed in Genesis 6:16. Simms also placed rooms in the ark (Genesis 6:14) and placed some animals inside for scale. As a teaching point, he also made some of the walls "see through" so observers can get an idea of the scale. Such things are mysteriously absent from many of the bathtub arks and other inaccurate depictions of the ark today.

I can tell Simms also thought about the "window." The window is difficult for us to understand, being that it is translated as "window," but the Hebrew word is typically translated as "noon" or "midday" elsewhere in Scripture. The "window" was something meant to allow ventilation and lighting in the ark. Though Simms placed several windows in the ark "a cubit from above" (Genesis 6:16) to serve this purpose, they are not at the noon or midday position. Today, we prefer a centrally located "midday" window finished a cubit from *above* the roof — a closer match to the biblical

---

2. Of course, there is debate over which cubit to use, be it the shorter or the longer cubit, but for more information on that subject see, "How Long Was the Original Cubit?" http://www.answersingenesis.org/articles/am/v2/n2/original-cubit.

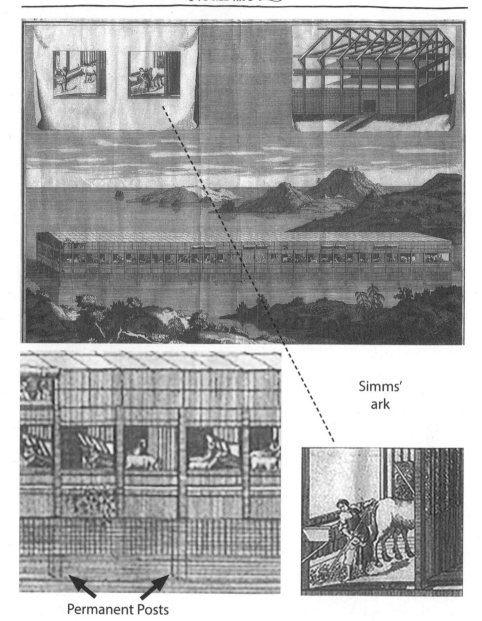

Simms'
ark

Permanent Posts

description and a more water-resistant design resembling a deck hatch. But in 1760, Simms was clearly trying to let Scripture guide his design, unlike modern bathtub mythological arks!

He also thought about the roof construction. In the upper right, he postulated how the ark may have been constructed with an angled roof and overhang to prevent water leakage from water sitting on the roof. He even considered the footings of how the ark could have been elevated on certain pillars to allow water underneath until the time of liftoff.

However, Simms' considerations for the water were hardly necessary. Water would have had no trouble getting underneath the ark. The pillars (which happened to be about as high as a human) would have allowed humans access underneath the ark. At the world famous *Ark Encounter* something similar has been done. This is much more important for a wooden vessel where planks need to be accessible, unlike the modern system of construction where modules are welded together in a single weld line across the ship. Many ships today are actually built above ground *and then* placed in the water. Noah probably did not have that luxury, and so Simms considered the pillars a viable option.

The ark may have been too large for picking up and placing into the water like a small boat (not to mention that Noah was shut in the ark by the Lord), so the only options comparable to modern shipbuilding are either launching on a slipway or flooding in a dry-dock. In Noah's case, rising floodwater is very similar to flooding a dry-dock, except not nearly as controllable.

One interesting detail in Simms' ark is the permanent posts. They are integral in the structure, so it looks like Mr. Simms was expecting the pillars to act the same way when the ark was beached at the end of the voyage.

It would be difficult to ensure that so many extended posts remained waterproof, as they would be very vulnerable to any bumps and scrapes. A glancing blow against something hard, and they would loosen up somewhat and let the water in. But at least he was thinking about it and coming up with ideas.

He even considers feeding, watering (even a bucket and pulley system), loading (with the ramp), perhaps human living quarters (middle thatched area on the image), and cleaning options too. Though obviously not perfect, he thought about it in his image.

Mr. Simms' ark is unique, because many ark pictures from Simms' time equated the ark with the ocean vessels *of his day* (think of the sailing ships carrying people to the Americas during the age of exploration).

Other Thoughtful Ark Depictions

Simms was not alone, nor the first to think through the ark's features. Back in 1554, Johannes Buteo published the first serious study of Noah's ark, investigating its construction, capacity, and the number of animals and food and provisions required.[3] His illustration was still rather basic. But even so, his ark was standing against some incredibly false shapes of Noah's ark permeating in his day. His ark was the basic rectangular box-shaped ark we often see.

More than a century later, Athanasius Kircher published his *Arca Noë* in 1675, with lavish illustrations depicting a rectangular ark of biblical proportions.

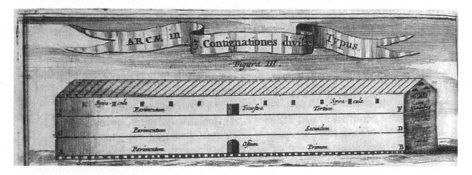

Kircher ark depiction

In 1707, a German Bible had an image of Noah's ark that also had been carefully considered. Famed Baptist commentator Dr. John Gill included it in his commentary on Genesis in 1748–63[4] (see following page).

Of course, there have been structural studies, animal studies, and so on for Noah's ark since the 1960s, mostly inspired by the recent return to biblical authority that was triggered by the book *The Genesis Flood* in the early 1960s by Drs. Henry Morris and John Whitcomb.

Since Simms and these others, more research has been done on ancient ships and technology of wooden vessels. Structural studies and designs have been discussed in detail in modern times. Some details about Noah's ark are believed to be different from these earlier images.

Was Noah's Ark Box-Shaped?

The dimensions for Noah's ark are given in length, width, and height. Does that mean it was shaped like a box? The dimensions given in Genesis 6:15

---

3. Tim Griffith and Natali Monnette, translators, "Johannes Buteo's On the Shape and Capacity of Noah's Ark," *Issues in Creation*, no. 2, February 28, 2008.

4. John Gill, *An Exposition of the First Book of Moses, Called Genesis* (Springfield, MO: Particular Baptist Press, 2010) (originally Aaron Ward Publishing, London, England, 1763–1766), p. 121.

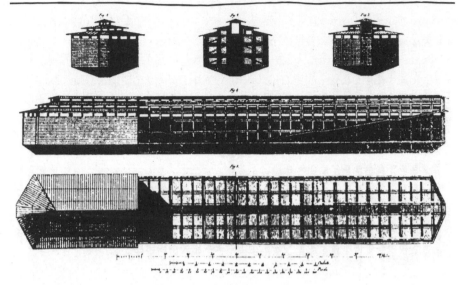

The John Gill ark depiction

are 300 x 50 x 30 cubits, which translate on the *long* or *royal* cubit as roughly 510 x 85 x 51 feet (see the previous chapter for a discussion on cubits). Some argue for a box shape while others argue for something that looked more like a ship. The basis for this comes from the scant information given in Genesis:

> Make yourself an ark of gopherwood; make rooms in the ark, and cover it inside and outside with pitch. And this is how you shall make it: The length of the ark shall be three hundred cubits, its width fifty cubits, and its height thirty cubits. You shall make a window for the ark, and you shall finish it to a cubit from above; and set the door of the ark in its side. You shall make it with lower, second, and third decks (Genesis 6:14–16).

This ratio of dimensions is extremely well placed. According to researchers, this ratio sits nearly central between strength, comfort, and stability.[5] Even some ocean-going vessels were designed based on this ratio because it is ideal.

But keep in mind that the Bible *doesn't* say the ark was a box shape. A box-shape *is assumed* by taking the length, width, and height of the ark and merely making it into a box. However, this was likely not the case, as ship dimensions are typically given as length, width, and height. This is common

---

5. Gon et al, "Safety Investigation of Noah's Ark in a Seaway," *Technical Journal*, vol. 8, no. 1, April 1994, p. 26–36, https://answersingenesis.org/noahs-ark/safety-investigation-of-noahs-ark-in-a-seaway/.

for other things as well. For example, a Corvette ZR1's dimensions were once given as the following:

Overall length (in / mm): 176.2 / 4476
Overall width (in / mm): 75.9 / 1928
Overall height (in / mm): 49 / 1244

Are we to assume the Corvette is a box shape given only its length, width, and height? Not at all. Noah's ark was a ship; therefore, it likely had features that ships would commonly have. These are not at all unreasonable assumptions.

Noah was 500–600 years old and knew better than to make a simple box that would have had significant issues in a global Flood (e.g., forces on the sharp corners would be too destructive, it could capsize if it was not facing into the wind and waves, and so on). The common way that a floating boat would keep from being turned perpendicular with the wind and waves is by having features on the front and back that naturally utilize the wind and waves to point it into the wind and waves. This would eliminate the need for sharp corners as well.

The word for ark in Hebrew is *tebah*, which is also the word for the bulrush basket in which Moses was laid as a child and then placed in the Nile (Exodus 2:3[6]).[7] Furthermore, *tebah* is not the same word used for the ark of the testimony or ark of the covenant — that Hebrew word is *'arown*.

The word *tebah* in some modern lexicons yields the definition of *box*, but is more properly *chest* and related to the Egyptian word for *coffin*. I'm sure that being in the ark for nearly a year must have felt like being in a coffin! Recognized Hebrew lexicons such as *Brown, Driver, and Briggs* yield the meaning of *tebah* regarding Noah's ark and the basket of Moses as a *vessel*, not a box.[8]

Why has the box shape persisted for so long? Well, it is *easy* — and little thought was required to do a box/rectangle. Besides, for the better part of the past, the question was about fitting animals on board the ark, so the structure wasn't seen as that big of a deal.

---

6. But when she could no longer hide him, she took an ark of bulrushes for him, daubed it with asphalt and pitch, put the child in it, and laid it in the reeds by the river's bank.

7. "Moses baskets" have become a novelty in certain places today and they are not a box shape either, but rather rounded. Their dimensions are commonly 30 in. x 12 in. x 9 in. Of course, since the Bible does not provide the dimensions of the ark in which Moses was placed we cannot state with any certainty what the size may have been.

8. *The Brown Driver and Briggs Hebrew and English Lexicon*, 9th printing (Peabody MA: Hendrickson Publishers, 2005), p. 1061.

Bodie Hodge on a "bathtub ark" ride

The response was usually, "Let's make a box and then see if we can fit the required animals on the ark." After years of research, that question has been answered sufficiently (see the next chapter for highlights). The skeptical questions are now shifting. Instead of asking how the animals fit on the ark (that question does still persist among those not learned on the subject), they ask how the box-shaped ark could survive the Flood. They point out that sharp corners would not be able to handle the stresses and would break, and the ark would flood and sink, for example.

So in recent times, this research has been focused on the shape and structure of Noah's ark. This has led to what is called the Lovett design. The basic design that was used for the *Ark Encounter* is from ship researcher Tim Lovett, a mechanical engineer.

The Lovett design

Is this the best design? Great question. But it is one of the most thought-through structural designs throughout the ages. And based on experimental data, it is stable in wind and waves and even rights itself in rough waters/windy air so that it doesn't capsize. The *Ark Encounter* design is a variation of the Lovett design.

The Ark Encounter (Photo: Ken Ham)

30 | DID THE ANIMALS FIT ON NOAH'S ARK?

BODIE HODGE

Of the birds after their kind, of animals after their kind, and of every creeping thing *of the earth* after its kind, two of every kind will come to you to keep them alive (Genesis 6:20, emphasis mine).

The first order of business is to point out that it was representative kinds of land-based creatures on the ark. No aquatic creatures like fish or trilobites needed to be on the ark. Much sea life died in the Flood — it was a violent Flood after all. But the kinds of *water*-based creatures could easily survive the *watery* Flood.

KINDS VS. SPECIES

To understand how many animals went on the ark, some preliminary information is needed. This brings us to the question of "What is a kind?"

Kinds are not necessarily species, genus, family, or order by our modern classification system. In a general sense, it is probably *closer* to the family level in most instances, but a few can still be at a species (like humans), genus, or even order level depending on what we are looking at.

Kinds are like the dog sort (including dingoes, wolves, coyotes, domestic dogs, etc.), cat sort (including lions, tigers, cougars, bobcats, domestic cats, etc.), horse sort (ponies, Clydesdales, donkeys, zebras, etc.), and so on. There is variation within these kinds especially since the Flood, but not evolution where one kind changes into a totally different kind over long periods of time — which is not observed anyway (e.g., amoebas turning into dogs).

Species is an arbitrary dividing line and becomes a paradox, hence the famous *"Species Problem"* when trying to define it. Some claim that if creatures can interbreed, then they are the same "species"; but clearly that is not always the case, since various species of dogs can and do interbreed — yet they are still considered different species.

The same is true of cats. For instance, we have a blinx (bobcat father with a linx mother hybrid), ligers (lion father-tiger mother mix), tigons (offspring of a male tiger and female lion), etc.

As stated, most kinds are closer to a family level, but in some cases they could be genus, species, or in the event of the elephant kind, is likely at the level of order, including the extinct families of elephants such as mammoths and mastodons, for example.

The point of all of this is that one cannot try to tally *species* on board Noah's ark or they will have a gross exaggeration. All the land-dwelling, air-breathing species we have today are the descendants of the representative kinds that were aboard the ark. Ocean-based creatures are not required on the ark (e.g., trilobites). But let's look at the other information in Scripture that further limits what went onboard Noah's ark.

FLESH, INSECTS, LAND-DWELLING, AND AIR-BREATHING . . . WHAT?

> And all flesh died that moved on the earth: birds and cattle and beasts and every creeping thing that creeps on the earth, and every man. All in whose nostrils was the breath of the spirit of life, all that was on the dry land, died. So He destroyed all living things which were on the face of the ground: both man and cattle, creeping thing and bird of the air. They were destroyed from the earth. Only Noah and those who were with him in the ark remained alive (Genesis 7:21–23).

What we learn in this passage is that the animals aboard the ark were further limited by being *air-breathing through the nostrils* as well as being *land-dwelling*. Naturally, creatures that are air-breathing and yet lived in the ocean need not be required (e.g., whales and dolphins). They can survive outside the ark.

Insects use tubes in their exoskeleton to take in oxygen, not nostrils. Therefore, many researchers do not have insects onboard Noah's ark.[1] They

---

1. Even if insects were on the ark, due to their extremely small size, they could have easily fit. If a million individuals were taken, it would still be a small footprint in the ark.

could easily survive on driftwood; or at the very least their eggs could survive on rafted wood and debris.

We also learn that all *flesh* that moved on the earth had died (Genesis 7:21, see also Genesis 6:13–19). This Hebrew word for flesh is *basar*. Insects were never considered flesh or *basar* in the Bible, which is a further confirmation that their residence wasn't required on the ark during the Flood. Furthermore, the Hebrew terms used for *behemah* and *remes*[2] in Genesis 6:19–20[3] were never used of insects in the Bible.

So we are left with land-dwelling, air-breathing (through their nostrils) kinds that were considered flesh or *basar*. What are the numbers?

Minimum Figures

What are the minimum figures for animals on the ark? Researcher Arthur Jones, writing in the *Creation Research Society Quarterly* in 1973, simply put these qualifications at a family level and did the numbers.[4] He arrived at about 1,000 families (and equated this with kinds). This would be about 2,000 individuals taken on the ark.

This includes the number of clean animals that came in by sevens. Even so, this is likely a minimum figure as some kinds are at a genus and species level (in a few instances). Consider one simple reason. We have found more animals since 1970. Many are within current families, but some are not. So naturally the numbers will have gone up a little. Thus, Jones' numbers would be a minimum figure.

Maximum Figures

Researcher John Woodmorappe decided to go a different route in 1996. He wanted to calculate maximum figures for animals and also included food and even water on board Noah's ark.[5]

To do this, Woodmorappe decided to use the smaller-sized ark (based on the short cubit of 18 inches). This would be an ark about 450 feet long.

2. *The Theological Wordbook of the Old Testament* says of *remes*: "The root encompasses all smaller animals but seems to exclude the large grazing animals, whales, birds, and insects," William White (Chicago, IL: Moody Press, 1999), p. 850.

3. And of every living thing of all flesh you shall bring two of every sort into the ark, to keep them alive with you; they shall be male and female. Of the birds after their kind, of animals [*behemah*] after their kind, and of every creeping thing [*remes*] of the earth after its kind, two of every kind will come to you to keep them alive.

4. Arthur J. Jones, "How Many Animals in the Ark?" *Creation Research Society Quarterly*, vol. 10, no. 2, September 1973, p. 102–108.

5. John Woodmorappe, *Noah's Ark: A Feasibility Study* (Dallas, TX: ICR Publications, 2009).

Then, instead of a *family* level for the kind (although he recognized the kind was closer to the family level), he used a *genus* level for all the kinds! So instead of one dog kind, there would be more than ten dog kinds represented in his numbers since there are more than 10 levels of genus within the dogs!

For the sake of maximum figures, John Woodmorappe still did 14 *of each genus* of the clean animals, which again was still not that many!

What he found was under 8,000 kinds and about 16,000 (15,745) individuals maximum, based on this genus level and calculations. With a smaller ark and this maximum number of animals and their required floor space/cages/rooms, this came out to be about 46.8% of the ark used to hold the animals! Remember, this is maximum figure. But Woodmorappe didn't stop there.

Then, Woodmorappe calculated various types of foodstuffs on the ark for this maximum number of animals. He calculated various numbers, but it is doubtful that Noah took *loose hay* (which takes a lot of space) as a feeding stuff for all animals to eat! The reasonable numbers are:

	Foodstuff	Ark space required
1	Lightly compressed dried hay pellet	16.3 %
2	Doubly compressed hay pellet	12.5%
3	Pelleted horse food	7.0%
4	Dried fruits/vegetables	6.8%

Let's use the highest number here (16.3%). Even though Noah and his family could have harvested water for part of their duration on the ark, Woodmorappe decided to calculate fresh water and put it in storage on board the ark. He found that it would take about 9.4% of the ark.

Putting all this together with the smaller ark and maximum number of animals, maximum amount of food, and maximum amount of water, this would be about 72.5% of the ark. Of course, this number could reduce depending on the types of foodstuff. Keep in mind that Noah likely used the long (older) cubit and took far fewer animals.

During the voyage, some animals reproduced (surely rabbits, right?). When God called the animals off the ark, it was now by their *families*, not two by two (Genesis 8:19[6]).

---

6. Every animal, every creeping thing, every bird, and whatever creeps on the earth, according to their families, went out of the ark.

Ark encounter figures

The Ark Encounter is basically using the Lovett design, which utilizes the older long cubit (20.4 inches), and this makes a longer and bigger ark (510 feet long). So the ark has much more space. This needs to be kept in mind with Ark Encounter figures.

When it comes to the animals on board, the Ark Encounter uses "reasonable maximums" — in engineering this is basically equated with a *safety factor or over engineered!* The project is intentionally trying to err on the high end but not to the degree that Woodmorappe did with a genus level. The purpose is to avoid being accused of trying to have intentionally lower numbers to fit on the ark.

So the Ark Encounter is using 14 of the clean animals and 14 of *all* birds. They also *split* animals when determining kinds as opposed to *lumping*. In other words, the current secular "family" lists are all being equated with a separate kind, unless otherwise warranted. More on this in a moment.

A few discussion points need to be understood prior to giving the tentatively final Ark Encounter numbers.

2 or 4 and 7 or 14?

Let's discuss 7 and 14 in more detail. Was it 2 of each unclean kind or 4 of each sort that went on the ark? Was it 7 of each clean animal and bird of the air kind or 14 of each that went on the ark?

> You shall take with you seven each of every clean animal, a
> male and his female; two each of animals that are unclean, a male
> and his female; also seven each of birds of the air, male and female,
> to keep the species alive on the face of all the earth (Genesis 7:2–3).

Furthermore, the animals went on by pairs, a male and its mate, and in some cases (i.e., the clean kinds) 7 went on board. The list of clean birds and animals in the Old Testament is found in Leviticus 11 and Deuteronomy 14.[7]

The Ark Encounter is erring on the side of caution in having 14 of each clean animal and *all* birds/winged creatures to maximize the number

---

7. Clean animals in the New Testament now differ in that Christ declared all foods clean by His power (e.g., Mark 7:19). This was demonstrated by both Peter (Acts 10:9–16) and Paul (e.g., 1 Corinthians 6:12–13; 1 Timothy 4:1–4; and Colossians 2:16), thus returning essentially to the diet given in Genesis 9:3 not by merely going backward to eat all foods clean *and unclean,* but by eating *only clean* foods, as all food is now made clean.

of animals on the ark, though they are only taking 2 of the unclean animals. However, this may not be the *actual* case.

The reason for the confusion is the way it is worded. Genesis 7:2–3, 7:9,[8] and 7:15[9] use wording that is uncommon in English. When the word is translated as *two* or as *seven*, the Hebrew behind it is [two two] or [seven seven in Genesis 7:2-3]. This type of construct is not normal to English, though, it is common in Hebrew.

Let me explain. The Hebrew is essentially "two two" and "seven seven," which is translated as "two" and "seven," denoting that they are paired when possible — remember Noah sacrificed of the clean animals after the Flood (Genesis 8:20[10]).[11] These are called supernumary animals — those meant for sacrifice, not requiring a female mate for the purpose of reproduction after the Flood.

Think of it as if we were to say *"pair of two."* "Pair of two" still indicates only 2 (not two plus two). We see this pairing in Exodus 36:30[12] (i.e., "two sockets under each of the boards" is "two two" implying that it was two total, but that it was paired with the socket above).

It is indicative of pairing. In other words, [two two] would be 2 in the form of a pair (i.e., a male and his female). Likewise, it would be 7 in the form of pairs when possible with a supernumary sacrificial animal. So it isn't doubled or multiplied. Why do I suggest this?

First, the immediate context called out 2 of each kind twice in Genesis 6:19-20[13] and Genesis 7:2 in reference to the same critters that are also denoted later as "two two." Thus, we know that two two is merely 2 in a paired form. Both "two" and "two two" were in reference to the same pair, male and female of unclean creatures.

---

8. Two by two they went into the ark to Noah, male and female, as God had commanded Noah.

9. And they went into the ark to Noah, two by two, of all flesh in which is the breath of life.

10. Then Noah built an altar to the LORD, and took of every clean animal and of every clean bird, and offered burnt offerings on the altar.

11. John Calvin writes: "Moreover, the expression, by sevens, is to be understood not of seven pairs of each kind, but of three pairs, to which one animal is added for the sake of sacrifice." John Calvin, *Commentaries on the First Book of Moses called Genesis*, translated by John King, reprint (Grand Rapids, MI: Baker Books, 2003), commentary notes on Genesis 7:2, p. 267.

12. So there were eight boards and their sockets — sixteen sockets of silver — two sockets under each of the boards.

13. Of the birds after their kind, of animals after their kind, and of every creeping thing of the earth after its kind, two of every kind will come to you to keep them alive.

As discussed elsewhere in Scripture, it uses the construct of [two two] as 2 (not doubled) as well. Exodus 36:29–30[14] also discusses pairs or couples of sockets under a board. So if you are looking for maximum figures, you can go with 14 and 4, but it makes more sense to remain with 2 and 7. Famed commentator H.C. Leupold concurs when he writes:

> The Hebrew expression "take seven seven" means "seven each" (Koenig's *Syntax* 85; 316b; Gesenius' *Grammatik* rev. by Kautzsch 134q). Hebrew parallels support this explanation. In any case, it would be a most clumsy method of trying to say "fourteen." Three pairs and one supernumery makes the "seven." As has been often suggested, the supernumary beast was the one Noah could conveniently offer for sacrifice after the termination of the Flood.[15]

It would have been very easy to say 14 (Hebrew *arba*) if that were meant. Seven animals has made sense to most commentators throughout the years. Why 7 clean? After the Flood, Noah sacrificed of each of the clean animals and perhaps this was to leave a breeding stock for Noah's three sons. This is a possibility.

7 of all Birds or 7 of the Clean Birds?

Another debate that presents itself at the Ark Encounter is the question of how many birds? The Bible says:

> You shall take with you seven each of every clean animal, a male and his female; two each of animals that are unclean, a male and his female; also seven each of birds of the air, male and female, to keep the species alive on the face of all the earth (Genesis 7:2–3).

Commentators recognize that when it says in Genesis 7:3, "seven each of birds of the air" that it is tied to the backdrop of *clean* creatures in Genesis 7:2. Contextually, this doesn't mean all birds came by 7 but instead that it is limited to 7 of the *clean* birds. Leupold writes:

---

14. And they were coupled at the bottom and coupled together at the top by one ring. Thus he made both of them for the two corners. So there were eight boards and their sockets — sixteen sockets of silver — two sockets under each of the boards.

15. H.C. Leupold, *Exposition of Genesis*, commentary notes on Genesis 7:2, as quoted by Drs. Henry Morris and John Whitcomb, *The Genesis Flood* (Phillipsburg, NJ: Presbyterian and Reformed Publishing Company, 1961), 44th printing, p. 65.

In v. 3 the idea of "the birds of the heavens" must, of course, be supplemented by the adjective "clean," according to the principle laid down in v. 2.[16]

Dr. John Gill agrees when discussing the birds. He says:

That is, of such as were clean; seven couple of these were to be brought into the ark, for the like use as of the clean beasts, and those under the law."[17]

Commentator Matthew Poole agrees:

Of clean fowls, which he leaves to be understood out of the foregoing verse.[18]

Even so, the Ark Encounter is inserting 14 of each bird regardless of whether it was clean or unclean. So this increases the number dramatically to help maximize the numbers on the ark.

Splitting and Lumping

Another factor that the Ark Encounter has used when researching kinds is *splitting* rather than *lumping*. What does that mean? When it comes to a group of animals that have many similarities, should they be lumped together as one kind or should they be left separated into separate kinds?

Although other factors may be involved, the key biblical factor to determine if two creatures are the same kind is if they can interbreed (though some may have lost the ability). But if they can have offspring together, then they are the same kind.

For example, a coyote, wolf, dingo, and a Great Dane can interbred. Thus, they are the same kind, so they can be lumped together. Camels and llamas can interbreed, so they can be lumped together. Finches and sparrows can interbreed, so they can be lumped together.

But some animals have never been brought into contact with each other to know if they can have offspring — this is clearly the case with creatures that have died out (e.g., dinosaur kinds!). Consider that there are several

16. Ibid.
17. John Gill, *An Exposition of the First Book of Moses, Called Genesis* (Springfield, Missouri: Particular Baptist Press, 2010 edition (original publication: London: Aaron Ward publisher, 1763–1766), p. 128.
18. Matthew Poole, "Commentary on Genesis 7:3," *Matthew Poole's English Annotations on the Holy Bible*, 1685, //www.studylight.org/commentaries/mpc/genesis-7.html.

sauropod dinosaur families because some have longer tails/necks or are buried in Flood sediment that is higher up in the rock record.[19] Realistically, they could be one kind, but we cannot get hybridization data for them since they are no longer around, so we are stuck with the secular family divisions. Thus, they are split into several families.

Therefore, even if they have many similarities and might be part of the same kind, they were split and each family was left as its own kind, unless data is found to lump them together. For example, all bats may be of the same kind and at minimum could only require two on board the ark. However, since studies of interbreeding among bats has not been documented as of the opening of the Ark Encounter, then they potentially have over 300 of them. This also causes numbers to be significantly (and purposely) higher at the Ark Encounter.

Ark Encounter Final Numbers

Using the maximums discussed, the Ark Encounter estimation is about 1,400 kinds. This is translated to about 6,700 individuals on the ark. This number maximizes the animals but should likely go down with more research into new hybrids as they come to light.

ReaLISTIC FIGures Are MUCH LeSS

Realistic numbers are clearly much lower. For example, having only 7 individuals of the *clean* birds rapidly reduced the number of birds/winged creatures on the ark. Bringing certain animals together that may be in the same kind, like sauropods, would reduce the number too. Also having *7 instead of 14* of the clean birds and beasts, and so on, would reduce the number of kinds and significantly reduce the number of individuals on the ark. The actual is likely less than 3,200 creatures.

Jones' minimum number of about 1,000 kinds and the Ark Encounter's maximum number of about 1,400 kinds gives us a decent range. From here, researchers can build and hone in on more realistic numbers.

19. In the secular mindset, these layers would be separated by millions of years and thus is also used so separate sauropods into different families. Creationists don't necessarily agree to this standard but for the sake of a starting point, the Ark Encounter is using this suite of criteria.

31 | HOW COULD NOAH GET AND CARE FOR ALL THE ANIMALS?

BODIE HODGE

GATHERING THE ANIMALS – THE EASY PART!

Some have pondered how Noah was capable of finding all the animals that needed to be on the ark. The task would be unthinkable (especially when you are in the middle of building the ark and gathering food for the ark's voyage). However, this was an easy task for Noah because *God* brought the animals to Noah.

> And of every living thing of all flesh you shall bring two of every sort into the ark, to keep them alive with you; they shall be male and female. Of the birds[1] after their kind, of animals after their kind, and of every creeping thing of the earth after its kind, two of every kind will come to you to keep them alive (Genesis 6:19–20).

God brought them in pairs, a male and its mate (female) of each kind (think dog kind, cat kind, elephant kind, etc.). Many are aware that seven of the clean animals and birds went aboard the ark. The Bible says:

> You shall take with you seven each of every clean animal, a male and his female; two each of animals that are unclean, a male and his female; also seven each of birds of the air, male and female, to keep the species alive on the face of all the earth (Genesis 7:2–3).

---

1. Bird here is *owph* in Hebrew, which means winged creature, so it would also include bats, pterosaurs, etc.

Interestingly, the Bible never says God brought seven of each kind to Noah, so it is possible they already had the 5 extra clean animals and birds (which is a small list per Leviticus 11 and Deuteronomy 14) in their possession. The clean animals could be used for sacrifice, leather, milk, and so forth. Recall, that it was not until after the Flood that meat eating was permissible for man (Genesis 9:3[2]).

Noah likely had been given the numbers by the Lord so that he could prepare the cages/rooms for them in the ark. It also allowed him to know the approximate amount of food to gather.

Loading The Animals

The animals went on the ark in pairs — a male and its mate. The loading could have taken upward of a week. Scripture says:

> Then the LORD said to Noah, "Come into the ark, you and all your household, because I have seen that you are righteous before Me in this generation. You shall take with you seven each of every clean animal, a male and his female; two each of animals that are unclean, a male and his female; also seven each of birds of the air, male and female, to keep the species alive on the face of all the earth. For after seven more days I will cause it to rain on the earth forty days and forty nights, and I will destroy from the face of the earth all living things that I have made (Genesis 7:1–4).

So Noah had listened to the Lord and built the ark just as God commanded. It was ready. Noah had it stocked with food (Genesis 6:21[3]) and likely initial water too.

Then the Lord gave permission to come aboard with the animals. Essentially, this was like a permit. When builders prepare a building, it has to be up to code. Noah's work on the ark had to be up to code as well. God agreed that Noah was in compliance (Genesis 6:22: "Thus Noah did; according to all that God commanded him, so he did"). Therefore, Noah received permission to inhabit the ark.

This is when Noah began the loading process (as well as taking their personal belongings) on the ark. He took the animals by twos, a male and its

---

2. "Every moving thing that lives shall be food for you. I have given you all things, even as the green herbs.
3. And you shall take for yourself of all food that is eaten, and you shall gather it to yourself; and it shall be food for you and for them.

mate (Genesis 7:8–9[4]). Keep in mind that of the clean animals' sacrifice was required after the Flood. So this would be the extra male[5] without a mate since it would not be required to mate and repopulate the earth afterward.

Those that entered the ark *in pairs* were for the purpose of repopulating their kind after the Flood. This is why the female is paired with it. But the sacrificial clean animals were obviously not required to go in pairs as they had no mates and their function was not to keep their kinds alive after the Flood (Genesis 7:3[6]).

Sacrifice costs the *sacrificer* something. If not, it really isn't a sacrifice. King David later recognized this (2 Samuel 24:24[7]). It makes sense that the sacrificial animals were those owned by the family and were taken aboard the ark. In other words, it was not to be counted from the pairs that God brought to Noah. The Bible simply doesn't give us details of *when* the sacrificial animals boarded, just as the Bible doesn't tell exactly when the food was loaded.

It is possible the sacrificial animals were among the first-born offspring of the clean animals taken aboard the ark. When the animals came off the ark, they came by their families (Genesis 8:19[8]), implying that many had likely borne offspring.

Caring for the Animals on the Ark

Caring for the animals aboard the ark may have been easier than initially thought. If operational designs were planned correctly for food and water dispensing, waste management, etc., this task would be quite easy.

Keep in mind that the ark is *not* a zoo, nor is it a permanent vessel meant for 20 years of service. Automatic watering systems and feeding systems could make the job almost too easy. Some animals could have hibernated.

---

4. Of clean animals, of animals that are unclean, of birds, and of everything that creeps on the earth, two by two they went into the ark to Noah, male and female, as God had commanded Noah

5. In most cases in the Old Testament, the sacrificial animals were male. There are a few cases where it could be either male or female (e.g., Genesis 15:9; Leviticus 3:1–6), but they are the exception, not the norm.

6. Also seven each of birds of the air, male and female, to keep the species alive on the face of all the earth.

7. Then the king said to Araunah, "No, but I will surely buy it from you for a price; nor will I offer burnt offerings to the LORD my God with that which costs me nothing." So David bought the threshing floor and the oxen for fifty shekels of silver.

8. Every animal, every creeping thing, every bird, and whatever creeps on the earth, according to their families, went out of the ark.

As a farmer in my (Bodie) youth, my experiences lend a little light to this subject. I never scooped poop from the hogs, cattle, chickens, etc., everyday. In fact, cleaning out the barn or chicken coup was rarely done. The point is that there are ways of collecting waste from animals or at least neutralizing it so that you don't have to scoop waste all the time. When properly done, once a year was sufficient. Who knows what sophisticated ideas people had developed before the Flood.

With Noah's voyage being about a year, they may not have had to scoop the waste overboard at all. It would surprise me if Noah and his family had to clean out the waste even once. They could have had drop floors for waste to pass through. They could have thick straw covering the floors to collect waste and cancel out effects of ammonia, and so forth. Noah's ark was only needed for about a year and then it was time to exit.

DIDN'T THE DINOSAURS EAT THE OTHER ANIMALS ON THE ARK?

Carnivorous animals, as we know them today, weren't always like that. Sharks eat kelp, spiders eat pollen, bears eat more plants than animals, and some cats have refused to eat meat. Originally, all animals were vegetarian (Genesis 1:30[9]), so having a vegetarian diet on the ark is not a problem. In fact, the animals that God brought to the ark may have been animals that were still vegetarian — even though flesh of all sorts — including animals — was corrupted on the earth (Genesis 6:12[10]).

Even if some ark inhabitants had begun to be carnivores by eating meat by the time of the ark's voyage, they could still eat vegetarian foods when they became hungry enough. Keep in mind that animals were separated into their rooms/cages, so trying to eat other animals would be a moot point anyway.

CONCLUSION

Getting the animals was the easy part, since God did that. Loading the animals and caring for them during the voyage was likely much easier than we are commonly led to believe. These issues really aren't a big deal when we think through the subject.

---

9. "Also, to every beast of the earth, to every bird of the air, and to everything that creeps on the earth, in which there is life, I have given every green herb for food"; and it was so.

10. So God looked upon the earth, and indeed it was corrupt; for all flesh had corrupted their way on the earth.

32 | COULD NOAH REALLY BUILD THE ARK BY HIMSELF?

KEN HAM AND BODIE HODGE

"How could Noah build that ark *by himself*?" is a question we hear far too often! Research into the subject reveals a lot of information. First, Noah wasn't by himself. He had three sons — Shem, Ham and Japheth. The Bible says:

> And Noah was five hundred years old, and Noah begot Shem, Ham, and Japheth (Genesis 5:32).

NOAH'S THREE SONS . . . TRIPLETS?

No, they were not triplets. Genesis 5:32 indicates that Noah was 500 when his first son was born. Listings such as these are rarely an indication of ages but shows that Noah *began* having children when He was 500. We see the same thing when Terah gave birth to his sons, Abram, Nahor, and Haran (Genesis 11:26[1]).

The listing of children often started with the most important one (through Shem we receive the blessing of Christ). Those with a greater godly legacy are listed first, being the most important. Consider that Jesus has a name above all other names (Philippians 2:9–10[2]).

By doing further research in the Bible, we know the relative ages of each of Noah's sons.

---

1. Now Terah lived seventy years, and begot Abram, Nahor, and Haran.
2. Therefore God also has highly exalted Him and given Him the name which is above every name, that at the name of Jesus every knee should bow, of those in heaven, and of those on earth, and of those under the earth.

> Unto Shem also, the father of all the children of Eber, the brother of Japheth the elder, even to him were children born (Genesis 10:21; KJV).

> When Noah awoke from his wine and knew what his youngest son [Ham] had done to him (Genesis 9:24; ESV).

Genesis 10:21 indicates that Japheth was the oldest and thus was born when Noah was 500 years old. We are informed that Ham is the youngest, as indicated in Genesis 9:24, after Ham's inappropriate actions to his father. Therefore, Shem had to be born in between Japheth and Ham. Shem wasn't born as a triplet or twin of Japheth when Noah was 500, as shown by Genesis 7:6 and Genesis 11:10.

> Noah was six hundred years old when the floodwaters were on the earth (Genesis 7:6).

> These are the generations of Shem. When Shem was 100 years old, he fathered Arphaxad two years after the flood (Genesis 11:10; ESV).

Noah was 600 when the floodwaters came on the earth, and two years later Shem was 100. Therefore, Shem had to be born to Noah when he was 502. We are not sure of Ham's exact age in Scripture, but he had to be born after Shem. Thus, Genesis 5:32 introduces us to Noah's sons all together, and other passages give more detail about their birth order and age. Now back to the point at hand — these three sons were there with Noah to help as well.

LAMECH AND METHUSELAH

Also consider that Lamech and Methuselah — Noah's father and grandfather were around to help too — that is, for a certain amount of time, though both died prior to the Flood. Lamech died about five years before the Flood and Methuselah died the year of the Flood.

Methuselah, being raised by a godly parent, Enoch (who walked with God and was translated to heaven without death), was surely righteous as well (Hebrews 11:5[3]). His death surely preceded the Flood unlike what is portrayed in the unbiblical movie *Noah* with Russell Crowe and Darren Aronofsky.

---

3. By faith Enoch was taken away so that he did not see death, "and was not found, because God had taken him"; for before he was taken he had this testimony, that he pleased God.

Some have suggested that Methuselah died immediately before the Flood and hence a seven-day mourning period was in order. This possibly makes sense of why Noah was given seven days until the Flood came (e.g., Genesis 7:4[4]). Whether this is true or not, we cannot be certain.

God's instruction for Noah and His family to board the ark seven days in advance was for several reasons. Obviously, one reason was to complete the final phase of loading the animals (Genesis 7:2–9), and a second was a final test of faith for Noah and his family, the final boarding being on the seventh day (Genesis 7:11–16).

Keep in mind that it was common for prominent people to be honored with designated times of mourning after they passed (e.g., Genesis 27:41,[5] 50:4–5[6]; Deuteronomy 34:8[7]; 2 Samuel 11:27[8]). However, there were surely many who had mourning periods that are simply not mentioned in the Bible. Was this a mourning period for Methuselah? Whether this is true or not, we cannot be certain, but it would make a good "cap" to the life of Methuselah.

Regardless, Methuselah and Lamech would have been available for help for some time during the ark's construction. Their ability to do certain things may have been limited by their age however.

RIGHTEOUS PEOPLE WHO WERE KILLED?

Let us also not forget the potential number of people who were righteous due to Noah's preaching (2 Peter 2:5[9]) who may have been killed or murdered leading up to the Flood. These are a possibility.

---

4. "For after seven more days I will cause it to rain on the earth forty days and forty nights, and I will destroy from the face of the earth all living things that I have made."

5. So Esau hated Jacob because of the blessing with which his father blessed him, and Esau said in his heart, "The days of mourning for my father are at hand; then I will kill my brother Jacob."

6. And when the days of his mourning were past, Joseph spoke to the household of Pharaoh, saying, "If now I have found favor in your eyes, please speak in the hearing of Pharaoh, saying. 'My father made me swear, saying, "Behold, I am dying; in my grave which I dug for myself in the land of Canaan, there you shall bury me." Now therefore, please let me go up and bury my father, and I will come back.' "

7. And the children of Israel wept for Moses in the plains of Moab thirty days. So the days of weeping and mourning for Moses ended.

8. And when her mourning was over, David sent and brought her to his house, and she becam'e his wife and bore him a son. But the thing that David had done displeased the LORD.

9. And did not spare the ancient world, but saved Noah, one of eight people, a preacher of righteousness, bringing in the flood on the world of the ungodly.

With the passing of Methuselah, and the recent passing of Lamech, we pause to realize that there were not many righteous people left on earth. After all, fewer than ten people were saved on the ark. Consider Abraham's discussion with the Lord over the destruction of Sodom (Genesis 18:26–32). Abraham did not proceed to a number fewer than ten righteous people when pleading for Sodom. He may have believed that judgment would come if there were fewer than ten — perhaps a reflection of his knowledge of the Flood.

Methuselah and Lamech had recently died, and this left eight. So, judgment was coming, but the Lord also prepared a means of salvation for Noah and his family on the ark, just as He did by sending the angels to rescue Lot and his family from Sodom.

Hired Hands/Contractors

Also, there is nothing wrong with Noah having hired hands or contractors to do specific work, gather wood, process wood, make specialized tools, food delivery, and so forth.

Noah could easily contract with unrighteous farmers or carpenters of his day to produce a certain amount of food or joists (etc.) since he was too busy with other aspects of the ark. I've often thought that if the Lord had blessed Noah as he did people like Abraham, Isaac, and Jacob, or David or Solomon, then Noah may have had the wealth to hire the manpower to get things done correctly and in a timely fashion.

Noah's Special Blessing

In a world full of wickedness and violence, did it ever worry Noah about the danger his family would be in during the trials of building the ark? Noah was righteous and standing against that wicked world. One would think he was a "target" or perhaps his family was a "target" for evil motives and possibly murder. But consider this wonderful verse of assurance given to Noah:

> But I will establish My covenant with you; and you shall go
> into the ark — you, your sons, your wife, and your sons' wives
> with you (Genesis 6:18).

This was told to Noah when he was first informed to build the ark. Noah was told that his wife, his sons, and his sons' wives would be on board the ark. Noah knew this information in advance. His family would not be murdered or killed during this ordeal. This prophecy given to Noah was a blessing of reassurance that his family would be safe. Thus, Noah had no need of concern or worry over his family. He knew in advance that they would be on the ark.

Some have wrestled with this verse, holding that it means that Noah knew that his preaching would be in vain and that the ark was not to be built as a sufficient rescue vessel for mankind, just designed for his family alone, though we don't see it that way. We see it as a guarantee that Noah could know that *at least* his family would be on it.

Think of it this way. In the same way, Christ's sacrifice on the Cross is sufficient means of salvation for all to receive the blood of Christ to be saved (1 John 2:2[10]; Hebrews 7:27[11]; Romans 6:10[12]). That doesn't mean all will receive (e.g., Matthew 7:13[13]) in the same way it doesn't mean that all would enter the door of the ark, but Noah was comforted in knowing that at the very least, his immediate family was going to be aboard.

---

10. And He Himself is the propitiation for our sins, and not for ours only but also for the whole world.
11. Who does not need daily, as those high priests, to offer up sacrifices, first for His own sins and then for the people's, for this He did once for all when He offered up Himself.
12. For the death that He died, He died to sin once for all; but the life that He lives, He lives to God.
13. "Enter by the narrow gate; for wide is the gate and broad is the way that leads to destruction, and there are many who go in by it.

33 | WAS THERE A CANOPY AROUND THE EARTH UNTIL THE FLOOD?

BODIE HODGE

PRELIMINARY COMMENTS

If there is one thing you need to know about biblical creationists . . . they can be divided on a subject. This isn't necessarily a bad thing. Though we all have the same heart to follow Christ and do the best we can for the sake of biblical authority and the cause of Christ, we can have differences when it comes to details of models used to explain various aspects of God's creation. Models though are subject to change, but what Scripture teaches is not subject to change!

When divisions occur over scientific models, this helps us dive into an issue in more detail and discover if that model is good, bad, needs revision, and so on. But note over *what* we are divided; it is not the Word of God nor is it even theology — it is a division over a *scientific model.*

This is where Christians can rightly be divided on a subject and still do so with Christian love, which I hope is how each Christian would conduct themselves. These "iron-sharpening-iron" dealings on a model can occur while still promoting a heart for the gospel (Proverbs 27:17[1]).

The debate over a canopy model is no different — we are all brothers and sisters in Christ trying to understand *what the Bible says and what it doesn't say* on this subject (2 Timothy 2:15[2]). It is the Bible that reigns

---

1. As iron sharpens iron, so a man sharpens the countenance of his friend.
2. Be diligent to present yourself approved to God, a worker who does not need to be ashamed, rightly dividing the word of truth.

supreme on the issue, and our scientific analysis on the subject will always be subservient to the Bible's text.

Introduction

For those familiar with creation, you may also be familiar with a particular scientific model that has dominated creation circles for about 50 years. This model has been denoted as the canopy theory or canopy model(s). In this science model, there was supposed to be a canopy of water (solid, liquid, or gas) that may have surrounded the earth from creation until its alleged dissipation at the Flood.

The reason for this model was to try to explain a better atmosphere prior to the Flood and possible health benefits for man, animals, and plants. After all, man before the Flood was living to great ages. So this model was proposed based on the "waters above" in Genesis 1.

For those familiar with creation, you may also know that many people no longer hold to this particular model. And you may be asking the question, what is going on with the canopy model? Let's evaluate the situation. Furthermore, since this is still a sensitive subject to many, a little more time will be spent in this chapter.

What Is The Canopy Model(s)?

There are several canopy models, but they all have one thing in common.[3] They all interpret the "waters above" the expanse (firmament) in Genesis 1:7 as some form of water-based canopy surrounding the earth that endured from creation until the Flood.

> Then God said, "Let there be a firmament [expanse] in the midst of the waters, and let it divide the waters from the waters." Thus God made the firmament [expanse], and divided the waters which were under the firmament [expanse] from the waters which were above the firmament [expanse]; and it was so (Genesis 1:6–7).

---

3. This is not to be confused with canopy ideas that have the edge of water at or near the end of the universe (e.g., white hole cosmology), but instead the models that have a water canopy in the atmosphere, e.g., like those mentioned in John C. Whitcomb and Henry M. Morris, *The Genesis Flood*, originally published c. 1960. Also see J.C. Dillow, *The Waters Above: Earth's Pre-Flood Vapor Canopy* (see footnote 4 in this chapter) or John C. Whitcomb, *The World that Perished*.

Essentially, the waters above are believed to have formed either a vapor, water (liquid), or ice canopy around the earth. It is the vapor canopy that seemed to dominate all of the proposed models.[4] It is suggested that this canopy was responsible for several things such as keeping harmful radiation from penetrating the earth, increasing the surface atmospheric pressure of oxygen, keeping the globe at a consistent temperature for a more uniform climate around the globe, and providing one of the sources of water for the Flood.

Some of these factors, like keeping radiation out and increasing the surface atmospheric pressures of oxygen, were thought to allow for human longevity to be increased from its present state (upward of 900 years or so as described in Genesis 5). So this scientific model was an effort to explain several things, including the long human lifespan prior to the Flood.

Other potential issues solved by the models were to destroy the possibility of large-scale storms with reduced airflow patterns for less extreme weather possibilities, have a climate without rain (such as Dillow's model, see below) but instead merely dew every night, and reduce any forms of barrenness like deserts and ice caps. It would have higher atmospheric pressure to possibly help certain creatures fly that otherwise may not be able to.

A Brief History of Canopy Models

Modern canopy models can be traced back to Dr. Henry Morris and Dr. John Whitcomb in their groundbreaking book *The Genesis Flood* in 1961. This book triggered a return to biblical authority in our age, which is highly commendable, and much is owed to their efforts. In this volume, Whitcomb and Morris introduce the possibility of a vapor canopy as the waters above.

The canopy models gained popularity thanks to the work of Dr. Joseph Dillow,[5] and many creationists have since researched various aspects of these scientific models such as Dr. Larry Vardiman with the Institute for Creation Research.

Researchers have studied the possibility of solid canopies, water canopies, vapor canopies, thick canopies, thin canopies, and so on. Each model

---

4. This is in large part due to the influence of Joseph Dillow, whose scientific treatise left only the vapor models with any potential: "We showed that only a vapor canopy model can satisfactorily meet the requirements of the necessary support mechanism." J.C. Dillow, *The Waters Above: Earth's Pre-Flood Vapor Canopy*, revised edition (Chicago, IL: Moody Press, 1981), p. 422.

5. J.C. Dillow, *The Waters Above: Earth's Pre-Flood Vapor Canopy*, revised edition (Chicago, IL: Moody Press, 1981).

has the canopy collapsing into history at the time of the Flood. Researchers thought it could have provided at least some of the water for the Flood and was associated with the 40 days of rain coming from the "windows of heaven" mentioned along with the fountains of the great deep at the onset of the Flood (Genesis 7:11).

However, the current state of the canopy models have faded to such an extent that most researchers and apologists have abandoned the various models. Let's take a look at the biblical and scientific reasons behind the abandonment.

BIBLICaL ISSUES

Though both will be discussed, any biblical difficulties that bear on the discussion of the canopy must *trump* scientific considerations, as it is the authority of the Bible that is supreme in all that it teaches.

Interpretations of Scripture Are Not Scripture

The necessity for a water-based canopy about the earth is not directly stated in the text. It is an *interpretation* of the text. Keep in mind that it is the *text* that is inspired, not our interpretations of it.

Others have interpreted the water's above as something entirely different from a water-based canopy about the earth. Most commentators appeal to the waters above as simply being the clouds, which are water droplets (not vapor) in the atmosphere, for they are simply "waters" that are above.

Most do not limit this interpretation as simply being the clouds, but perhaps something that reaches deep into space and extends as far as the *Third Heaven* or *Heaven of Heavens*. For example, expositor Dr. John Gill in the 1700s said:

> The lower part of it, the atmosphere above, which are the clouds full of water, from whence rain descends upon the earth; and which divided between them and those that were left on the earth, and so under it, not yet gathered into one place; as it now does between the clouds of heaven and the waters of the sea. Though Mr. Gregory is of the opinion, that an abyss of waters above the most supreme orb is here meant; or a great deep between the heavens and the heaven of heavens.[6]

---

6. John Gill, *Exposition of the Bible*, Genesis 1:7.

Gill agrees that clouds were inclusive of these waters above but that the waters also extend to the heaven of heavens, at the outer edge of the universe. Matthew Poole noted this possibility as well in his commentary in the 1600s:

> . . . the expansion, or extension, because it is extended far and wide, even from the earth to the third heaven; called also the firmament, because it is fixed in its proper place, from whence it cannot be moved, unless by force.[7]

Matthew Henry also concurs that this expanse extends to the heaven of heavens (third heaven):

> The command of God concerning it: Let there be a firmament, an expansion, so the Hebrew word signifies, like a sheet spread, or a curtain drawn out. This includes all that is visible above the earth, between it and the third heavens: the air, its higher, middle, and lower, regions — the celestial globe, and all the spheres and orbs of light above: it reaches as high as the place where the stars are fixed, for that is called here the firmament of heaven Ge 1:14,15, and as low as the place where the birds fly, for that also is called the firmament of heaven, Ge 1:20.[8]

The point is that a canopy model about the earth is simply that . . . an interpretation. It should be evaluated as such, not taken as Scripture itself. Many respected Bible interpreters do not share in the interpretation of the "waters above" being a water canopy in the upper atmosphere of earth.

Stars for Seasons and Light and Other Implications

Another biblical issue crops up when we read in Genesis 1:14–15

> Then God said, "Let there be lights in the firmament [expanse] of the heavens to divide the day from the night; and let them be for signs and seasons, and for days and years; and let them be for lights in the firmament [expanse] of the heavens to give light on the earth"; and it was so.[9]

The stars are intended by God to be used to map seasons. And they were also to "give light on the earth." Though this is not much light, it does help

---

7. Matthew Poole, *A Commentary on the Holy Bible*, Genesis 1:7.
8. Matthew Henry, *A Commentary on the Whole Bible*, Genesis 1:7.
9. See also Genesis 1:17.

significantly during new moon conditions — that is, if you live in an area not affected by light pollution.

Water

If the canopy were liquid water, then in its various forms like mist or haze it would inhibit seeing these stars. How could one see the stars to map the seasons? It would be like a perpetually cloudy day. The light would be absorbed or reflected back to space much the way fog does the headlights of a car. What little light is transmitted through would not be sufficiently discernable to make out stars and star patterns to map seasons. Unlike a vapor canopy, clouds are moving and in motion; one can still see the stars to map seasons when they move through. Furthermore, if it was water why didn't it fall?[10]

Ice

If it were ice, then it *is* possible to see the stars but they would not appear in the positions one normally sees them, but still they would be sufficient to map seasons. But ice, when kept cool (to remain ice), tends to coat at the surface where other water molecules freezes to it (think of the coating you see on an ice cube left in the freezer). This could inhibit visibility, as evaporated water from the ocean surface would surely make contact — especially in a sin-cursed and broken world.

Vapor

If an invisible vapor canopy existed in our upper atmosphere, then it makes the most sense, but there could still turn out to be a problem. As cooler vapor nears space, water condenses and begins to haze, though as long as the vapor in the upper atmosphere is kept warm and above the dew point, it could remain invisible. But there are a lot of "if's." In short, the stars may not serve their purpose to give light on the earth with some possibilities within these models.

Consider that if there were a water *vapor* canopy, what would stop it from interacting with the rest of the atmosphere *that is vapor*? Gasses mix to equilibrium and that is the way God upholds the universe.[11] If it was a vapor, then why is it distinguished from the atmosphere, which is vapor?

10. Would one appeal to the supernatural? If so, it defeats the purpose of this scientific model that seeks to explain things in a naturalistic fashion.
11. Again, would one appeal to the supernatural? If so, it defeats the purpose of this scientific model that seeks to explain things in a naturalistic fashion.

The Bible uses the terms *waters* above, which implies that the temperature is between 32°F and 212°F (0°C and 100°C). If it was meant to be vapor, then why say "waters" above? Why not say vapor (*hebel*), which was used in the Old Testament?

Where Were the Stars Made?

If the canopy really was part of earth's atmosphere, then all the stars, sun, and moon would have been created within the earth's atmosphere.

Why is this? A closer look at Genesis 1:14[12] reveals that the "waters above" may very well be much farther out — if they still exist today.

The entirety of the stars, including our own sun (the greater light) and moon (lesser light) were made "*in* the expanse." Further, they are obviously not in our atmosphere. Recall that the waters of verse 7 are above the expanse. If the canopy were just outside the atmosphere of the young earth, then the sun, moon, and stars would have to be in the atmosphere, according to verse 14.

Further, the winged creatures were flying *in the face of* the expanse (Genesis 1:20[13]; the NKJV accurately translates the Hebrew), and this helps reveal the extent of the expanse. It would likely include aspects of the atmosphere as well as space. The Bible calls the firmament "heaven" in Genesis 1:8,[14] which would include both. Perhaps our understanding of "sky" is similar or perhaps the best translation of this as well.

Regardless, this understanding of the text allows for the stars to be in the expanse, and this means that any waters above, which is beyond the stars, is not limited to being in the atmosphere. Also, 2 Corinthians 12:2[15] discusses three heavens, which are likely the atmosphere (airy heavens), space (starry heavens), and the heaven of heavens (Nehemiah 9:6[16]).

Some have argued that the prepositions in, under, above, etc. are not in the Hebrew text but are determined from the context, so the meaning

---

12. Then God said, "Let there be lights in the firmament of the heavens to divide the day from the night; and let them be for signs and seasons, and for days and years."
13. Then God said, "Let the waters abound with an abundance of living creatures, and let birds fly above the earth across the face of the firmament of the heavens."
14. And God called the firmament Heaven. So the evening and the morning were the second day.
15. I know a man in Christ who fourteen years ago — whether in the body I do not know, or whether out of the body I do not know, God knows — such a one was caught up to the third heaven.
16. You alone are the LORD; You have made heaven, the heaven of heavens, with all their host, the earth and everything on it, the seas and all that is in them, and You preserve them all. The host of heaven worships You.

in verses 14 and 17 is vague. It is true that the prepositions are determined by the context, so we must rely on a proper translation of Genesis 1:14.[17] Virtually all translations have the sun, moon, and stars being created *in* the expanse, not *above,* as any canopy model would require.

In Genesis 1, some have attempted to make a distinction between the expanse in which the birds fly (Genesis 1:20[18]) and the expanse in which the sun, moon, and stars were placed (Genesis 1:7[19]); this was in an effort to have the sun, moon, and stars made in the second expanse. This is not a distinction that is necessary from the text, and is only necessary if a canopy is assumed.

From the Hebrew, the birds are said to fly "across the face of the firmament of the heavens." Looking up at a bird flying across the sky, it would be seen against the face of both the atmosphere and the space beyond the atmosphere — the "heavens." The proponents of the canopy model must make a distinction between these two expanses to support the position, but this is an arbitrary assertion that is only necessary to support the view and is not described elsewhere in Scripture.

Expanse (Firmament) Still Existed Post-Flood

Another issue that is raised from the Bible is that the waters above the heavens were mentioned *after* the Flood, when it was supposedly gone.

> Praise Him, you heavens of heavens, and you waters above the heavens! (Psalm 148:4).

> So an officer on whose hand the king leaned answered the man of God and said, "Look, if the LORD would make windows in heaven, could this thing be?" And he said, "In fact, you shall see it with your eyes, but you shall not eat of it" (2 Kings 7:2; see also 2 Kings 7:19[20]).

> "Bring all the tithes into the storehouse, that there may be food in My house, and try Me now in this," says the LORD of

---

17. Then God said, "Let there be lights in the firmament of the heavens to divide the day from the night; and let them be for signs and seasons, and for days and years."
18. Then God said, "Let the waters abound with an abundance of living creatures, and let birds fly above the earth across the face of the firmament of the heavens."
19. Thus God made the firmament, and divided the waters which were under the firmament from the waters which were above the firmament; and it was so.
20. Then that officer had answered the man of God, and said, "Now look, if the LORD would make windows in heaven, could such a thing be?" And he had said, "In fact, you shall see it with your eyes, but you shall not eat of it."

hosts, "If I will not open for you the windows of heaven and pour out for you such blessing that there will not be room enough to receive it" (Malachi 3:10).

The biblical authors wrote these in a post-Flood world in the context of other post-Flood aspects. So it appears that the "waters above" and "windows of heaven" are in reference to something that still existed after the Flood. The "waters above" can't be referring to a long-gone canopy that dissipated at the Flood and still be present after the Flood. This is complemented by:

> The fountains of the deep and the windows of heaven were also stopped, and the rain from heaven was restrained (Genesis 8:2)

Genesis 8:2 merely points out that the two sources were stopped and restrained, not necessarily *done away* with. The verses above suggest that the windows of heaven remained after the Flood. Even the "springs of the great deep" were stopped but did not entirely disappear, but there may have been residual waters trapped that have slowly oozed out since that time, clearly not in any gushing spring-like fashion.[21]

Is a Canopy Necessary Biblically?

Finally, is a canopy necessary from the text? At this stage, perhaps not. It was promoted as a scientific model based on a possible interpretation of Genesis 1 to deal with several aspects of the overall biblical creation model developed in the mid-1900s. I don't say this lightly for my brothers and sisters in the Lord who may still find it appealing. Last century, I was introduced to the canopy model and found it fascinating. For years, I had espoused it, but after further study, I began leaning against it, as did many other creationists.

Old biblical commentators were not distraught at the windows of heaven or the waters not being a canopy encircling the earth. Such an interpretation was not deemed necessary in their sight. In fact, this idea is a recent addition to scriptural interpretation that is less than 100 years old. The canopy model was a scientific interpretation developed in an effort to help explain certain aspects of the text to those who were skeptical of the Bible's accounts of earth history, but when it comes down to it, it is not necessary and even has some serious biblical issues associated with it.

---

21. I would leave open the option that this affected the ocean sea level to a small degree, but the main reasons for changing sea level were via the Ice Age.

SCIENTIFIC ISSUES (SEMI-TECHNICAL)

Clearly, there are some biblical issues that are difficult to overcome. Researchers have often pointed out the scientific issues of the canopy model, as well. A couple will be noted below.

This is no discredit to the *researchers* by any means. The research was valuable and necessary to see how the model may or may not work with variations and types. The development and testing of models is an important part of scientific inquiry and we should continue to do so with many models to help us understand the world God has given us. So I appreciate and applaud all the work that has been done, and I further wish to encourage researchers to study other aspects to see if anything was missed.

Temperatures

To answer the question about how the earth regulates its temperature without a canopy, consider that it may not have been that much different than the way it regulates it today — by the atmosphere and oceans. Although there may have been much water underground prior to the Flood, there was obviously enough at or near the surface to sustain immense amounts of sea life. We know this because of the well-known figure that nearly 95 percent of the fossil record consists of shallow-water marine organisms. Was the earth's surface around 70 percent water before the Flood? That is a question creationist researchers still debate.

An infinitely knowledgeable God would have no problem designing the earth in a perfect world to have an ideal climate (even with variations like the cool of the day — Genesis 3:8[22]) where people could have filled the earth without wearing clothes (Genesis 2:25,[23] 1:28[24]). But with a different continental scheme, that contained remnants of a perfect world (merely cursed, not rearranged by the Flood yet), it would surely have been better equipped to deal with regulated temperatures and climate.

A vapor canopy, on the other hand, would cause major problems for the regulation of earth's temperature. A vapor canopy would absorb both

---

22. And they heard the sound of the LORD God walking in the garden in the cool of the day, and Adam and his wife hid themselves from the presence of the LORD God among the trees of the garden.
23. And they were both naked, the man and his wife, and were not ashamed.
24. Then God blessed them, and God said to them, "Be fruitful and multiply; fill the earth and subdue it; have dominion over the fish of the sea, over the birds of the air, and over every living thing that moves on the earth."

solar and infrared radiation and become hot, which would heat the surface by conduction downward. The various canopy models have therefore been plagued with heat problems from the greenhouse effect. For example, solar radiation would have to decrease by around 25 percent to make the most plausible model work.[25] The heat problem actually makes this model very problematic and adds an additional problem rather than helping to explain the environment before the Flood.[26]

The Source of Water

The primary source of water for the Flood was the springs of the great deep bursting forth (Genesis 7:11[27]). This water in turn likely provided some of the water in the "windows of heaven" in an indirect fashion. There is no need for an ocean of vapor above the atmosphere to provide for extreme amounts of water for the rain that fell during the Flood.

For example, if Dillow's vapor canopy existed (40 feet of precipitable water) and collapsed at the time of the Flood to supply, in large part, the rainfall, the latent heat of condensation would have boiled the atmosphere! And a viable canopy would not have had enough water vapor in it to sustain 40 days and nights of torrential global rain as in Vardiman's model (2–6 feet of precipitable water). Thus, the vapor canopy doesn't adequately explain the rain at the Flood.

Longevity

Some have appealed to a canopy to increase surface atmospheric pressures prior to the Flood. The reasoning is to allow for better healing as well as living longer and bigger as a result. However, increased oxygen (and likewise oxidation that produces dangerous free radicals), though beneficial in a few respects, is mostly a detriment to biological systems. Hence, antioxidants (including things like catalase and vitamins E, A, and C) are very important to reduce these free radicals within organisms.

---

25. For more on this see "Temperature Profiles for an Optimized Water Vapor Canopy" by Dr. Larry Vardiman, a researcher on this subject for over 25 years at the time of writing that paper, http://static.icr.org/i/pdf/technical/Temperature-Profiles-for-an-Optimized-Water-Vapor-Canopy.pdf.

26. Another issue is the amount of water vapor in the canopy. Dillow's 40 feet of precipitable water, the amount collected after all the water condenses, has major heat problems. But Vardiman's view has modeled canopies with 2 to 6 feet of precipitable water with better temperature results and we look forward to seeing his latest results.

27. In the six hundredth year of Noah's life, in the second month, the seventeenth day of the month, on that day all the fountains of the great deep were broken up, and the windows of heaven were opened.

Longevity (and the large size of many creatures) before and after the Flood is better explained by genetics through the bottlenecks of the Flood and the Tower of Babel as opposed to pre-Flood oxygen levels due to a canopy. Not to belabor these points, this idea has already been discussed elsewhere.[28]

Pre-Flood Climate

Regardless of canopy models, creationists generally agree that climate before the Fall was perfect. This doesn't mean the air was stagnant and 70°F every day, but instead had variations within the days and nights (Genesis 3:8[29]). These variations were not extreme but very reasonable.

Consider that Adam and Eve were told to be fruitful and multiply and fill the earth (Genesis 1:27–28[30]). In a perfect world where there was no need for clothes to cover sin (this came after the Fall), we can deduce that man should have been able to fill the earth without wearing clothes, hence the extremes were not as they are today or the couple would have been miserable as the temperatures fluctuated.

Even after the Fall, it makes sense that these weather variations were minimally different, because the general positions of continents and oceans were still the same. But with the global Flood that destroyed the earth and rearranged continents and so on, the extremes become pronounced — we now have ice caps and extremely high mountains that were pushed up from the Flood (Psalm 104:8[31]). We now have deserts that have extreme heat and cold and little water.

Biblical Models and Encouragement

I continue to encourage research and the development of scientific and theological models. However, a good grasp of all biblical passages that are relevant

---

28. Ken Ham,ed., *New Answers Book 2* (Green Forest, AR: Master Books, 2008), p. 159–168; Bodie Hodge, Tower of Babel (Green Forest, AR: Master Books, 2013), p. 205–212.

29. And they heard the sound of the Lord God walking in the garden in the cool of the day, and Adam and his wife hid themselves from the presence of the Lord God among the trees of the garden.

30. So God created man in His own image; in the image of God He created him; male and female He created them. Then God blessed them, and God said to them, "Be fruitful and multiply; fill the earth and subdue it; have dominion over the fish of the sea, over the birds of the air, and over every living thing that moves on the earth."

31. The mountains rose; the valleys sank down to the place which You established for them (NASB).

to the topic must precede the scientific research and models, and the Bible must be the ultimate judge over all of our conclusions.

The canopy model may have a glimmer of hope still remaining, and that will be left to the proponents to more carefully explain, but both the biblical and scientific difficulties need to be addressed thoroughly and convincingly for the model to be embraced. So we do look forward to future research.

In all of this, we must remember that scientific models are not Scripture, and it is the Scripture that we should defend as the authority. While we must surely affirm that the waters above were divided from the waters below, something the Bible clearly states, whether or not there was a canopy must be held loosely lest we do damage to the text of Scripture or the limits of scientific understanding.

34 | DID NOAH NEED OXYGEN ON THE ARK?

BODIE HODGE

INTRODUCTION

If the waters of the Flood covered the highest mountains, does that mean the ark's inhabitants needed oxygen supplies?

Why would someone ask this question? Let's back up and look at this from a big picture. Consider what the Bible says about the voyage of the ark:

> The water prevailed more and more upon the earth, so that all the high mountains everywhere under the heavens were covered. The water prevailed fifteen cubits higher, and the mountains were covered. (Genesis 7:19–20)[1]

People then look at the earth *today* and note that the highest mountain is Mt. Everest, which stands just over 29,000 feet above sea level. Then they put two and two together and say that Noah's ark floated at least 15 cubits above Mt. Everest — and at such high altitude, people need oxygen!

It sounds like a straightforward argument, doesn't it? But did you notice that I emphasized the word *today*? In light of this, the solution is quite simple: the Flood did not happen on today's earth, but rather on the earth of nearly 4,300 years ago. The world today is not the same as it was before the Flood, or even *during* the Flood. For instance, if the mountains, continents, and ocean basins of today's earth were more leveled out, the planet's surface

---

1. Scripture in this chapter is from the New American Standard Bible (NASB).

243

water alone would cover the earth to a calculated 1.66 miles deep — about 8,000 feet. Yet when I visited Cusco, Peru, which is around 11,000 feet above sea level, I didn't need an oxygen tank.

Furthermore, atmospheric air pressure is relative to sea level. So as rising sea levels pushed the air column higher, the air pressure at sea level would stay the same. So again, oxygen tanks are unnecessary.

PSALM 104:6-9: CREATION OR THE FLOOD?

Beginning on day 150 of the Flood, mountains began overtaking the water again as the mountain-building phase had begun (Genesis 8:2–4[2]). Poetic Psalm 104 gives further hints of this possible mountain building as the valley basins sank down:

> You covered it with the deep as with a garment; the waters were standing above the mountains. At Your rebuke they fled, at the sound of Your thunder they hurried away. The mountains rose; the valleys sank down to the place which You established for them. You set a boundary that they may not pass over, so that they will not return to cover the earth (Psalm 104:6–9).

This section of the Psalm is obviously speaking of the Flood, as water would no longer *return* to cover the earth — if this passage were speaking of creation week (as some commentators have stated), then God would have erred when the waters covered the whole earth during the Flood.

Consider this overview of the entire Psalm as it continues down through history:

Psalm 104:1–5	Creation Week
Psalm 104:6–9	Flood
Psalm 104:10–35	Post-Flood

It makes sense that, because the Psalm is referring to the earth and what is in it, it begins with earth history (creation week). But mentions of donkeys (verse 11) and goats (verse 18) show variation within the created kind, which shows this would have taken place *after* the Flood. Also, a post-Flood

---

2. The fountains of the deep and the floodgates of the sky were closed, and the rain from the sky was restrained; and the waters receded steadily from the earth, and at the end of one hundred and fifty days the waters decreased. In the seventh month, on the seventeenth day of the month, the ark rested upon the mountains of Ararat.

geographic location is named (Lebanon, verse 16) as well as ships (verse 26) that indicate this Psalm was not looking strictly at creation week.

LOST IN Translation?

While everyone agrees that Psalm 104:1–5[3] is referring to creation week, what of the argument — made by many commentators from the 1600s onward — that attributes Psalm 104:6–9 to creation week also? One could suggest that much of this is due to the translation being viewed. Two basic variants of the translation of the Hebrew in Psalm 104:8 read:

1. They went up over the mountains and went down into the valleys.
2. Mountains rose and the valleys sank down.

In fact, a variety of translations yield some variant of one of these two possibilities.

Table 1. Translations of Psalm 104:8a[4]

Translation	Agrees with: "They went up over the mountains and went down into the valleys"	Agrees with: "Mountains rose and the valleys sank down"
New American Standard		X
New International Version	X	
King James Version	X	
New King James Version	X	
English Standard Version		X
Holman Christian Standard		X
English translation of the Septuagint	X	

3. Bless the Lord, O my soul! O Lord my God, You are very great: You are clothed with honor and majesty, covering Yourself with light as with a cloak, stretching out heaven like a tent curtain. He lays the beams of His upper chambers in the waters; He makes the clouds His chariot; He walks upon the wings of the wind; He makes the winds His messengers, flaming fire His ministers. He established the earth upon its foundations, so that it will not totter forever and ever.

4. Data was taken from two sources: Charles Taylor, "Did Mountains Really Rise According to Psalm 104:8?" *TJ* 12(3), 1998, 312–313, and Online Bible, Larry Pierce, February 2009, or looked up separately.

Revised Version (UK)	X	
Amplified Bible		X
Good News Bible	X	
New English Bible	X	
Revised Berkley		X
J.N. Darby's		X
Living Bible		X
New Living Translation		X
Jerusalem Bible	X	
R.G. Moulton	X	
Knox Version		X
The Holy Scriptures according to the Masoretic Text (a new translation by the Jewish Publication Society)		X
Revised Standard Version		X
Young's Literal Translation	X	
King James 21st Century Version	X	
Geneva Bible		X
New Revised Standard Version	X	
Webster's Bible	X	
New International Children's Version		X
Interlinear Bible		X

Obviously, there is no consensus on translation among these English versions. Looking at other languages, we see how the Hebrew was translated.

Table 2. Some Foreign Translations of Psalm 104:8a[5]

Foreign translation	Agrees with: "They went up over the mountains and went down into the valleys"	Agrees with: "Mountains rose and the valleys sank down"

5. Ibid.

Luther's German		X
Menge's German		X
French Protestant Bible (Version Synondale)		X
Italian Edizione Paoline		X
Swedish Protestant		X
Spanish Reins Valera		X
Latin Vulgate (by Jerome)		X
La Bible Louis Segond 1910 (French)		X
Septuagint (Koine Greek)		X

Notice that there doesn't seem to be a discrepancy. Of course, there are many translations, so one cannot be dogmatic, but the point is that foreign translations agree with "mountains rising and valleys sinking down."

Hebrew

In Hebrew, which reads right to left, the phrase in 104:8a is basically *biq'ah yarad har 'alah*. Translated into English, the phrase in question is:

biq'ah	yarad	har	'alah
valleys	down go/sink	mountains	up go/rise

Take note that there are no prepositions like "over" or "into." It is literally "up go mountains, down go valleys." It makes sense why many translations, including non-English translations, use the phrase "mountains rose and the valleys sank down" — this is what it should be.

Why Would Commentators Miss This?

Commentaries could easily misinterpret this passage if they were based on translations that agree with "they went up over the mountains and went down into the valleys." For example, the most popular English translation for several hundred years, the King James Version, reads this way.

Furthermore, from a logical perspective, water doesn't flow uphill over mountains, but rather the opposite. Given language like this, commentators likely attributed this to a miraculous event during creation week, when many miracles were taking place anyway; also, creation week was referenced earlier in the chapter. Of course, the problems came when reading the rest of the context. One excellent commentator, Dr. John Gill, to whom I have appealed many times, regarding verse 9 and the waters not returning to cover the earth, stated:

> That they turn not again to cover the earth; as they did when it was first made, Psalm 104:6 that is, not without the divine leave and power; for they did turn again and cover the earth, at the time of the flood; but never shall more.[6]

Gill was forced to conclude that the waters did return to cover the earth, and he justified their return on "divine leave and power"! Yet this would mean that God breaks promises. Because we know that God does not break promises, this must be referring to the end of the Flood; so on this point, I disagree with Gill.

That said, we should understand the difficulty in commenting on the passage: it is a psalm of praise to God, and thus it is not as straightforward as literal history. It is difficult to determine where the shift from creation to the Flood occurs and where the shift from Flood to post-Flood occurs. However, there are a few more hints in the text.

A FEW MORE COMMENTS

We should use clear passages in Scripture to help interpret unclear passages. Consider that God's "rebuke" would not exist in a perfect world, where nothing would need rebuking or correcting. Remember, a perfect God created a perfect world — Genesis 1:31,[7] Deuteronomy 32:4.[8] One should expect nothing less of such a God. It was due to man's sin that the world is now imperfect and fallen.

Therefore, during creation week when everything was good, there would be no need for any rebuking. If Psalm 104:6–9 were referring to creation week (specifically day 3), then why the rebuke in Psalm 104:7? This implies an imperfect, *not* very good creation. But if Psalm 104:6–9 is referring to

---

6. http://biblehub.com/commentaries/psalms/104-9.htm.
7. God saw everything that He had made, and behold, it was very good. And there was evening and there was morning, the sixth day.
8. "The Rock! His work is perfect, for all His ways are just, a God of faithfulness and without injustice, righteous and upright is He.

the Flood, then of course a rebuke would exist in a fallen world where the judgment of water had overtaken the earth.

Additionally, note that Psalm 104:9 is clearly referencing Genesis 9:8–16 in saying that the waters would not return to cover the earth.

Some have asked how mountains and valleys could move up and down when the foundations are identified as immovable in Psalm 104:5. Keep in mind that mountains and valleys are not the foundation, but like the seas that sit well above the foundation. In fact, continents shifting and mountains rising do no damage to the foundation that is immovable.

Last, note that when the land appeared in Genesis 1 on day 3, the land that was being separated from the water was *dry*, not wet. The text in Genesis says that the waters were gathered into one place *and then* the dry land appeared. It says nothing of water flowing over the land to make it wet; otherwise, wet land would have appeared and then *became dry*, but during the Flood, the land was indeed overtaken by water that eventually stood above the land.

conclusion

The Hebrew phrase in Psalm 104:8a is the basis for the correct translation of mountains rising and valleys sinking. This shows that mountains and valleys during the Flood were not the same height as they are today. Even today mountains and valleys are changing their height; volcanic mountains, for instance, can grow very quickly, such as Surtsey (a new island) or Paricutin (a volcanic mountain in Mexico that formed in 1943).

Therefore, with mountains and continents leveled out and ocean basins nowhere near the depth they are today, it makes perfect sense that Noah was not at the height of modern-day Mt. Everest. Noah and those aboard the ark would not have required oxygen.

35 WHERE DID THE WATER FOR THE FLOOD COME FROM, AND WHERE DID IT GO?

KEN HAM AND BODIE HODGE

INTRODUCTION

Just like the last chapter, one of the main reasons people ask this question is because of Mt. Everest. Yes, you read this correctly. It is from Mt. Everest, which is the highest mountain peak in the world (over 29,029 feet, or 8,848 meters).

The question is often framed like this, "Where did all the water come from to cover Mt. Everest and where did all that water go?" You need to understand that when people ask this question, they are making the assumption that the Flood didn't affect the earth or the terrain such as Mt. Everest today. They merely assume that Mt. Everest was basically the same height before and after the Flood.

MISCONCEPTION ABOUT THE FLOOD

Once again, this is a rather naïve understanding of the Flood *and* Mt. Everest. It is *because of* the Flood that Mt. Everest now exists in the first place! In other words, Mt. Everest didn't exist before the Flood but is the result of mountainous uplift associated with the Flood that formed Mt. Everest, as well as other mountain ranges and peaks we have today![1]

When people falsely presume that Mt. Everest existed before the Flood and was the same basic height as today, they struggle with understanding where all the water was to cover that peak! But this is based on a false understanding of the Flood and mountains that formed as a result of the Flood.

---

1. We have seen a handful of mountains grow or form since the Flood like the volcano Paricutin in Mexico. Though these few are minute in comparison to the majority that formed in the Flood.

IS THE WATER (AND MOUNTAINS) A PROBLEM?

If we take ocean basins and bring them up and take mountain ranges and continents and bring them down to a level position, there is enough water to cover the earth 1.6 miles deep (2.57 km deep), so there is plenty of water on the earth for a global Flood.

1.6 miles deep! (2.57 kilometers)

Yet there was only the need for the highest underwater peak *during the Flood* to be covered by 15 cubits (22.5 feet or ~6.8 meters based on the short cubit to 25.5 feet or ~7.8 meters based on the long cubit) per Genesis 7:20.[2]

By the 150th day of the Flood (Genesis 8:3–4[3]), the mountains were already in the process of being built, likely by tectonic plate collisions on the earth's outer shell. For example, when two plates collide (called "convergent plate boundaries"), one plate goes up and the other plate goes under (called a "subduction zone").[4]

We know the mountains of Ararat existed by the 150th day of the Flood; thus, we also know that the plate collisions that formed this range were essentially completed at this time. Of course, residual effects likely occurred for some time — we still feel some earthquakes today!

By the 150th day, much of the rapid plate movement would largely begin to cease since the mechanism to move such plates had now ceased as well — springs of the great deep, rain, and windows of heaven were restrained (Genesis 8:2) and thus geological mechanisms associated with these would begin to cease as well.

The mountains of Ararat are part of the larger mountain chain called the *Alpide Belt* or *Alpine-Himalayan Belt*. This range extends from Spain and North Africa, through the Alps and Middle Eastern ranges (like the mountains of Ararat), and through the Himalayas down the Malay Peninsula and Indonesia, almost reaching Australia. It makes sense that these Alpine mountain ranges were all formed about the same time during the Flood's mountain-building,

---

2. The waters prevailed fifteen cubits upward, and the mountains were covered.
3. And the waters receded continually from the earth. At the end of the hundred and fifty days the waters decreased. Then the ark rested in the seventh month, the seventeenth day of the month, on the mountains of Ararat.
4. There are other plate interactions like "transform plate movements" (when plates go beside each other), or "divergent plate boundaries" (when they are going away from each other) — think mid-Atlantic Ridge.

which coincides with the valley sinking phase (ocean basins going down).

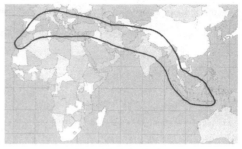

The Alpide Belt

Psalm 104:6–9 says:

> You covered it with the deep as with a garment; the waters were standing above the mountains. At Your rebuke they fled, at the sound of Your thunder they hurried away. The mountains rose; the valleys sank down to the place which You established for them. You set a boundary that they may not pass over, so that they will not return to cover the earth (NASB).

Mt. Everest's initial formation, being in the Alpide Belt, was about the same time as the mountains of Ararat or very shortly thereafter — since they involve much the same continental collisions. Naturally, Mt. Everest would be pushed up near its current height, though a little less. Mt. Everest still rises a little each year, merely due to residual effects that extend back to the Flood.

so Where did all the Water come From?

The majority of the water was subterranean (came from under the earth). The Bible says:

> In the six hundredth year of Noah's life, in the second month, the seventeenth day of the month, the same day were all the fountains of the great deep broken up, and the windows of heaven were opened (Genesis 7:11; KJV).

> The fountains also of the deep and the windows of heaven were stopped, and the rain from heaven was restrained (Genesis 8:2; KJV).

The fountains or springs of the great deep were the source of the majority of the waters for the Flood. The *windows of heaven* were also a source of water, though fully saturated clouds would not be sufficient for the initial 40 days rain until the ark raised up (Genesis 7:17,[5]) nor the continued rain until the

---

5. Now the flood was on the earth forty days. The waters increased and lifted up the ark, and it rose high above the earth.

150th day (Genesis 8:2).[6] So its contribution was likely smaller initially but continually renewed from the springs of the great deep that supplied water to the sky.

Also, there may be more to the meaning of "windows of heaven." This phrase is used in a metaphorical fashion in Malachi. The text says:

> Bring the whole tithe into the storehouse, so that there may be food in My house, and test Me now in this," says the LORD of hosts, "if I will not open for you the windows of heaven and pour out for you a blessing until it overflows (Malachi 3:10; NASB).

It basically means that something was poured out from God in abundance — whether blessing, as in the case of Malachi, or water, as in the case of the Flood! Think of it like this: The springs of the great deep burst forth and it was "raining cats and dogs!" In our English language, this phrase "raining cats and dogs" doesn't mean it was raining literal cats and dogs, but instead raining immensely. This could easily be the meaning of "windows of heaven" in Genesis 7:11 and 8:2, though, the windows of heaven may be in reference to the physical clouds and vapor in the sky too. Either option yields to the text.

WHERE DID ALL THE WATER GO?

The obvious answer is that the water is in the oceans, lakes, rivers, and so on that we have today! Some water may have seeped and again become subterranean (we do observe *springs* today), though most of that initial subterranean water from the Flood has now been exhausted. The continental shifting during the Flood did away with the original water "storehouses" that supplied the fountains of the great deep.

Any initial oceans before the Flood were likely much more shallow with a few deep areas. Keep in mind that about 95 percent of all fossils are from shallow marine organism — so this makes sense. Our current post-Flood oceanography has some areas that are shallow, but most is quite deep.

Consider that oceans cover about 70 percent of the earth surface today. At one point the whole earth was covered with the Floodwater. It was very kind of the Lord to give us 30 percent of land surface back.

---

6. See the chapter in this volume as to why an alleged canopy of water or vapor is not what is in view here.

36 | HOW DID ANIMALS GET TO PLACES ALL OVER THE WORLD LIKE AUSTRALIA?

BODIE HODGE

Obviously, when animals came off the ark in the Middle East, they could progress throughout Europe, Asia, and Africa rather easily, since those areas are connected by land. Of course, they would have had hurdles such as mountains and rivers to go around or cross, among other issues with terrain.[1]

Naturally, these obstacles would not be such a hindrance for birds and other flying creatures. It only took starlings (a type of bird) about 100 years to cover the entire North American continent when about 60 were released in New York City in 1890. With this in mind, it probably did not take long for many places to be populated with flying creatures after the Flood. Many birds can transverse great distances over lakes, seas, and oceans.

Some birds and other flying creatures may have *lost* the ability to fly due to mutations or breeding (particularly inbreeding) since the Flood. This could have occurred *after* migrating long distances. On the farm where I grew up, we had some giant white turkeys. They were so large, awkward, and had such poor feathers that with one look at them you would be able to discern they could never fly. In fact, I've thought the same thing when I first saw an emu, kiwi, ostrich, and some others — surely, they could never fly! But is their current look the result of mutations and breeding? It is possible.

---

1. Keep in mind that the weather patterns and climates for places may not have been established yet and were still under constant flux at this time, so many rivers may have been smaller in places and larger in others (like areas that later became deserts). For example, many areas that are deserts today would not have been so right after the Flood. Instead, they were likely the results of later weather patterns (e.g., Genesis 12:10, 26:1).

We also had wild turkeys where I lived. I often frightened them so that they took flight, and they could fly very well. I once spooked a few turkeys into flight to such a degree that one of them flew immensely high; I could hardly see it! It was much higher than the high-flying vultures that dominated our area. And it flew so far that it was miles before it descended.

The giant white turkeys that could never fly resulted from recent breeding of wild turkeys to be large supermarket specials. Considering this, it is easy to see how other birds may have *lost* their ability to fly. I would also leave this option open with other flightless birds.

Land Animals

In general, placental animals would move slower than marsupials, which can collect their young (e.g., in pouches) and continue migrating. Many placental animals need to stop and settle for a time to raise their young but, theoretically, great varieties of land animals could have gone to any region of Europe, Asia, and Africa. Still, this doesn't mean they did, nor does it mean they thrived there (they may have died out). Is it possible that kangaroos made it to Europe and died out? It is possible, and we would leave open such an option. What we do know is that kangaroos have thrived in Australia, where they currently live. In other words, marsupials can travel farther and faster than many placentals. This may help explain why marsupials dominated Australia.

Some may have migrated to certain areas but not to others. In other instances, some of these animals may have made it to a particular area and become extinct for various reasons — ultimately due to sin, of course! One objection to this is that we should find fossils of them if they lived in an area, but this is fallacious.[2] Paul Taylor states the following regarding this subject on fossils:

> But the expectation of such fossils is a presuppositional error. Such an expectation is predicated on the assumption that fossils form gradually and inevitably from animal populations. In fact, fossilization is by no means inevitable. It usually requires sudden, rapid burial. Otherwise the bones would decompose before permineralization. One ought likewise to ask why it is that, despite the fact that

---

2. Many fossils can be determined if they are in situ or were transported. But many are still difficult to ascertain. If something is found fossilized someplace, the one thing we can be certain about is its final burial place.

millions of bison used to roam the prairies of North America, hardly any bison fossils are found there. Similarly, lion fossils are not found in Israel even though we know that lions once lived there.[3]

Even recently, researchers at IUCN (International Union for Conservation of Nature) have tentatively declared that the West African Black Rhinoceros has gone extinct.[4] However, other rhinoceroses have continued in different areas of Africa and Asia. This is a good example of how a species can die out while another member of the same kind remains in other parts around the world. Could this have happened with other animals?[5] Surely it has.

Ice Age and Land Bridges to the Americas and Australia?

But how did they get to Australia? How did animals get to the Americas or remote islands?

Most creationists believe there was an Ice Age (see chapter 22).[6] If the globe simply cools down, that does not cause an ice age; instead, it causes a cool globe. An ice age requires warmer oceans and cool summers. Here is why: with warmer oceans there is more evaporation, which provides greater accumulation of snow during winter months.

With cool summers, it does not heat up enough to melt off the previous winter's snow accumulation. So during the next winter even more snow layers accumulate, their weight causing the previous winter's snow layers to compact into ice layers, thus eventually causing an ice age.

Most believe the Flood of Noah triggered the Ice Age. The rising magmas, lavas, and hot waters associated with continental plate movements would have caused ocean temperatures to rise. Also, fine ash from volcanic eruptions probably lingered in the upper atmosphere in post-Flood years, which, unlike a greenhouse effect, would reduce the sunlight for cooler summers. So the mechanism for such a rare event was in place due to Genesis 6–8.

---

3. *The New Answers Book 1*, Ken Ham, Gen. Ed., chapter by Paul Taylor: "How Did Animals Spread All Over the World from Where the Ark Landed?", Master Books, Green Forest, AK, 2006, page 144.
4. Matthew Knight, Western Black Rhino Declared Extinct, CNN, November 6, 2013, http://www.cnn.com/2011/11/10/world/africa/rhino-extinct-species-report/.
5. There are slim possibilities that they could be living elsewhere in remote areas, but the point is that many animals are going extinct even today, despite conservation efforts.
6. Ice Age is capitalized so as not to confuse it with the alleged numerous ice ages that supposedly occurred several times hundreds of millions of years ago, for which there isn't unequivocal evidence. The only Ice Age was triggered by the global Flood in Noah's day.

But what happens in an ice age? A lot of water is taken out of the ocean and deposited on land, so the ocean level drops.[7] This exposes land bridges. One well-known land bridge was the one that crossed what we call today "the Bering Strait" from Alaska to Russia, so it is easily feasible for animals to have walked from Asia to North and South America.

Other land bridges could also have connected the British Isles to the mainland. Much of the North Sea was formerly known as *Doggerland* or

Dogger Hills, including later shallow danger areas as it appears on old maps such as the one included here.

Other land bridges could have connected Japan to Korea, and potentially Japan to the mainland as well. It is possible that Australia could have been connected to Southeast Asia, although today this route is much deeper and may not have been open as long.

That area is known for tectonic activity, and we still see consequences of plate movements from the many earthquakes in Southeast Asia (e.g., consider the earthquake and

(Map by Guillaume De L'Isle in 1730 entitled *Les Isles Britannique ou font le Royaumes D'Angleterre*)

resultant tsunami in 2004). So the depth today may well be a result of activity *since* the Flood and Ice Age. But let's look at this in more detail.

OTHER NATURAL EFFECTS

We also need to keep in mind that tectonic activity has been occurring since the time of the Flood, causing earthquakes and other issues, and we have seen examples even today when faults shift — some even cause tsunamis. Two large earthquakes and resultant tsunamis have recently occurred in Eastern Japan in 2011 and Southeast Asia in 2004 that were due to ocean floor shifting.

---

7. Some estimates as low as 350 feet (~107 meters) lower than the current ocean level.

It is possible that some land bridges sank or were destroyed by these movements of the earth and ocean floor. Could this be the case with the connection between Australia and Southeast Asia since the time of the Ice Age? It seems to be a bit deeper today than what it likely was many years ago. Also, Scripture often records earthquakes (e.g., Amos 1:1[8]; Matthew 28:2[9]), and we need to keep in mind that many are not felt in other parts of the world — even very large ones! If tectonic activity reduced this bridge so that it wasn't open as long, this helps explain the following concept.

If this Southeast Asia–Australia land bridge was not in existence for as long as others, like the Bering Strait Bridge, that could explain why marsupials dominated the continent. Recall that marsupials travel farther faster compared to some placental animals, which lag behind. Marsupials could have made it across the land bridge during the migratory period, prior to the arrival of most placentals.

This makes much more sense than the common evolutionary model where marsupials evolved in Australia, which can't explain why marsupials like opossums came to North and South America. The common explanation that Australia and South America were linked is much harder to believe than a short-lived land bridge to Southeast Asia. Furthermore, if South America and Australia were linked (barring any global Flood, as the secularists teach), then why doesn't South America abound with marsupials?

The Ice Age may also have contributed something else to animal migrations. Generally speaking, reptiles are found in larger numbers and greater varieties in warmer climates, potentially like most dinosaurs, and would not thrive as well in the cold. It makes sense that they strayed from colder areas, died out, or their numbers were at least reduced. It also makes sense that mammals would thrive in colder climates.

Many believe that the post-Flood era has more extreme weather patterns (e.g., colder winters, higher elevations in area). In line with this, Adam and Eve did not wear clothes originally in the Garden of Eden, and God's creation was declared to be "very good." So, hypothetically speaking, it makes sense that people should have been able to fill the earth without much need for clothes, if any. After sin and the Curse, things changed, but the continent(s)

---

8. The words of Amos, who was among the sheepbreeders of Tekoa, which he saw concerning Israel in the days of Uzziah king of Judah, and in the days of Jeroboam the son of Joash, king of Israel, two years before the earthquake.

9. And behold, there was a great earthquake; for an angel of the Lord descended from heaven, and came and rolled back the stone from the door and sat on it (KJV).

and arrangements were not affected at the Curse (that we know of). So at least the pre-Flood topography was a little closer to a perfect world. The world after the Flood is a demolished remnant of the pre-Flood created continent(s).

Our current arrangements of continents and topography makes some areas colder and some hotter, due to different elevation, latitude, etc. Then there is Antarctica sitting at the South Pole! Many ideal habitats could have been completely eradicated during the Flood, never to be replaced. Insects that grew large in the past now die out by winter in many parts of the world before reaching maturity. Therefore, it is possible that the ones that matured more quickly, although they were smaller, laid their eggs prior to winter, and thus had a better chance of surviving.

Even desertification may have been triggered by changes in the weather. The new conditions could have wiped out populations in those areas or permitted a select few to survive. With variations of creatures after the Flood, they had to find a new niche or die out. The Ice Age and new weather patterns surely helped solidify where they lived and flourished from that time until now.

Could animals have migrated to a part of the world they were previously familiar with (latitude and longitude)? We've always wondered this. If a continent ended up at a particular place on the globe, and migratory animals thrived in those former areas before continental movement, is it possible that some attempted to migrate back to that original latitude and longitude? We would leave that option open.

In some cases, animals could have ridden on floating debris to make it to islands or other far-reaching places. Consider tsunamis, hurricanes, or other storms that force animals near coasts to grab onto things for their survival. They may be whisked out to sea only to arrive at another place to make their home.

WHAT WE SEE TODAY

Let's not forget another major factor to animal distribution — humans! Humans have been involved since the Flood. In fact, due to the ark, land animals and birds exist today.

Although rats had already traveled to many parts of the world, by the age of exploration (A.D. 1400–1800), these stowaways were easily distributed around the world in all the European exploits and trade. They were commonplace on most ships and ended up all over the world because men accidentally transported them. Think how many insects were surely taken to various places in the same manner.

Throughout history, people have brought plants and animals to new locations, and those organisms have become permanent populations, interacting with the original creatures. For example, it is claimed that the Romans brought pheasants (members of the chicken kind) to England, and they have since been regular inhabitants of various habitats. In fact, the Romans redistributed organisms from one side of the Roman Empire to the other.[10] When we were in Australia, and went out to Green Island, we found out that the coconuts that grew there were planted to provide food for shipwrecked people. Horses, wild boars, fallow deer, and wild goats are well-known examples of animals introduced to North America.

The point is that many animals and plants have been redistributed to places all over the world by mankind. Many were pets and went wild (such as dingoes); many were introduced as potential food sources (e.g., pigs), and so on. Imagine how much of this redistribution was done prior to the years when we actually started keeping track!

Conclusion

We know that a host of factors were involved with getting animals to various places. In fact, there are likely options that were not explored in this chapter.

The Bible gives us a framework in which to interpret this topic even though little is given by way of specifics. When it comes to answering questions like this, it is always best to uphold the Bible as our authority and reject ideas that are inconsistent with God's Word.

---

10. BBC Nature Wildlife website, "Pheasant," 2012, http://www.bbc.co.uk/nature/life/Common_Pheasant.

37 | Has Noah's Ark Been Found?

Bodie Hodge

Introduction

As with many questions, there are always debates, and the questions surrounding the search for Noah's ark are no different. However, one debate most people are probably *somewhat* familiar with, or have at the very least considered, is "Has Noah's Ark been found?" There is actually much more to this than meets the eye.

Entire volumes could be written on this subject of the ark, and some have been written already. However, the aim here is to provide some concise answers to the best of our ability to the many questions about the ark in an overview format.

Biblical Data

The Bible gives some information about the ark[1]:

- Its overall dimensions were 300 by 50 by 30 cubits (Genesis 6:15). Using the short or common cubit (~18 inches), it would have been about 450 feet long; or using a longer royal cubit (~20.4 inches), it would have been around 510 feet long[2]

---

1. Footnotes of the passages in the bulleted tabulation will not be given — most can be looked up easily in chapter 2.
2. Bodie Hodge, "How Long Was the Original Cubit?" *Answers* magazine, April–June 2007, p. 82, http://www.answersingenesis.org/articles/am/v2/n2/original-cubit.

- It was made of wood (gopher)[3] — Genesis 6:14
- It was covered with pitch inside and out — Genesis 6:14
- The ark had rooms — Genesis 6:14
- It had three decks — Genesis 6:16
- The ark had a covering — Genesis 8:13
- It had a window (Hebrew: *tsohar*, which means "noon"), which was finished to a cubit from above (think of something like a "ridge vent" on houses today for ventilation and lighting) and could be opened and shut (though Noah did not open it until 40 days after they landed on the mountains of Ararat — Genesis 6:16, 8:6
- The ark was made/fabricated, and done so with godly fear — Genesis 6:14–15, 6:22; Hebrews 11:7
- One of its purposes was to house land-dwelling, air-breathing animals during the Flood with a male-female pair from each of the representative kinds[4] of the unclean animals and seven individuals (or pairs — the meaning is debated) of the clean animals (likely three breeding pairs of these clean animals, as well as sacrificial individuals for after the Flood) — Genesis 6:20, 7:2–3, 21–23, 8:20
- Eight people survived on the ark: Noah, Shem, Ham, Japheth, and their respective wives — Genesis 7:7, 13; 2 Peter 2:5; 1 Peter 3:20
- It had a door, which was likely in the center deck as implied by the wording "lower, second, and third decks"; that is, one deck was lower than the door — Genesis 6:16
- The Lord shut the door to the ark from the outside (and it is probable that it too was sealed with pitch like the rest of the ark; otherwise, the rest of the pitch was pointless with these untreated seals) — Genesis 7:14, 16

---

3. Scholars have debated whether this was a particular type of wood or a means of processing wood (similar to the process of making plywood or pressed wood). Many ancient ships of antiquity had intricate wood that had been processed to make it stronger and more durable. Was that technology passed down through Noah and his sons? It is possible.

4. It is important to note that a kind is not necessarily what we know today as a "species." For more information, see Georgia Purdom and Bodie Hodge, "What are 'Kinds' in Genesis?" in *The New Answers Book 3*, Ken Ham, ed. (Green Forest, AR: Master Books, 2010), p. 39–48.

- The unrighteous sinners who did not go on the ark did not realize their doom, even up to the day that Noah boarded the ark — Matthew 24:38; Luke 17:27

- The ark was lifted off the ground by or on the fortieth day of the Flood and then floated high above land surface on the waters — Genesis 7:17

- It landed in the mountains of Ararat on the 150th day of the Flood (confirmed by calculating from Genesis 7:11 with a 360-day year) — Genesis 8:3–4

- The ark survived the Flood and Noah's family and the animals came out of the ark — Genesis 8:18–19

- They had remained on the ark for 370 days (or 371, depending on whether half days are rounded as full days or not) — Genesis 7:11, 8:14–16

- Noah's family left the ark and settled where there was fertile soil for Noah, who became a farmer — Genesis 8:19, 9:1, 20. This first settlement would have been in an east/west direction from Babel, the later place of rebellion — Genesis 11:2[5]

Notice that very little information is given about the ark's resting place (simply "mountains of Ararat"). However, there are some deductions and inferences that can be made from the Scriptures, which leads to the debate over the ark's landing site.

Where Are the Mountains of Ararat?

If someone had asked me years ago which mountain Noah's ark landed on, my response would have been a naïve, "Mt. Ararat, of course, because that is what the Bible says." However, a reading of Genesis 8:4 reveals no such thing. Instead, the text says the "mountains of Ararat," which refers to a range of mountains, not a specific mountain.

And this raises an important point. Christians always need to check information with the Scriptures. Let God be the authority, rather than man, on any subject. Believers know Noah's ark existed, and they can be certain of that because of God's Word, regardless of whether or not any remains of the

---

5. There could be more information from the biblical text, but this should be sufficient to give us the relevant highlights of ark information from the Bible.

ark are found. The all-knowing God says in His Word that the ark existed. There is no greater authority on this subject to whom one can appeal.

So where are the mountains of Ararat? The mountains of Ararat form a mountain range named after the Urartu people who settled in that region after the dispersion event at the Tower of Babel. In Hebrew, Ararat and Urartu are even spelled the same way. Hebrew does not have written vowels, so both are essentially spelled *rrt*.

Josephus, a Jewish historian living about 2,000 years ago, said that Armenia was made up of the descendants of Hul through Aram and Shem.[6] Armenia is the *later name* of the region of Urartu/Ararat, which is a specific part of the Armenian highlands. So it is understandable why Josephus used the later name, whereas Moses used the earlier name.

When Moses wrote Genesis around 1491–1451 B.C.,[7] he had been educated in Egypt as royalty (and he had been inspired by the Holy Spirit), so it is to be expected that he understood the geography of the peoples in the Middle East. In fact, other Bible writers like Isaiah and Jeremiah, who lived well after Moses but well before Josephus, were also familiar with the Ararat land and people:

> Now it came to pass, as he was worshiping in the house of Nisroch his god, that his sons Adrammelech and Sharezer struck him down with the sword; and they escaped into the land of Ararat. Then Esarhaddon his son reigned in his place (Isaiah 37:38).

> Set up a banner in the land, blow the trumpet among the nations! Prepare the nations against her, call the kingdoms together against her: Ararat, Minni, and Ashkenaz. Appoint a general against her; cause the horses to come up like the bristling locusts (Jeremiah 51:27).

This ancient region is basically in the eastern part of modern-day Turkey, Armenia, and western Iran.

THE DEBATE OVER WHICH MOUNTAIN

One of the most heated debates on this subject, though, is over which specific *mountain* the ark landed on within the mountain range. Of course, the

6. Bodie Hodge, "Josephus and Genesis Chapter Ten," Answers in Genesis, http://www. answersingenesis.org/articles/aid/v4/n1/josephus-and-genesis-chapter-ten#fnList_1_1.

7. James Ussher, *The Annals of the World*, Larry and Marion Pierce, eds. (Green Forest, AR: Master Books, 2003), p.39–47.

Bible does not say the ark landed on a specific mountain, but this is inferred. It is possible it landed in a lower area within the mountains of Ararat. However, the two most popular sites are:

> Mt. Ararat (Agri Dagh)
> Mt. Cudi (or Cudi Dagh; Cudi sounds like "Judi")

Many ark landing sites have been proposed over the years. One that has been rejected as a geological formation by most scholars in recent years is the Durupinar or Akyayla site in Turkey, near the Iran and Turkey border. That site consists of something akin to a boat-shaped feature that is readily recognizable (think of a football field-sized "footprint" in the shape of a boat).[8] The area contains several of these geological features and that is really all that it is.

Other sites that have attained some popularity but have been largely rejected by archaeologists, geologists, and researchers are Mt. Salvalon and Mt. Suleiman in Iran. It is unreasonable for these mountains to be included in the region of Ararat. There are other problems associated with them too.[9]

Ararat

The discussion following will focus on the debate over these two primary alleged resting places, Cudi and Ararat. Key verses in the Scriptures need to be consulted before proceeding:

> Then the ark rested in the seventh month, the seventeenth day of the month, on the mountains of Ararat. And the waters decreased continually until the tenth month. In the tenth month, on the first day of the month, the tops of the mountains were seen (Genesis 8:4–5).

The tops of the surrounding mountains were seen 74 days after the ark landed in the mountains of Ararat. This gives the impression that the mountain the ark landed on was much higher than the others. So the obvious choice is Mt. Ararat, which today towers excessively over all the other mountains in the region.[10]

---

8. Dr. Andrew Snelling, "Special Report: Amazing 'Ark' Exposé," *Creation ex nihilo*, Sept. 1, 1992, p. 26–38, http://www.answersingenesis.org/articles/cm/v14/n4/special-report-amazing-ark-expose.

9. Gordon Franz, "Did the BASE Institute Discover Noah's Ark in Iran?" Associates For Biblical Research, February 16, 2007, http://www.biblearchaeology.org/post/2007/02/Did-the-BASE-Institute-Discover-Noahs-Ark-in-Iran.aspx#Article.

10. This does not take into account the fact that some mountains of the region may have been raising and lowering during this transitional period of the Flood (Psalms 104:8–9).

Mt. Ararat is a large volcano that extends to a height of 16,854 feet! This is higher than any mountain in the 48 contiguous United States (Alaska does have a few mountains that are taller). Lesser Ararat (also known as Little Ararat) is another volcano that stands adjacent to Mt. Ararat and is 12,782 feet high, which is similar in height to a number of impressive peaks in the Rocky Mountains in the United States.

Many say that if the ark landed on Mt. Ararat, then it would have taken another two and one-half months for the water to reveal other surrounding mountain peaks. This seems logical. In fact, this is one reason some scholars argue that Mt. Ararat is the resting place for the ark.

Nevertheless, this is not the main reason why the search for the ark has focused on Ararat. The primary reason is because of the eyewitness accounts of ark sightings in recent times. B.J. Corbin wrote a book on the search for Noah's ark, which is helpful to anyone wanting to find out the details of various expeditions on Ararat. The book also discusses Mt. Cudi, the other proposed site. In the preface of the second edition, Corbin states:

> The only major reason to consider Mount Ararat is because of the few documented eyewitnesses. . . . There is a number of intriguing statements from individuals who indicate that there may be a barge-like or boat-like structure high on modern day Mount Ararat. These statements are really the primary basis for the search on Mount Ararat.[11]

Corbin, who has also been involved in the ark search on Ararat, confirms that the primary reason for the search on Ararat is because of the eyewitness accounts. There have been quite a few accounts including many reputable people in the 20th century, and Corbin in the preface to his book documents these as well. Furthermore, Ararat is covered with ice and glaciers all year, so this is an ideal hiding place (i.e., more difficult to locate) for an ark.

Even in some older literature, such as in the writings of Byzantine historian Philostorgius in the fifth century, Ararat was suggested as the ark's landing site. After the 13th century A.D., more sources affirm this mountain as the landing site.[12]

---

11. B.J. Corbin, *The Explorers of Ararat* (Long Beach, CA: Great Commission Illustrated Books, 1999), p. 8.
12. Richard Lanser, "The Case for Ararat," *Bible and Spade*, Fall 2006, p. 114–118.

Considering the scriptural basis of the highest mountain, the eyewitness accounts, and the historical sources, why would anyone look elsewhere for the landing site?

The Debate Gets Heated

On the other side of the debate, there are some objections to consider. First, even with all the eyewitness accounts of purportedly seeing something like the ark on Ararat, there has never been anything of substance ever found or documented to prove the ark landed on Ararat.

Also, the Bible does not explicitly say that it was *only* due to the water's recession (which all sides agree is indeed a factor) as to why mountaintops were seen. The text says "the tops of the mountains were seen" (Genesis 8:5). This involves two things: water level (1) *and* visibility (2).

This second factor that is often overlooked is the conditions that may affect visibility. The warmer ocean water (which is expected from the Flood with continental shifting, rising basalts from the mantle, and possibly some nuclear decay would surely generate heat and volcanism) gives off vapors and mists that form low-lying fog and clouds. Hence, visibility would likely be rather low. Genesis 8:5 may well be discussing the state of visibility and atmospheric condition regarding clouds and fog from the heated ocean just as much at it discusses water level.

One way or another, this passage (Genesis 8:5[13]) cannot be so easily used to affirm a landing spot on the highest peak. It *may* still be the highest peak, but one cannot be dogmatic. Another factor needs to be considered here too — if it were the highest peak, what was the highest peak *at this time*?

One common objection is that if the ark landed at such a high altitude, how did the animals get off the ark and make their way down from this deadly mountain? And how did man and the animals at that high altitude survive all that time without sufficient oxygen after striking ground (day 150) until being called off the ark (day 370)? Oxygen tanks would not be necessary when floating on the surface of the water, because oxygen percentages are based on sea level (about 21 percent at sea level). If the ark were at 16,000 feet above sea level, then when the water receded, oxygen would be

---

13. And the waters decreased continually until the tenth month. In the tenth month, on the first day of the month, the tops of the mountains were seen.

a requirement because serious problems can occur due to lack of oxygen at altitudes over 12,000 feet.[14]

Another oft-used argument is that pillow lavas should be found on Mt. Ararat if it formed underwater. For those unfamiliar with pillow lavas, they are formed when a volcanic eruption occurs underwater. The lavas that come in contact with water cause it to harden quickly in masses that look "like a pillow."[15]

Some believe there may possibly be some pillow lavas on Ararat, as reported by Corbin[16] and through observation attributed specifically to Clifford Burdick. However, if this volcano was formed in the Flood before day 150 when the ark ran aground, then such pillow lavas should have extensively covered it. But this is not the case. Rather, there is a severe lack of evidence that this mountain was ever covered by water. There are some pillow lavas on Ararat at very high altitudes (e.g., 14,000 feet)[17], but the same characteristic features of pillow lavas also form when lavas meet ice and snow, which may be a better explanation of these specific pillow lavas at high altitudes on Ararat where it is capped in snow and ice.[18]

Another argument must also be considered: Mt. Ararat and Lesser Ararat are volcanoes. They have been identified as having been formed after the Flood because they sit on top of fossil-bearing sediment from the Flood.[19] Classed as Pleistocene rock, Ararat is regarded by most creation researchers as post-Flood continuous with the Ice Age that followed the Flood.[20]

---

14. It is possible that this volcano was much smaller originally and later post-Flood eruptions are what caused it to become so large and so high. But if this were the case, eruptions should have burned the wooden vessel to oblivion, so no remains of the ark should ever be found on Ararat. It is possible that petrification of the wood could take place at such temperatures; however, being coated in pitch, which is typically rather flammable, and being made of seasoned dry wood, it makes more sense that the ark would be burned in the presence of volcanic heat, not petrified.

15. There are also other underwater geological evidences that should be present such as interbedded water-deposited volcaniclastics and pyroclastics, but these do not cover the mountain either.

16. Corbin, *The Explorers of Ararat*, p. 326.

17. Ibid., p. 326.

18. "Ararat," NoahsArkSearch.Com, http://www.noahsarksearch.com/ararat.htm.

19. Y. Yilmaz, Y. Güner, and F. Şaroğlu, "Geology of the Quaternary Volcanic Centres of the East Anatolia," *Journal of Volcanology and Geothermal Research* 85 (1998): 173–210.

20. For more on the post-Flood Ice Age see Michael Oard, "Where Does the Ice Age Fit?" in *The New Answers Book 1*, ed. Ken Ham (Green Forest, AR: Master Books, 2006).

By this argument, these volcanoes *did not exist* at the time the ark landed. When viewing these volcanoes from above, one can readily see the lava and volcanic flow from the volcanoes *overlaying* the foothills and plains that make up part of the region of the mountains of Ararat. From the account of Scripture, the mountains of Ararat were made by day 150 of the Flood (Genesis 8:4) and the ark landed on day 150 of the Flood (Genesis 8:4), so these volcanoes had to come *after* both the mountain formation and ark landing to have their volcanic flows sitting aloft on the foothills of the mountains of Ararat today.[21]

Furthermore, fossils are readily found within the mountains of Ararat, but they are rare or absent entirely on Mt. Ararat. Some claim to have found some, but there is no documentation for *in situ* (in their original place) fossils on Ararat. The layers on Ararat are volcanic, not sedimentary.

Habermehl has reviewed the search for Noah's ark.[22] Though we do not agree with all of Habermehl's assertions,[23] she does provide a thorough review of evidences and arguments regarding Ararat and Cudi.

Cudi

The other potential mountain that has long been proposed is Mt. Cudi. Crouse and Franz point out that this mountain has gone by various names

---

21. It is possible these volcanos were smaller at the time of the Flood and further eruptions have covered or destroyed any remains of the ark at the previous height of the mountains, but if this were the case, the ark did not come to rest on Ararat as we know it, nor would we know if it were taller than any other mountain in the range at that time.

22. Anne Habermehl, "A Review of the Search for Noah's Ark," in *Proceedings of the Sixth International Conference on Creationism*, ed. Andrew A. Snelling (Pittsburg, PA: Creation Science Fellowship; Dallas, TX: Institute for Creation Research, 2008), p. 485–502.

23. As one example, she holds the position that Noah and his family settled rather close to the ark and hence uses Genesis 11:2 as a basis to relocate Babel to an east-west direction of the ark landing site. Many scholars have pointed out the fallacy in this east-west direction, as this is in reference to Noah's *first* settlement after the Flood (see footnote 7 or Adam Clarke's Commentary on Genesis 11:2, http://www.sacred-texts.com/bib/cmt/clarke/gen011.htm). Noah's initial settlement is unknown, but it was a place that was fertile enough to farm. Noah and his family were also able to live in tents. One cannot assume this was essentially still at the ark landing site, as Noah and his immediate family were told to come off the ark (Genesis 8:16) and fill the earth (Genesis 9:1.) It was not until Noah had (in some cases) great, great, great, great grandsons that the rebellion occurred at Babel. Also, why live in tents when there is a huge wooden mansion to live in (i.e., the ark) or, at the very least, wood enough to build a proper shelter? Furthermore, Noah had his pick of the new world, so why remain at or near the rough mountainous area of the ark landing site and not find a place to start a new beginning, especially somewhere suitable for farming?

such as Judi, Cardu, Quardu, Kardu, Ararat, Nipur, Gardyene, and others.[24] Cudi, being in the mountains of the Ararat region, also sits in a "specified" range of mountains known as the Gordian, Kurdish, Gordyene, and others.

This is important to know, as many ancient sources say the ark landed on this specific portion of the mountains. Both Ararat and Cudi are in the basic region of where the Urartu lived, but whereas Ararat is referred to in some early literature (5th century at the earliest) as the ark's landing site, Mt. Cudi is referred to as the landing site in many more and far earlier sources.

In *Bible and Spade*, there were cases presented for Ararat (Lanser) and for Cudi (Crouse and Franz), along with other pertinent articles on the subject.[25] Crouse and Franz did an extensive historical review referring to numerous ancient and modern sources that point to Cudi. These include direct and indirect allusions to Cudi from Jewish (e.g., Josephus, Targums, Book of Jubilees, and Benjamin of Tudela), Christian (e.g., Theophilus of Antioch of Syria, Julius Africanus, Eusebius, and several others), pagan (e.g., Berossus and The Epic of Gilgamesh), and Muslim sources (e.g., Koran [Qur'an], Al-Mas'udi, Zakariya ibn Muhammad al Qazvini).

Cudi is much lower in elevation, being about 6,800 feet high, so it would not have been so difficult to herd animals down the mountain. There would have been no problems with low oxygen levels, and this mountain is not a volcano that is resting upon the top of the mountains of Ararat (like volcanic Ararat is). But it was easily in a place where pieces could be looted or taken as relics. According to Crouse and Franz, the Muslims claimed to have taken the last of the major beams for use in a mosque.[26]

The legends and lore associated with this mountain still persist in the area as well. Christians, Jews, Muslims, and others still came together for a yearly celebration in honor of the sacrifices made by Noah after the Flood as

---

24. Bill Crouse and Gordon Franz, "Mount Cudi — True Mountain of Noah's Ark," *Bible and Spade*, Fall 2006, p. 99–111, http://www.biblearchaeology.org/publications/bas19_4.pdf.
25. Ibid.
26. One also has to consider the amount of deterioration the wooden vessel underwent over 4,350 years. If kept frozen or in a dry, arid climate, a wooden ark could last quite a long time. However, in mid-temperate areas with alternating wet-dry conditions, it should not last long at all (think of a barn in the Midwest; one must work hard to keep such a thing for even 200 years). Being coated with pitch helps, but even that is not a perfect preservative. A perfectly engineered ark would have the pitch's usefulness end at the end of the Flood (~370 days).

recorded by a historian nearly 100 years ago (W.A. Wigram).[27] There is even a place on Cudi that is the traditional landing spot of the ark on a particular ridge. So is this the absolute landing site? We simply do not know.

CONCLUSION

Has Noah's ark been found? The obvious answer is that people would not be asking this question if Noah's ark really had been found! It would likely be the find of a lifetime.

Both Ararat and Cudi have had their share of popularity over the years. And both have strong supporters on their side. When viewing the evidence through the lenses of Scripture, the more logical choice is that of Cudi, not modern-day, volcanic Mt. Ararat that sits on top of fossil-bearing sediment from the Flood.

But would we be dogmatic that Cudi was the landing spot? Not at all. The Bible simply does not say, and though many ancient sources point to Cudi, these sources are not absolute, while Scripture is. The fact is that there has been no indisputable evidence of Noah's ark having been found anywhere (outside of Scripture, which itself is sufficient proof that the ark existed, as there is no greater authority on any subject than God). But is such external evidence needed? Not at all.

To summarize, there was so much more that could have been discussed, but with such limitations, a brief overview of the debate is the best that can be hoped for in a single chapter of a book. My hope is that this brief introduction will encourage you to learn more about the subject, and that you will give glory to God when doing so. Much more research on the topic of the ark's landing site needs to be done, be it on Ararat, Cudi, or other places.

Would undisputed evidence of the ark be of value? Absolutely. But is it necessary for one's faith? Not in the least. So do not forget this point: the Bible is true, and Christ is who He says He is, regardless of whether anyone finds the remains of the ark or not.

Further Reading:

1. Bible and Spade Debate: http://www.biblearchaeology.org/publications/bas19_4.pdf.
2. *The Explorers of Ararat*, B.J. Corbin (Long Beach, CA: Great Commission Illustrated Books, 1999).

---

27. Habermehl, "A Review of the Search for Noah's Ark."

3. Noah's Ark Search website: http://www.noahsarksearch.com/.

4. Rick Lanser of the Associate for Biblical Research has published a four-part series on the group's website entitled "The Landing-Place of Noah's Ark: Testimonial, Geological and Historical Considerations," parts 1–4, available at http://www.biblearchaeology.org/category/flood.aspx.

I would like to extend a special thanks to Dr. Andrew Snelling for his guidance on this chapter.

38 | WHAT ABOUT THE WINDOW, PITCH, DOOR, 'GOPHER' WOOD, AND OTHER ARK FEATURES?

KEN HAM AND BODIE HODGE

The size and shape of Noah's ark are not the only things unbelievers tend to attack. I've seen hosts of attacks on a variety of features and aspects of the ark. Some attacks are completely without warrant and not worth comment. However, some need to be addressed. So let's "dive in!"

WINDOW OF THE ARK

The Bible says there is a window on the ark. The Bible says:

> You shall make a window for the ark, and you shall finish it to a cubit from above; and set the door of the ark in its side. You shall make it with lower, second, and third decks (Genesis 6:16).

> So it came to pass, at the end of forty days, that Noah opened the window of the ark which he had made (Genesis 8:6).

Many criticisms of the ark designs were summed up in this question: "Where is the little window at?" As you look at the design, you might concur, and say, "I don't see the window either, so what is going on."

This is because most people don't realize what the "window" is. The Hebrew word for window is *tsohar*. It means "noon" or "midday." We simply translate it as "window." This *window* is something that runs along the *overhead* position (top, middle) of the ark that allows lighting and ventilation into the ark, while keeping bad weather out!

We do something similar when we build many houses today. We put a ridge vent on the top to do the very same thing.

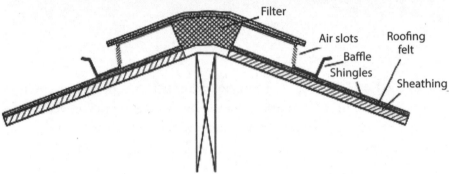

So the window is what you see along many ark images that run the course of the top middle and that is finished to "a cubit from above." Noah can easily open this area up for a better view too when he is analyzing the post-Flood world.

DOOR OF THE ARK

Few unbelievers question that there was a door in the ark, so that is not the criticism. But we do receive other questions like, *In what level of the three decks of the ark was the door? Was it under the water level? How did Noah seal up the door of the ark with pitch, when he was inside of it?* Let's briefly *swim* through these questions!

What Level Was the Door Placed?

The Bible says:

> You shall make a window for the ark, and you shall finish it
> to a cubit from above; and set the door of the ark in its side. You
> shall make it with lower, second, and third decks (Genesis 6:16).

Obviously, the door was in the *side* of the ship, not the front nor back. Also by the terminology of "lower," second, and third decks, it sounds as though the door was on the second level. So as you come into the ark at the door, there is one level that is "lower."

Was the Door under the Water Level?

It makes more sense to have the door above the *draft* level (sometimes spelled *draught*). *Draft* is how much of the ship is below the water level. A ship can't float if the water depth is less than the *draft*; otherwise the ship runs aground.

With this in mind, would the door of the ark on the second level be above the draft? The dimensions of the ark, based on the long cubit, are 510 x 85 x 51 feet. This is 51 feet of total vertical height of the ark from the keel to the window.

Just doing a remedial calculation for three decks, this is 51 divided by 3, which equals 17 feet per deck. If the lower deck is 17 feet, then the door must be higher than 17 feet (this is a minimum). Is this feasible?

Let's compare this to a big, heavy cruise ship. The *Emerald Princess* cruise ship is an 113,000-ton ship. Its height is 195 feet but it only has a draft of 26 feet![1] Naturally, it can vary depending on weight. But only about 13 percent of this ship is under the water line!

If this same percentage (13 percent) is applied to the ark, then that would only be about 6–7 feet of draft! Even with variation in the weight, this is still no problem, being well above 17 feet. Though there are many factors to calculate a proper draft, I expect it to be a bit more than this. But the second level of the ark for the door is perfectly reasonable.

Some have suggested that draft was 15 cubits (half of the ark) because of Genesis 7:20,[2] where the water covered the mountains by at least 15 cubits, though we're not convinced that we can directly relate this to the draft. Even so, let's say the draft level had the door under the water line. It was *the Lord* who shut them in. So it is still *not* a problem, as such a remedial job by the Creator God would be done perfectly (Deuteronomy 32:4[3]).

---

1. Linda Garrison, "Emerald Princess Cruise Ship," About Travel website, accessed, October 9, 2015, http://cruises.about.com/od/princesscruises/ig/Emerald-Princess.-1wQ/index.htm.
2. The waters prevailed fifteen cubits upward, and the mountains were covered.
3. He is the Rock, His work is perfect; for all His ways are justice, a God of truth and without injustice; righteous and upright is He.

HOW CAN NOAH SEAL UP THE DOOR OF THE ARK WITH PITCH (GENESIS 6:14, TO WATERPROOF IT) . . . WHEN HE WAS INSIDE OF THE ARK?

This question is rather easy to answer. Consider what we just read (it was the Lord's job to shut them in!) and what the Bible says:

> So those that entered, male and female of all flesh, went in as God had commanded him; and the LORD shut him in (Genesis 7:16).

The Lord shut Noah and his family in the ark. So *Who* sealed up the door with pitch to shut Noah in? The Lord. Is the answer that simple? Yes. The Bible doesn't say, but Noah likely did the final pitching for the *inside* of the door, since the ark was coated with pitch inside and out (Genesis 6:14[4]).

PITCH

Where did the pitch come from to seal up the ark in the first place? We make pitch today mainly from petroleum products, but it can also be made from plants.

Regarding petroleum pitch, is this a problem? Many unbelievers tend to think it is. They argue that Christians point out that petroleum was largely formed during the Flood. But the Flood hadn't occurred yet, so where did this pitch come from?

Petroleum Pitch

It is possible that a certain amount of petroleum was in existence from creation or developed due to pre-Flood processes. And Noah could have utilized this, although we tend to think Noah didn't. More on this in a moment.

The bulk of the petroleum we have today was from the Flood. Think of it like this — organic material from the ocean and land was buried by sediment-rich water (think vegetation, microorganism, algae and animals, shells, fish, etc.).[5] As this water seeped down into the earth, it transported the organic material elsewhere and replaced the organic material (in things like trees, shells, and so on) to produce fossils. These fossils are now the

---

4. Make yourself an ark of gopherwood; make rooms in the ark, and cover it inside and outside with pitch.
5. Coal wasn't fossilized into things like limestone and thus it retained much of the organic material.

remains of once organic things that are now made of material like limestone. The organic material from micro-organisms, marine organisms, trees, algae, etc. accumulates in trapped pools under the surface and is essentially what we call crude oil/petroleum. They are simply hydrocarbons.

The Flood buried the world's supply of most organic material at the time of Noah so that is where most petroleum that we tap into comes from today. Though pitch can be made from petroleum (and coal tar), Noah likely used a different kind of pitch.

Plant Pitch

Pitch can also be made from plants. It is also called *resin* and in some cases *rosin*. A number of ancient wooden ships were covered with pitch, and even canoes were often sealed with plant pitch like that made from balsam fir. This is quite logical with wooden ships to help seal them up.

The Bible points out that when Noah was building the ark, he was to cover it with pitch, inside and outside. Why inside? During longer construction periods, having things pitched on the inside helped preserve the integrity of the wood from weathering. This could be one reason for the command as well as the fact that internal pitching adds another layer of sealing from the water outside the ark.

There were plenty of plants pre-Flood as witnessed from the Flood sediment, so plant-based pitch was likely what Noah used as opposed to petroleum-based pitch.

Gopher Wood

What is gopher wood? Great question. In the past, many thought this may have been a type of tree (think of oak, pine, hickory, etc.). However, many now lean against that interpretation.

The prevailing thought now is that it was a way the wood was *processed*. Processed wood is nothing new. Though many of you may be familiar with some processed wood and may not realize it! Did you know that *plywood* or *pressed wood/particleboard* or *wood veneer* is merely processed wood. Most houses built today utilize processed wood — even processed particleboard beams such as floor joists!

Working with wood like this was common in the past. Certain ancient ships also utilized incredible types of wood processing technology. There have been ancient ships found with some almost unbelievable planking styles that helped make the ship structurally sound, lighter, and even proved to be superior in waterproofing! Ark researcher Tim Lovett comments:

> Ancient shipbuilders usually began with a shell of planks (strakes) and then built internal framing (ribs) to fit inside. This is the complete reverse of the familiar European method where planking was added to the frame. In shell-first construction, the planks must be attached to each other somehow. Some used overlapping (clinker) planks that were dowelled or nailed, others used rope to sew the planks together. The ancient Greeks used a sophisticated system where the planks were interlocked with thousands of precise mortise and tenon joints. The resulting hull was strong enough to ram another ship, yet light enough to be hauled onto a beach by the crew.[6]

The Age of Exploration by Europeans lost much of this technology when ships were made via carvel planking techniques, which were simple and quick but prone to problems. We suggest that many of these incredible planking styles may have been carry-overs from the technology Noah and his three sons had. It could easily have been passed along to subsequent generations. Keep in mind that Noah lived 350 years after the Flood (Genesis 9:28[7]) and Shem lived 500 years after the Flood (Genesis 11:10–11[8]). I am not sure how long Japheth and Ham lived after the Flood; it could have been as long or even much longer than Shem!

Free For All' In The Ark?

Certain portrayals of the ark have animals in a "free for all" going all over the ark — bathtub arks especially! However, the Bible indicates the ark had rooms. The Bible says:

> Make yourself an ark of gopherwood; make rooms in the ark, and cover it inside and outside with pitch (Genesis 6:14).

---

6. Tim Lovett, "Thinking Outside the Box," Answers in Genesis, https://answersingenesis.org/noahs-ark/thinking-outside-the-box/.

7. And Noah lived after the flood three hundred and fifty years.

8. This is the genealogy of Shem: Shem was one hundred years old, and begot Arphaxad two years after the flood. After he begot Arphaxad, Shem lived five hundred years, and begot sons and daughters.

So the animals were divided in the ark. Many could have shared rooms with others. Originally, all animals were vegetarian (Genesis 1:30[9]), and even though all flesh had corrupted itself on the earth (Genesis 6:12[10]), the Lord brought specific animals to Noah for survival. It makes more sense that God sent animals to Noah that were still in accordance with Genesis 1:30,[11] thus conflicts of carnivory may not have been what many think they were on board the ark. Nonetheless, the animals were separated into rooms/cages.

Some animals can destroy wood cages easily — like rabbits and woodpeckers! I grew up on a farm, and rabbits would chew through wood cages quickly without the wire mesh affixed in the cages. But having cages reinforced with iron is not a problem. Iron working had preceded the ark for quite some time (Genesis 4:22[12]). Thus, cages with some iron reinforcements are not a problem. Keep in mind that many animals could have hibernated as well during the voyage for safekeeping.

Iron Tools

If the Iron Age were after the Flood with Noah's descendants, then where would Noah get the tools necessary to build the ark? This is a misconception based on the world's story of origins. In the world's story, people have to become smart enough to develop the technology to do iron working. This is based on the evolutionary story where man supposedly evolved from apes and had to get smarter.

However, in the Christian account, iron and bronze working was well before the Flood (Genesis 4:22[13]). This technology passed through the Flood and what occurred next was why some peoples lost this technology and had to regain it — that was the scattering at Babel.

Not every family at Babel knew iron or bronze working; just like today, not every family alive knows iron working or bronze working! So at the scattering at Babel, those who had a family member who knew the art could

---

9. "Also, to every beast of the earth, to every bird of the air, and to everything that creeps on the earth, in which there is life, I have given every green herb for food"; and it was so.
10. So God looked upon the earth, and indeed it was corrupt; for all flesh had corrupted their way on the earth.
11. See footnote 9.
12. And as for Zillah, she also bore Tubal-Cain, an instructor of every craftsman in bronze and iron. And the sister of Tubal-Cain was Naamah.
13. Ibid.

easily retain it for his descendants wherever they initially moved from Babel. Once they were on their feet and settled in, they could pick it back up.

Others, who did not know the art of iron or bronze working, would lose that technology for their families until later contact with those who did have active iron or bronze working that would permit them to regain this technology. But with all this in mind, Noah likely used iron or bronze-based tools.

PLANTS/SEEDS ON THE ARK?

Did Noah take plants and seeds on the ark? The Bible does not say directly. Though the foodstuffs for Noah's family and many animals were surely grains, those are seeds (Genesis 6:21[14]), and many of those could have been utilized after the Flood.

Noah surely planned ahead. He knew they would come off the ark and have to begin again. If you were thrust into that situation, would you take seeds and plants (bulbs, saplings, some potted planted, domestic plants, etc.) to be ready to start again? I suggest Noah was prepared by taking seeds and plants for the new world (particularly food plants).

Keep in mind that Noah became a farmer once he settled. The Bible says:

> And Noah began to be a farmer, and he planted a vineyard (Genesis 9:20).

Seeds would have been extremely valuable at this stage of human history. Surely Noah was prepared.

---

14. "And you shall take for yourself of all food that is eaten, and you shall gather it to yourself; and it shall be food for you and for them."

39 | HOW MANY PEOPLE DIED IN THE FLOOD?

KEN HAM AND BODIE HODGE

INTRODUCTION

For years, we've heard this question. We think it is more of a *curious* question rather than a question that attacks the authority of God's Word. Whatever answer we give is speculative because the Bible simply doesn't tell us — though an educated guess may be in order here.

BIBLICAL INFORMATION

The Bible reveals information that is useful to the discussion. For example, the Bible indicates there are ten generations from Adam to Noah. We also know that the timeline from Adam to the Flood was 1,656 years.[1] We also know that the lineage from Adam through Cain to Naamah (in Genesis 4) was only eight generations.

We also know that generation times seemed far slower than today — consider that Noah did not have children until he was 500 years old! Other patriarchs often waited to have children as well.

POPULAR ESTIMATES

As you can see from the following table, estimates for the pre-Flood population are based on very little information, since Genesis 1–6 doesn't give extensive family size and growth information. Genesis also indicates that in

---

1. By adding up the ages of the sons from creation week to Noah's oldest son Japheth (born when Noah was 500 years old), we get 1,556. The Flood began when Noah was 600 years old, so add 100 years to 1,556 and you get 1,656.

283

Patriarchal Tables*

Patriarch	Age	Age of Son**	Bible Reference
Adam	930	130	Genesis 5:3–4
Seth	912	105	Genesis 5:6–8
Enosh	905	90	Genesis 5:9–11
Cainan	910	70	Genesis 5:12–14
Mahalalel	895	65	Genesis 5:15-17
Jared	962	162	Genesis 5:18–20
Enoch	365 (translated)	65	Genesis 5:21–23
Methuselah	969	187	Genesis 5:25–27
Lamech	777	182	Genesis 5:28–31
Noah	950	500	Genesis 5:32, 9:29

* Bible verse footnotes are not given for the table.

** In the lineage of Adam to Japheth; Japheth was Noah's oldest born when Noah was 500 years old. Shem was born when Noah was 502 being that he was 100, two years after the Flood.

Noah's lineage children were being born when their fathers were between the ages of 65 (Enoch to Methuselah) to 500 (Noah to the first of his three sons).

How many generations were there in other lineages outside of Cain's recorded lineage to Naamah? We don't know. We know the line from Adam to Noah was living upward of 900 years, but we can't be certain everyone lived this long. How often and how many children were born? We don't know? What were the death/mortality rates? We don't know.

Despite this lack of information, some estimates have been done. Tom Pickett gives a range of about 5 to 17 billion people.[2] This is based on various population growth rates and generations of 16–22 prior to the Flood. Recall that Noah was in the 10th generation and Naamah was the 8th generation, so this may be well beyond the higher end of the population maximum.

Consider that we have had about 100 generations or less *since* Noah and our world population is only about 7 billion in A.D. 2015,[3] so these numbers seem considerably high.

---

2. Tom Pickett, "Population of the Pre-Flood World," www.ldolphin.org/pickett.html.

3. I, Bodie, have a continuous lineage (long and short) from Adam to Noah, through Japheth down through Woden to Alfred the Great down to Edward the Longshanks and his son Thomas the Earl of Norfolk down to my mother. The long yields Noah as my 90th great grandfather; the short yields Noah as my 74th great grandfather, both through Japheth.

More reasonable numbers come from Dr. Henry Morris who had conservative estimates as low as 235 million people. He also calculated rates based on modern population growth, giving about 3 billion people.[4] John Morris reports estimates that there were about 350 million people pre-Flood.[5] Based on these estimates, pre-Flood populations could have peaked from the low hundred millions to 3 billion people.

These would be reasonable peak or maximum numbers pre-Flood, though we still tend to think these are rather high for the population at the time of the Flood. As we have seen, there were only eight generations from Adam through Cain to Naamah. So if this stat were used instead of ten generations, the numbers would go down much further.

Did you realize that one of the few commands given to mankind through Adam was "to be fruitful and multiply" (Genesis 1:28[6])? If man had intense disobedience to God (e.g., Genesis 6:5,[7] 6:12[8]) 120 years prior to the Flood (Genesis 6:3[9]), are we to believe they were still being obedient to God's command here? Likely not!

Consider Joshua's Generation

We know of Joshua's genealogy, and he was contemporaneous with Moses, yet younger. His lineage is revealed in 1 Chronicles 7:22–27:

> Then Ephraim [1st generation] their father mourned many days, and his brethren came to comfort him. And when he went in to his wife, she conceived and bore a son; and he called his name Beriah [2nd gen.], because tragedy had come upon his house. Now his daughter was Sheerah, who built Lower and Upper Beth Horon and Uzzen Sheerah; and Rephah [3rd gen.] was his son, as well as Resheph, and Telah [4th gen.] his son, Tahan [5th gen.]

4. H. Morris, *Biblical Cosmology and Modern Science* (Grand Rapids, MI: Baker Book House, 1970), p. 77–78.
5. J. Morris, *The Young Earth* (Green Forest, AR: Master Books, 2002), p. 71.
6. Then God blessed them, and God said to them, "Be fruitful and multiply; fill the earth and subdue it; have dominion over the fish of the sea, over the birds of the air, and over every living thing that moves on the earth."
7. Then the Lord saw that the wickedness of man was great in the earth, and that every intent of the thoughts of his heart was only evil continually.
8. So God looked upon the earth, and indeed it was corrupt; for all flesh had corrupted their way on the earth.
9. And the Lord said, "My Spirit shall not strive with man forever, for he is indeed flesh; yet his days shall be one hundred and twenty years."

his son, Laadan [6th gen.] his son, Ammihud [7th gen.] his son, Elishama [8th gen.] his son, Nun [9th gen.] his son, and Joshua [10th gen.] his son.

Joshua was the tenth generation from Joseph (having his son Ephraim as the first generation). So Joshua, who was contemporaneous with Moses and yet was the tenth generation, led the fourth generation and their descendants into conquest of the Promised Land. But *note* that Joshua was the tenth generation — and Noah was in the tenth generation too.

The Bible reveals how many males of fighting age existed among the Israelites at the Exodus. There were 603,550 males over 20 years of age in Numbers 1:1–3,[10] 2:32,[11] though this is an exceptional growth rate.

Consider the Lord's prophetic promise to Abraham and then Isaac was that *God Himself* would increase them (Genesis 13:16,[12] 22:17,[13] 26:4[14]; Exodus 1:7[15]; Deuteronomy 1:10[16]) — and this came true.

God is the one responsible for multiplying Abraham's descendants, and this exceeding increase came to Israel. The Egyptians recognized this and wanted to do something about this population explosion occurring with the Israelites — hence enslaving them and trying to kill their baby boys in an effort to control them!

So this was an exceptional growth rate discussed in the Bible, but this would yield a population (if ~equal male to female) just over 1.2 million

---

10. Now the LORD spoke to Moses in the Wilderness of Sinai, in the tabernacle of meeting, on the first day of the second month, in the second year after they had come out of the land of Egypt, saying: "Take a census of all the congregation of the children of Israel, by their families, by their fathers' houses, according to the number of names, every male individually, from twenty years old and above — all who are able to go to war in Israel. You and Aaron shall number them by their armies."

11. These are the ones who were numbered of the children of Israel by their fathers' houses. All who were numbered according to their armies of the forces were six hundred and three thousand five hundred and fifty.

12. And I will make your descendants as the dust of the earth; so that if a man could number the dust of the earth, then your descendants also could be numbered.

13. Blessing I will bless you, and multiplying I will multiply your descendants as the stars of the heaven and as the sand which is on the seashore; and your descendants shall possess the gate of their enemies.

14. And I will make your descendants multiply as the stars of heaven; I will give to your descendants all these lands; and in your seed all the nations of the earth shall be blessed.

15. But the children of Israel were fruitful and increased abundantly, multiplied and grew exceedingly mighty; and the land was filled with them.

16. The LORD your God has multiplied you, and here you are today, as the stars of heaven in multitude.

people and their children in these ten generations. This almost sets an extreme upper limit, as the Lord was not increasing the people before the Flood, as He did with the Israelites. Thus, we tentatively suggest the pre-Flood population was far less than this at its peak — perhaps just a few hundred thousand. Allow us to elaborate.

OBEDIENT TO 'BE FRUITFUL AND MULTIPLY'?

Childbirths were likely reduced — people were making a name for themselves being *men of renown* (Genesis 6:4[17]), which means they would hardly care or have time for any children! With people living lives that are about themselves, they rarely care for children — even in our culture today!

With pre-Flood wickedness (Genesis 6:5[18]) abounding (which often includes sodomy/homosexuality — Genesis 13:13[19]; see also Judges 19–20), this would naturally reduce the possibility of children and population growth. This would be especially true if this population reduction were consistent in the century leading up to the Flood.

Let us also not forget who gets the brunt of an evil culture. It is almost always the children! This is how Pharaoh dealt with the Israelites — killing baby boys (Exodus 1:16,[20] 1:22[21]). The Canaanites were sacrificing their children (Leviticus 18:21,[22] 20:2–5[23]). This is what we saw with Herod —

---

17. The Nephilim were on the earth in those days, and also afterward, when the sons of God came in to the daughters of men, and they bore children to them. Those were the mighty men who were of old, men of renown (NASB).
18. Then the LORD saw that the wickedness of man was great in the earth, and that every intent of the thoughts of his heart was only evil continually.
19. But the men of Sodom were exceedingly wicked and sinful against the LORD.
20. And he said, "When you do the duties of a midwife for the Hebrew women, and see them on the birthstools, if it is a son, then you shall kill him; but if it is a daughter, then she shall live."
21. So Pharaoh commanded all his people, saying, "Every son who is born you shall cast into the river, and every daughter you shall save alive."
22. And you shall not let any of your descendants pass through the fire to Molech, nor shall you profane the name of your God: I am the LORD.
23. Again, you shall say to the children of Israel: "Whoever of the children of Israel, or of the strangers who dwell in Israel, who gives any of his descendants to Molech, he shall surely be put to death. The people of the land shall stone him with stones. I will set My face against that man, and will cut him off from his people, because he has given some of his descendants to Molech, to defile My sanctuary and profane My holy name. And if the people of the land should in any way hide their eyes from the man, when he gives some of his descendants to Molech, and they do not kill him, then I will set My face against that man and against his family; and I will cut him off from his people, and all who prostitute themselves with him to commit harlotry with Molech.

A sacrificed young girl in Peru

killing baby boys (Matthew 2:16[24]). Pagan cultures often sacrificed their children.

This is what we saw in modern times as well with Hitler when he killed upward of 13 million Jews, Poles, Slavs, and Gypsies, and their children were not exempt! This is what we see in our own modern secular culture where millions of babies are aborted (murdered through child sacrifice) every year through state-funded organizations like Planned Parenthood! The population of the USA has lost over 55 million people to abortion since the Supreme Court permitted the murder of babies in 1973 (and counting).

POPULATION INCREASING OR DECREASING AT THE FLOOD?

With these types of things occurring in the pre-Flood world for at least 120 years, it makes more sense that the population was declining not rising during this period. But what of other factors?

---

24. Then Herod, when he saw that he was deceived by the wise men, was exceedingly angry; and he sent forth and put to death all the male children who were in Bethlehem and in all its districts, from two years old and under, according to the time which he had determined from the wise men.

Did you realize the world was violent — very violent (Genesis 6:12–13[25])? Every thought was evil continually and the wickedness and violence (Genesis 6:5–6[26]) was unrestricted. Just imagine if half of the world were murderers . . . the world's population would cut in half in one day! Our humble suggestion is that the pre-Flood world's population was quite low — far less than suggested estimates listed above.

Was the Ark a Sufficient Means of Salvation?

We have had a number of people ask this question over the years. How does this relate to the pre-Flood population? It goes something like this, "If the ark was a type of salvation from the Flood, then how can we say it was a *sufficient* means of salvation if the population was too big to fit on the ark?"

In other words, the claim is that the ark wouldn't have been able to hold all the pre-Flood population; therefore, they claim that God's means of salvation was not adequate. "Couldn't people have rightly stated that the ark wouldn't have been good enough to save them?"

Besides the fact that this excuse is merely trying to blame God (for enacting justice upon their sin no less!), there are a couple of problems with this. Only eight people survived the Flood on the ark, so if someone pre-Flood really wanted to complain with that excuse, then they need to realize there was plenty of space for that one complainer — had they repented and become righteous!

But let's evaluate the other aspect. Was the ark sufficient to hold the pre-Flood world's population? Again, all we have are estimates. Is it possible that an unknown-sized population could have fit inside the ark, giving them no excuse? From the inductive argument given, the probability that the population size was rather small (perhaps only a matter of thousands), it is highly possible they could fit on the ark.[27]

But let's not forget one thing — God knew how many people would survive on the ark. So for the pre-Flood unrepentant sinners there is no excuse anyway.

---

25. So God looked upon the earth, and indeed it was corrupt; for all flesh had corrupted their way on the earth. And God said to Noah, "The end of all flesh has come before Me, for the earth is filled with violence through them; and behold, I will destroy them with the earth."

26. Then the Lord saw that the wickedness of man was great in the earth, and that every intent of the thoughts of his heart was only evil continually. And the Lord was sorry that He had made man on the earth, and He was grieved in His heart.

27. But consider another factor — if the world had repented of their sin, would the Flood have been necessary? Although certain "if" question are simply that . . . "if."

SO WAS THE ARK DESIGNED SIMPLY FOR THOSE EIGHT PEOPLE?

The Bible doesn't tell us. What we know is that when Noah was told to build the ark, the text says:

> But I will establish My covenant with you; and you shall go into the ark — you, your sons, your wife, and your sons' wives with you (Genesis 6:18).

Does this imply that *only* these eight people were given the privileged possibility of survival? The text did not say the ark was for them *alone*. It was for those eight people *at least*. Consider the same type of phrasing ("shall go into") in Amos:

> Their king shall go into captivity, He and his princes together," says the LORD (Amos 1:15).

Does this mean that others within the king's dominion had no possibility of going into captivity *with* the king and his family? By no means. We know they did!

What we learn subsequently is that no others came into the ark (confirmed by 2 Peter 2:5[28]), but we cannot say they didn't have the opportunity or possibility. The onus for their absence on the ark is entirely on their own sinful heads.

But some object and ask, what about the "innocent children" — if there were any left — at the time of the Flood? First they weren't innocent (Romans 3:23[29]). But again, the onus would be on the parents and guardians who refused to allow their evil children the possibility of survival on the ark!

Glance more closely at Genesis 6:18.[30] What the Bible says is that Noah *knew* that his wife, his sons, and his sons wives would indeed be on the ark. This passage is not only instructional but also comforting.

With this information told to Noah in advance, he had a reassurance that his family would not succumb to the murderous actions of the evil people on earth at the time. That was a guarantee for Noah's comfort like a "hedge of protection" around his family during this time. And this short bit

---

28. And did not spare the ancient world, but saved Noah, one of eight people, a preacher of righteousness, bringing in the flood on the world of the ungodly.
29. For all have sinned and fall short of the glory of God.
30. But I will establish My covenant with you; and you shall go into the ark — you, your sons, your wife, and your sons' wives with you.

of information was revealed to Noah in advance, even though God always knew how many would truly board the ark.

Noah, being a preacher of righteousness, was not preaching in vain (2 Peter 2:5[31]). Keep in mind *the heart* of Noah when doing this preaching . . . Noah surely lost brothers and sisters in the Flood. Consider:

> After he begot Noah, Lamech lived five hundred and ninety-five years, and had sons and daughters (Genesis 5:30).

There may have been some pre-Flood people who became righteous and were murdered well before the Flood began. Noah's preaching was surely a sign that he knew that there was a possibility of others becoming righteous. As it was, only the righteous warranted that final invitation from the Lord to board the ark (Genesis 7:1[32]).

---

31. See footnote 28.
32. Then the Lord said to Noah, "Come into the ark, you and all your household, because I have seen that you are righteous before Me in this generation.

Concluding Remarks

40 | OUR REAL MOTIVE FOR BUILDING ARK ENCOUNTER

KEN HAM

Throughout this book, we have discussed the Flood, the ark, and the alleged millions of years that permeate our culture. This is coupled with the building of a full-sized replica of Noah's ark — the Ark Encounter. I believe its opening is a historic moment in Christendom. It's the opening of one of the greatest Christian outreaches of our era: the life-size Noah's ark in Northern Kentucky.

ARK ENCOUNTER

As I read many of the secularist attacks on the Ark (and occasional criticisms from self-described Christians), I saw one theme coming up over and over again: our motive! Most secularists, who are in rebellion against God, just can't get their head around why we would build a replica of this massive wooden ship as described in the Bible. Many claim we must be doing it for the money!

Well, those of you who know Answers in Genesis understand that, while money is certainly needed to build and then maintain such a massive project and to construct future phases, money is not our motive in the slightest degree.

Some critics who say they are Christians declare that we're building an idol, supposedly because we are worshiping the Bible and not God! (We were even accused of that bizarre claim when building the Creation Museum.)

Of course, anyone who has visited the museum (and the same will be true for the life-size Ark) understands that this Bible-upholding center is not an idol in any way. The Creation Museum and Ark Encounter direct people to the Word of God and the gospel of Jesus Christ.

Others have accused us of building the Ark out of pride, claiming we just want to build something for the sake of getting our name in the news! Amazing!

THE JUDAS PROPOSITION: THE MONEY SHOULD BE SPENT ON THE POOR!

Others (some claiming to be Christians) say we shouldn't have built the Ark but should have spent the money on feeding the poor. There seem to be those habitual complainers who insist the money not be "wasted" this way. Such people either don't understand or don't seem to care about the millions who will be reached with the most important food in the universe — the spiritual food of the saving gospel — the very message that their eternal life depends on.

Before I address that, it is interesting to note that there are many projects underway in this nation that cost as much or enormous amounts more than the Ark Encounter. For instance, this project in Louisiana is costing about the same as the Ark project:

> Students at Louisiana State University will soon be able to soak up the sun in a manmade "lazy river," part of an $85 million leisure project under way despite the school's desperate financial situation.[1]

So where are all the naysayers complaining that the money for this "lazy river" should be spent on the poor? Or consider:

> One piece of art (Triptych) sold for $142 million.[2]

Where were all the naysayers saying the money would be best spent on the poor for that deal? In fact, there are thousands of multi-million dollar projects going on across the United States — and throughout the world. But it seems the Ark project is singled out — why?

I think it's as simple as this — it's the message! The Ark project (like the Creation Museum) is a professional, powerful, and gracious way to present the truth of God's Word and the gospel.

Yes, we do need to help the poor. And most Christians like me do that personally and through various ministries. Recently I encouraged people to give to the relief efforts in Nepal after the recent massive earthquake, and

---

1. Aalia Shaheed, "LSU's $85M 'Lazy River' Leisure Project Rolls on, Despite School's Budget Woes," Fox News, May 17, 2015, http://www.foxnews.com/us/2015/05/17/lsu-85m-lazy-river-leisure-project-rolls-on-despite-school-budget-woes.html.
2. Carol Vogel, "At $142.4 Million, Triptych Is the Most Expensive Artwork Ever Sold at an Auction," *The New York Times*, November 12, 2013, http://www.nytimes.com/2013/11/13/arts/design/bacons-study-of-freud-sells-for-more-than-142-million.html?_r=2.

Ken Ham and his daughter, Renee Hodge, in front of the Ark Encounter.

we provided a link to the donation page of Gospel for Asia, which has relief work going on there.

More directly, last year, through AiG's Vacation Bible School program, hundreds of thousands of meals were provided to needy children around the world. AiG worked with the Children's Hunger Fund — and we set a record for providing such meals.

At Answers in Genesis, our mission is to "proclaim the absolute truth and authority of the Bible with boldness, relate the relevance of a literal Genesis to the church and world today, and obey God's call to deliver the message of the gospel." So while it is important to help the poor and needy meet their physical needs (which we do), it is even more important to help meet their spiritual need — the need to come to know Jesus Christ, the Savior of the world — because lives — and eternity — hang in the balance.

The Ark Encounter will help us do that in a powerful, non-threatening way by simply sharing the truth of God's Word with visitors at the Ark concerning the historicity of Noah's ark, the Genesis Flood, and other authentic accounts of history revealed in the Scriptures, including the account of redemption weaved throughout the Bible.

Our motivation for the Ark project is to reach as many people as we can worldwide with the saving gospel message:

> And they sang a new song, saying, "Worthy are you to take the scroll and to open its seals, for you were slain, and by your blood you ransomed people for God from every tribe and language and people and nation" (Revelation 5:9; ESV).

Actually, the more I read such comments from the anti-Ark complainers, who are obviously inconsistent, it reminds me of how important the Ark Encounter is and how much the enemy doesn't want it happening!

For those people who say the money for building the Ark should be given to the poor, would these same critics give the money to the poor they have saved for their retirement? I bring this up because 65% of the funds to build the Ark are from a bond offering where people who support God's Word decided to use some of their funds to invest in interest-paying bonds for the sake of the Kingdom! Actually, for some of those who complain about money in regard to the poor, I wonder if they care about the poor very much. I'm reminded of the Judas Proposition found in Matthew 26:9–10, Mark 14:3–6, and John 12:3–8. John 12:3–8 says:

> Mary therefore took a pound of expensive ointment made from pure nard, and anointed the feet of Jesus and wiped his feet with her hair. The house was filled with the fragrance of the perfume. But Judas Iscariot, one of his disciples (he who was about to betray him), said, "Why was this ointment not sold for three hundred denarii and given to the poor?" He said this, not because he cared about the poor, but because he was a thief, and having charge of the moneybag he used to help himself to what was put into it. Jesus said, "Leave her alone, so that she may keep it for the day of my burial. For the poor you always have with you, but you do not always have me" (John 12:1–8; ESV).

Usually when people mimic the Judas Proposition, it shows they really don't care about the poor but, like Judas, have other motives.

WHAT IS OUR REAL MOTIVE FOR BUILDING THEMED ATTRACTIONS LIKE THE CREATION MUSEUM AND THE ARK ENCOUNTER?

A number of years ago in Australia, my wife Mally and I attended the commencement ceremony held at a secular university as one of our family members was graduating. A local judge gave the commencement address. Her speech went something like this: "Students, you are graduating from university. You're thinking of your future. Eventually you will die. So what do you do until you're dead?"

At this point, I turned to Mally and said, "Wow, this is going to be a message of hope and encouragement!"

Well, the judge went on to say, "In my life, there were books that greatly influenced my life." She named *Zen and the Art of Motorcycle Maintenance* and *The Hitchhiker's Guide to the Galaxy* (where a computer came up with the meaning of life as the number 42). The judge explained how these books influenced her life. She then encouraged students to find what would influence their lives to be impactful until they are dead!

She then sat down to a standing ovation by the faculty! I turned again to Mally and said, "If I were a student, I would feel compelled to jump off a cliff right now and get life over and done with." What a message of meaninglessness, hopelessness, and purposelessness she offered.

As a Christian, doesn't a speech like that make you want to stand up and declare to the audience that there is a message of real hope — not only for this life, but for eternity?"

What the judge presented was the ultimate message of the world. And sadly, it is being given daily to millions of students in public schools, universities, and through most of the media and the entertainment industry! Doesn't your heart ache when you think about this hopelessness? No wonder the suicide rate is rising in America and the Western World. No wonder younger generations turn to sexual immorality, drunkenness, and drugs.

I remember saying to Mally after the commencement speech, "I wish we had a way to get the Bible's teaching of the hope of the gospel to these students. How can we get out the message of truth concerning God's Word and our hope in Christ to this lost world?"

Really, what I shared that day with Mally sums up our motive! You see, every human being is one of our family — we're all related going back to Noah (and then back to Adam). We're all sinners in need of salvation. We're all under the judgment of death. But God reminds us:

> The Lord is . . . not willing that any should perish but that all should come to repentance (2 Peter 3:9).

> If you confess with your mouth that Jesus is Lord and believe in your heart that God raised Him from the dead, you will be saved (Romans 10:9; ESV).

Our real motive for building the Creation Museum, and the Ark, can be summed up in these verses:

> Go into all the world and preach the gospel to every creature (Mark 16:15).

> Go therefore and make disciples of all the nations (Matthew 28:19).

> But sanctify the Lord God in your hearts, and always be ready to give a defense to everyone who asks you a reason for the hope that is in you, with meekness and fear (1 Peter 3:15).

> Contend earnestly for the faith (Jude 3).

> Do business till I come (Luke 19:13).

Yes, our motive is to do the King's business until He comes. And that means preaching the gospel and defending the faith, so that we can reach as many souls as we can with the greatest message of purpose, hope, and meaning — that even though we rebelled against our Creator, He provided a way as a free gift so we can spend eternity with Him — through His shed blood on the Cross.

Oh, how we want to see as many as possible repent and receive this free gift of salvation! As a corollary to more people getting saved, there will be more who are motivated by Christ to help the poor.

I can't even describe how I feel right now contemplating that millions of souls will hear the most important message of all — not one of hopelessness from a human judge, but a message of hope from the holy, righteous Judge who, despite our sin, wants us to spend eternity with Him! Wow! Now that's a motive to build an Ark.

We need your prayers and support to keep the park's doors open to millions of guests who will learn the truth of God's Word and its life-changing gospel message.

The Ark Encounter at night

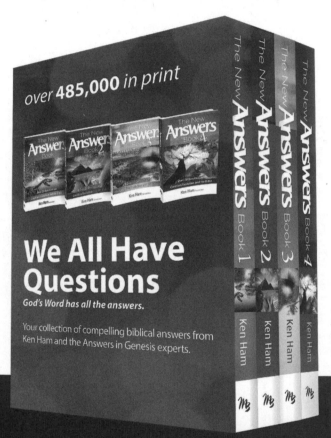

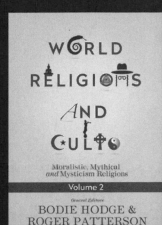

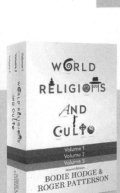